Hymn Introits
for the Liturgical Year
The Origin and Early Development
of the Latin Texts

Christoph Tietze

HillenbrandBooks

Chicago / Mundelein, Illinois

HYMN INTROITS FOR THE LITURGICAL YEAR: THE ORIGIN AND EARLY DEVELOPMENT OF THE LATIN TEXTS © 2005 Archdiocese of Chicago: Liturgy Training Publications, 1800 North Hermitage Avenue, Chicago IL 60622-1101; 1-800-933-1800, fax 1-800-933-7094, e-mail orders@ltp.org. All rights reserved. See our website at www.ltp.org.

On the cover: *Children Singing from a Choir Loft.* Sculpture by Luca della Kobbia the Elder (ca. 1400–1482). Cathedral of Florence. Photo by Erich Lessing/Art Resource.

Hillenbrand Books is an imprint of Liturgy Training Publications (LTP) and the Liturgical Institute at the University of Saint Mary of the Lake (USML). The imprint is focused on contemporary and classical theological thought concerning the liturgy of the Catholic Church. Available at bookstores everywhere, or through LTP by calling 1-800-933-1800 or visiting www.ltp.org. Further information about the **Hillenbrand Books** publishing program is available from the University of Saint Mary of the Lake/Mundelein Seminary, 1000 East Maple Avenue, Mundelein, IL 60060 (847-837-4542), on the web at www.usml.edu/liturgicalinstitute, or e-mail litinst@usml.edu.

Printed in the United States of America.

Library of Congress Control Number: 2004118209

ISBN 1-59525-011-5

HILY

Contents

Foreword

A view of the development of Western music during its first thousand years reveals that the force that precipitated that development was the somewhat rapid evolution of the liturgy and its ritual of the Roman Church. As the Church moved from the house church into the basilica, new ritual needs developed and music was utilized to fill those needs. The history of Chant and liturgy intertwine. More people, more space, more public prayer. Liturgy emerges with its own song.

One also sees how the music could dictate the manner in which the liturgy was understood and how it was to be celebrated. The concerted liturgies of the eighteenth and nineteenth centuries freely accepted the dominance of the musical form and its length as it shaped the rubrics. The priests with their deacons and sub-deacons simply sat down while the lengthy Glorias and Credos were sung; however, they sat down only after the priest recited sotto voce the text of the Gloria and the Creed. The music was the ruling factor.

The composers also sought to accommodate the reforms of eighteenth-century Josephenism, which demanded that all parts— proper and ordinary—were to be sung. We see composers such as Michael Haydn and Johann Matthias Kracher setting the texts of the graduals in typical eighteenth-century style incorporating orchestra and choir. Of course, that extended the length of the Mass, which frustrated the edict that the Mass must be under one hour. The musician seeks to comply, but with the language of his or her craft and time frame.

Dr. Tietze falls into this continuous tradition of music accommodating the liturgy and liturgy being influenced by the music. His launching point is the renewed interest in the proper texts of the Mass, more specifically, the entrance song—the introit.

With extensive and impeccable scholarship on the origins of the introit and its usage, he poses a solution of providing metrical settings of the entrance song. The proper text is variable for each Sunday and feast. New music for each introit would baffle even the most cultivated singing congregation and its leadership. The *swapping* of hymn tunes that would accommodate the variable texts is a giant step forward in cultivating a sung liturgy.

He is in good company. The use of metrical texts for sung prayers hearkens back to John Calvin and Isaac Watts. The setting of ritual texts to contemporary music practice points to the work of the eighteenth-century classical composers listed above. He utilizes the nearly universal practice of singing a metrical hymn as part of the entrance rite. He is, as the vernacular states, right on target.

He provides an immediate solution for a problem that liturgical musicians face every day. Do we sing at the liturgy or do we *sing* the liturgy? The monumental collection of texts and tunes for the Lectionary cycles bodes well for the tradition of *singing* the liturgy that fulfills the need that Catholic worship be *full, conscious, and active.*

Dr. Fred Moleck, Editor,
GIA Quarterly

Preface

This book is the fruit of a semester of sabbatical study and research work, undertaken during the Michaelmas Term 2002 at St. Benet's Hall, Oxford University. This sabbatical was a rebirth for me in two ways. Before I actually embarked on my study, I had the occasion to travel around Europe, and one of my visits was to the hospital in Cologne where I was born on Palm Sunday, 1956, and the hospital chapel where I was baptized on Easter Sunday of the same year. Right from the start of my life, I was destined to work with matters liturgical. This was the first rebirth, visiting these very special places for the first time since my birth and being reminded of my beginnings. The second rebirth was connected with my studies themselves, which gave me a deeper understanding of my Catholic liturgical roots. After my return, my understanding of the Holy Week liturgies had changed completely, and I felt for the first time a close connection with the early Christian community in Rome and generation after generation that followed.

Those who know me or work with me know that I am a methodical person. I like absolutes; I tend to draw lines and set boundaries; I am what you might call a black and white person. I do not like gray matter. At an early age, I began to take an interest in the absoluteness of the proper texts of the Mass. These are the texts that the Church sets as the norm for certain parts of the Mass, though they are rarely performed. The hymns or songs that are normally substituted for these texts at the entrance procession are what I would call gray matter. They are not the prescribed texts for that part of the Mass, and their use has always left me a bit disappointed. The black and white matter, however, the introit texts that the Church assigns to particular Sundays and feasts, sum up the theme of the feast day or the season in a couple of sentences and set the tone for the rest of the Mass. Moreover, by following these texts Sunday after Sunday, a thematic unity is established across the whole liturgical year. I suppose my disappointment with hymns and songs at the beginning of Mass has less to do with the lack of thematic unity of the particular Mass (as a matter of fact, hymns and songs can sometimes express the daily theme just as well, if not better) and more with their inability to express this unity across the year.

An early attempt at dealing with the introit texts was made by me in the early 1980s, when I was music director at St. Rose of Lima Church in Manhattan. I had been given a small budget to hire a vocal quartet for the Sundays of Lent and embarked on a project that would change the way the entrance rite was performed once and for all. Practical experience taught me the futility of this attempt and left me with a profound sense of humility. I set the antiphon texts in four-part harmony for the choir and attached psalms to each in simple Gregorian tones meant for congregational participation. While these were somewhat satisfying as musical compositions, the congregation, for some reason, did not heed my written instructions to sing the psalm tones, and the compositions ended up being choir pieces. With the end of that budget, both this experiment and any such future adventures were abandoned.

After this endeavor, I studied other people's attempts at dealing with the same subject, mainly John Ainslie's *Simple Gradual for Sundays and Holy Days,* Paul Ford's *By Flowing Waters,* and an as-yet incomplete project by Lynn Trapp and Delores Dufner, OSB. All three approach the subject from different angles. Ainslie's and Ford's books deal with the whole Mass proper, based on the seasonal texts as found in the *Graduale Simplex.* The introits in these publications are in responsorial chant style, where the verses are meant for choral or solo performance. The project by Lynn Trapp and Delores Dufner, OSB, sets the antiphon to a familiar hymn tune, intended for congregation, and the verse in well-crafted through-composed style meant for choir or cantor. An article calling for the application of introit texts through hymnody by Aidan Kavanagh, OSB, in the *GIA Quarterly* provided more food for thought.

In the early part of this century, Father John Talesfore of the Archdiocese of San Francisco planted the seed in my mind again, inspiring me to choose this project as a doctoral thesis at the Graduate Theological Foundation, and I began to think of another way to make these texts come alive for congregations, this time without the need of a choir or a cantor, something that would be truly congregational. I decided to follow Father Kavanagh's suggestion and explore metrical hymnody as the vehicle for achieving the desired result. But where were those familiar hymn tunes that could accommodate both an antiphon and psalm verses in a responsorial form? After all, the chant books instruct us to sing antiphon–verse 1–antiphon–verse 2–antiphon–and so on. Yet I could only think of a handful of somewhat familiar hymn tunes that could follow this form. After a feasibility study, which is fancy terminology for disguising some pretty wild experiments, usually at the expense of the congregation, I embarked on my studies in Oxford knowing less than I had before.

Fortunately, my initial research into the origin and early development of the introit dispelled the responsorial myth so eloquently expressed in official publications. The introit was, in fact, originally performed antiphonally: antiphon–several psalm verses–doxology–antiphon. In the Early Middle Ages, the psalm bore much more weight than it does today. As a matter of fact, today only the first verse of the psalm is published in the chant books, and the Sacramentary leaves the psalm out completely, reducing or eliminating any thematic connection between the psalm and the theme of the day. Ainslie, Ford, Trapp, and Dufner all use multiple verses, restoring the psalm to its original position of balance with the antiphon text. I decided to follow their laudable example and incorporate several verses of the psalm. I also decided at that point to set both antiphon and psalm verses to the same meter, so that they could be sung to the same hymn tune, and since a refrain was no longer needed, the list of available hymn tunes grew astronomically.

As far as metrical psalms go, there are several hundred metrical psalters, and in a way there was no lack of material for that part of the project. Christopher Webber's *New Metrical Psalter* was a valuable inspiration. This hymn tune psalter contains a great many psalms in contemporary, easy-flowing yet eloquent language. Some of the historic psalters tended to be largely unusable because of archaic and clumsy language, non-inclusivity, bad grammar, and so on, but on occasion even bad settings could be salvaged with a few Band-Aids. In addition, after gaining some experience, I enjoyed composing my own settings and even excelled at inventing some meters for which I could later find no tunes. For practical purposes, these settings are not included in this book.

Procedurally, I usually began with the psalm. If I found a suitable metrical psalm setting, I would go back to the translation of the antiphon and set it to the same meter. If I found no suitable psalm setting, I decided first on a meter that would accommodate the text of the antiphon and then composed my own psalm setting in the same meter. In that case, the length of the antiphon would dictate whether the setting would be in eight or four lines per verse, or somewhere in between. In dealing with particular meters, I tried to incorporate hymn tunes that are specific to feasts and seasons whenever possible (for example, Forest Green in the Christmas season or the Passion Chorale toward the end of Lent).

The entrance hymn or song is arguably the most important of all the sung parts of the Mass from the practical standpoint of facilitating congregational singing further on. In other words, if we can get people to sing at the very beginning, it is easier to continue that trend through the rest of the Mass. This is much more difficult when the congregation is presented with the challenge of singing an unknown hymn at the beginning. Conversely, choosing bad music for the sake of participation kills the spiritual values the music is supposed to impart, and this, too, has repercussions for the rest of the Mass. In suggesting tunes to my settings, I opted for music that was mostly familiar and of high quality. There are some tunes, however, that may be unfamiliar, but they are of such high quality that they are well worth learning and should be a boon to any congregation's repertoire.

A considerable portion of this work is devoted to the origin and early development of the introit. I felt that I needed to get to the root of the matter before embarking on a form about whose origin I knew very little. Thanks to the great resources of the Bodleian Library of Oxford University and the guidance of Dr. Emma Hornby, I was not only able to study this subject, but I believe that I made a significant contribution to the field by linking the non-psalmic Latin texts of the introit antiphons to Old Latin translations of the Bible, placing the introit's origin before 550. I also concluded that the introit should be performed antiphonally, and that there is considerable evidence showing that some parts of the Mass proper developed side by side with the chants of the monastic office.

A project of this type would not be possible without the help and inspiration of so many individuals who have taught, encouraged, and inspired me through my sabbatical and the following months: Father John Talesfore inspired me to take this project on as a doctoral project. Father Milton Walsh, also of the Archdiocese of San Francisco, and his interest in chant and the quality of liturgy instilled in me a love of the proper texts; he also helped me with the translation of some particularly nasty Latin texts. Archbishop Levada and Monsignor John O'Connor were very supportive of my sabbatical and helped make this study possible. Dom Henry Wansbrough, OSB, Master of St. Benet's Hall, tutored me on the psalms. He also assisted me in translating some "pretty rotten" Medieval Latin documents, and his candid remarks about some of my introit settings, while helping me to see them in a realistic light, aided me in improving them greatly. Moreover, without his help, I would probably not have been able to study at Oxford at all, and for this I am entirely in his debt. Dr. Emma Hornby of Christ Church College tutored me in the origin and early development of the introits, and her enthusiasm for the subject was contagious. In addition, she was the final proofreader of the first portion of the book. Brother Kees Pouderoijn, OSB, of the Congregation of Solesmes changed his travel plans to give me some helpful advice in the study of the introits. Father James Aylward of the Archdiocese of San Francisco also helped by proofreading and making helpful suggestions. Dr. Peter Roussakis of the Graduate Theological Foundation encouraged me to get this work published. Greg Labus, who happened to receive the manuscript purely by chance, encouraged the Liturgical Institute of Chicago to get involved; he also used some of the settings and gave valuable feedback by which I was able to improve them. Kevin Thornton of the Liturgical Institute helped me revise some portions, which greatly improved the book's usability. Mary Beth Kunde-Anderson, Alan Hommerding, and Tom Strickland of World Library Publications were responsible for the publication of the hymn texts with musical notation, and they also made some very helpful suggestions. A special thanks to Fred Moleck, editor of the *GIA Quarterly* and a good friend, who not only gave some advice on the finished product but who also wrote the introduction. Lastly, and most importantly, I wish to acknowledge with much love and admiration my wonderful wife Jeanette, and my darling children Helena (nine), Karl (six), and Elisabeth (three), who trotted along on the sabbatical and put up with my late hours at the computer and occasional outbursts of desperation over Amalar's Latin. Jeanette was an early proofreader and a constant source of encouragement, and to her I dedicate this work.

A Word about the Use of Psalters

For Part I, the numbering system of the Septuagint was used, since most original documents, as well as later sources dealing with research of the Early Middle Ages, adhere to that system. But since the numbering of the Hebrew psalter is becoming more prevalent in the Catholic Church, as it has been for centuries in the Protestant Churches, that system was applied to Parts II and III.

The purpose of Part III is to show how the official introit texts can be adapted in metrical form, so that they might be sung by congregations. Because they do not follow the official translations verbatim, the settings are not meant to be representations of the official introit texts, but only adaptations.

Acknowledgments

I gratefully acknowledge the use of some copyrighted material for this project, in particular:

The Gregorian Missal for Sunday. Solesmes: St. Peter's Abbey, and Paris-Tournai: Desclee, Copyright © 1990: English translations of the Latin introit texts in Part III.

Christopher L. Webber. *A New Metrical Psalter.* Copyright © 1986 Christopher Webber. Published by Church Publishing Corporation, New York, New York:

Antiphons: Ordinary Time 10 B, 16, 28, and 29.

Psalm Verses and Doxologies: Advent 3, 4, Christmas Vigil and Dawn, Holy Family, Christmas 2, Epiphany, Lent 2, 4, Holy Thursday, Easter 2, 7, Corpus Christi, Ordinary Time 3 AB, 10 B, 11, 16, 24, 28, 29, Annunciation, Ss. Peter and Paul Vigil, Transfiguration, Triumph of the Cross, Dedication of the Lateran Basilica.

Psalm 27 in Chapter 7 © 1999 Michael Morgan. All Rights Reserved. Reprinted with Permission.

Psalter Hymnal, Doctrinal Standards and Liturgy of the Christian Reformed Church. Copyright © 1976 Board of Publications of the Christian Reformed Church, Inc.

Psalm Verses: Christmas Midnight, OT 15, 18, 25.

These texts are in the public domain.

A special word of gratitude goes to World Library Publications (WLP), the owner and copyright holder of all metrical introit settings not mentioned above. WLP graciously agreed to have these texts be reproduced here and they will publish the complete set with musical notation concurrently with this volume. *Introit Hymns for the Church Year* Copyright © 2005 World Library Publications.

Part I

The Origin and Early Development of the Introit

Chapter 1

Introduction

EARLIEST MENTION OF THE INTROIT

The introit is the entrance chant of the Mass of the Catholic Church, sung to a prescribed text that is thematically linked to the season or the particular celebration. Ordo Romanus Primus (692–731), a directory for pontifical stational Masses, shows us for the first time a mature introit, performed by a well-established schola cantorum in a hierarchical ecclesiastical environment. This ordo became the basis for all succeeding Frankish ordines, as the Carolingian liturgical reform spread throughout the Frankish empire and much of Northern Europe in the eighth and ninth centuries and eventually came back to Italy. The persecuted Church, meeting in house churches, had no need for an elaborate entrance rite. We therefore must seek the introduction of the introit into the papal liturgy some time between 313, the Edict of Milan, and 731, the latest possible date of authorship of Ordo I.

There is little or no documentary evidence of introits earlier than Ordo I. However, from the textual structure and the texts themselves we can draw some conclusions. This book seeks to document the evidence for a pre-Gregorian (before 590) advent of this part of the Mass proper, examining in detail the musical structure of the introit, especially as it relates to monastic performance practice, the use of various translations of the Bible for introit antiphon texts, the placement of the introits within the stational system, and the utilization of the psalms.

The reader should keep in mind that I am dealing with the introits mainly as assigned texts and only secondarily as musical compositions. The whole subject of Gregorian versus Old Roman chant can be the subject of another book, but for now I am concentrating on the texts, drawing on the music only insofar as it helps to understand the context.

This treatise is not intended to answer questions definitively or to negate existing theories. It merely tries to open up a different way of looking at the evidence and to seek answers in fields that had not been sufficiently explored. As such, it will probably raise more questions than it answers.

Historical Background

For the discussion on the early history of the Church in Rome and the stational liturgy I am much indebted to the excellent research of John Baldovin, SJ, as found in his book on the urban character of Christian worship.

The early developments of the Mass proper are closely linked with the unfolding of the liturgical year. Any discussion of these early developments would not be complete without first elaborating on the historical context, especially in regard to the evolution of the stational Mass. As we will see, the history of the Eternal City, the development of the liturgical year, the organization of the stational system, and the assignment of liturgical texts to specific feasts went hand in hand. During the period when most liturgical changes took place, from the first to the eighth century, but especially the fourth through sixth, we cannot discuss one element without looking at the whole.

Early Christian worship in Rome took place in tituli, which were private residences named after the owner whose name was inscribed on a plaque (titulus) above the door. Nine of these are known to have been used before the fourth century, and three more were added between 300 and 313. Under Pope Miltiades (311), 11 tituli were in use, as opposed to 25 attributed to Pope Marcellus (308–309) in the *Liber pontificalis*. Each titulus was in or near a populous area.

Worship in these tituli was fairly simple. Because of space limitations in the homes and because of frequent periods of persecution, elaborate rites were impractical. Christians of Jewish roots followed the Jewish ritual in addition to the Christian liturgies, which were attended also by Gentile Christians. Coming from many different national, ethnic, and cultural backgrounds, Christians were

Table 1.1 Population of Rome

Year	Population
2nd century	1.5 million
300	800,000
500	100,000
560	30,000
600	90,000
9th century	35,000

mostly immigrants, and the most common liturgical language was Greek until the middle of the third century, when it became Latin. Many tituli were segregated according to national and cultural heritage. North Africa preceded Rome in the use of Latin as a liturgical language by about 50 years, and we shall later see that the advanced stage of biblical translations in North Africa had a profound impact on the choice of texts for the Mass propers.

In the first six centuries after Christ, the city of Rome experienced tremendous population shifts, especially in the monumental center (the forum and the area immediately surrounding it), because of invasions, epidemics, floods, and water supply (or lack thereof). Table 1.1 shows the population of Rome during that time.

The Aurelian walls, built from 272 to 279, did not separate the city from the countryside, and cemeteries were not considered discontinuous with the city, especially after the fourth century, when Christian public worship took place, among other locations, at burial places outside the walls. Christianity was officially tolerated by the Emperor Constantine in the Edict of Milan in 313 and became the state religion under Theodosius 66 years later in 379. Various social and economic factors forced the administrative center of the empire to shift North and East, and from the mid third century on, we see a decline in the importance of Rome. The establishment by Constantine of Constantinople as the new capital had a devastating effect on Rome. Much of the political and social elite went with the emperor and left a gaping void. This void was gradually filled by the papacy and the Church structure, beginning in 379. While the Eastern Church was very much influenced by the court in

Constantinople, the same cannot be said for Rome, where the papacy would develop into a temporal as well as spiritual power.

From the start, Constantine was concerned with the visibility of the Christian religion, and he sponsored several ambitious architectural endeavors that were to set the tone for Christian worship spaces in the following centuries. He took as a model the secular basilica, a place suitable for public gathering, and transformed this architectural type for use in sacred rites. The first to be erected was the Lateran Basilica (313), designed as the headquarters of the Christian community. This building is of monumental proportions, with a nave, four aisles, a transept, and an apse. There was also a processional walkway (solea), which reached from the inner East wall (facade) either to the chancel (schola cantorum) or the altar. This solea is most likely not Constantinian. "The axis of the building is longitudinal, providing the possibility of processional liturgy, and the existence of such a walkway making processional liturgy a certainty has been pinpointed to a period before the beginning of the 5th century."[1] The schola cantorum, an enclosed space in front of the sanctuary designated for the placement of the choir, is also most likely not original to the building, since choral singing had not sufficiently evolved within worship (more on this later).

Efforts to make the Lateran Basilica the center of Christian Rome were offset by the popularity of the shrine that marked the grave of Saint Peter. The first basilica there was begun in 329 and was ready for use in 337. Considerably larger than the Lateran, it was positioned so that it faced the rising sun over the city, which seems to have been important for the celebration of Christmas from the mid-fourth century on, but certainly so by the time of Leo the Great (440–461).

Other fourth-century basilicas were the Sessorian Basilica (Santa Croce in Gerusalemme), St. Paul's Outside the Walls (381), St. Lawrence, and Ss. Apostoli (originally named Basilica Julia, then rebuilt as the Basilica of Ss. Philip and James). Another Basilica Julia, later renamed Sta. Maria in Trastevere, replaced the titulus Callisti. The Liberian Basilica was renamed in honor of Mary (Sta. Maria Maggiore) after the Council of Ephesus under Sixtus (432–440). Decorations of worship spaces were known in pre-Constantinian times, but they were nothing compared to the splendor of the fourth- and fifth-century basilicas. The imperial donation to the Lateran consisted of 4390 solidi for lamps, 165 pounds of gold for liturgical vessels, and 1,600 pounds of silver.

Tituli continued to be used and were gradually transformed into basilicas of a smaller scale. One example is the Titulus Sabina on the Aventine, rebuilt as a basilica under Pope Celestine I (422–432). After the sack of Alaric in 410, this basilica was built on older foundations. It has a nave, two aisles, an apse, and a schola cantorum.

By the end of the fourth century, Rome had 20 tituli, either home churches or basilicas, none of them near the monumental center. There are two reasons for this: the center of Rome was largely unpopulated at that time, and there was some resistance from the pagan aristocracy to allow Christian worship centers in the area devoted to pagan rituals. The fourth and fifth centuries were a time of consolidation for the Roman Church. Much of the aristocracy had left for Constantinople, and the pagan aristocracy that was left behind experienced either massive conversion to Christianity or loss of power in the sacks of Alaric and the Visigoths. This void was filled by the Church, as Peter and Paul came to replace Romulus and Remus as the founders of the city.[2]

By the time of Leo the Great (440–461), five more tituli had been converted to basilicas, all of them in populous areas, and by the mid-fifth century, all of the tituli mentioned in the Lenten stational system existed as church buildings. Other churches which were added as stations were St. Stefano Rotondo (468–483) and Ss. Cosma e Damiano (530).

The Gothic wars of 536–555 were disastrous for Rome, as Byzantines and Goths fought for control of the city. Food supply dwindled, water supply was cut off, country estates were abandoned, and disease was rampant. The population, which at the beginning of the century still numbered 100,000, shrank to 30,000. By the end of the century, Rome was no longer viable as a political or economic center, but it retained its status as the symbolic center of the Western Church. By the time Gregory the Great ascended the papacy in 590, the population had grown to about 90,000, most of them refugees. Gregory reorganized the city, mostly with the help of monastic communities. The Byzantine influence made itself felt during the sixth century, which is shown in the architecture of three churches:

St. Maria Antiqua, St. Giovanni a Porta Latina (550), and the rebuilt
Ss. Apostoli (560). It was not until the beginning of the seventh
century that a pagan temple was transformed into a Christian Church.
By the end of that century, the Church had established welfare centers
for foreigners and the poor. Because of the increasing influx of pilgrims during the sixth and seventh centuries, the basilicas which were
outside the walls needed to be permanently equipped for liturgical
services. Welfare, politics, economy, and spirituality were all dominated
by the Church; Rome was indeed a Holy City.[3]

THE STATIONAL MASS—SOURCES

When we think of the way our liturgical year is structured, we think
of the celebration of liturgical seasons and feasts, the parochial daily
Mass, and assigned texts for each day. The bishop may be celebrating
Mass in his parish, the cathedral, or he may be at another church
for sacramental or administrative reasons. This situation was totally different in Rome before 800. The pope visited various basilicas on a predetermined, annually repeating cycle. This cycle became as much a
part of the liturgical year at Rome as the readings and other Mass texts
that came to be assigned to those days. Moreover, the pope's Mass
was not just another Mass; it was *the* liturgy. Considerable effort went
into each papal Mass, involving one-seventh of the Roman clergy.
Mass on the same day at other parishes would have been a certainty
for Sundays, but there is no documented evidence that daily Mass was
celebrated on stational, let alone other weekdays in churches other
than the stational church of the day.

 The stational system by which the Roman pontiff celebrated
Mass at different "stational" churches on particular feasts was not the
invention of any particular pope. Its roots can be traced back to the
second century, but the fully matured stational system does not appear
until shortly after Gregory the Great. There are several sources that
give us a glimpse at its evolution.

 The Philocalian calendar of 354 lists the dates of Easter, the
"depositiones" of martyrs and bishops, as well as their burial places
or places of commemoration,[8] and it fixes Christmas on December 25.
There is every indication that this calendar reflects liturgical usage.
Stations are not given, but these days were most likely eucharistic,

	Easter and Pentecost had been celebrated from apostolic times; Ember Saturdays and martyr feasts celebrated since the second century[4]
313	Edict of Milan, Emperor Constantine
320	Constantine moves capitol to Constantinople
325	Council of Nicea
336	Christmas celebrated in Rome, Mass of the Day; station: St. Peter
4th century	rapid spread of Christian singing[5]
4th century	Ascension added to calendar
Early 4th century	Epiphany celebrated in the East, late fourth century in Rome
Second half of 4th century	full Lent/Easter Cycle
354	The Philocalian Calendar includes 23 martyr feasts[6]
Late 4th century	three scrutinies in place on the Third, Fourth, and Fifth Sundays of Lent
The 4th-century	Roman liturgy began like the present Good Friday liturgy: prostration, then readings (Tertullian, Justin Martyr, Augustine)
410	Rome is captured by Alaric and sacked by the Goths
	In the fifth century, there were two main Latin liturgical families: Italy/North Africa and Gaul/North of the Alps
432	Pope Celestine institutes psalmody before the "sacrificium"
432–440	Sixtus institutes Christmas Midnight Mass (ad galli cantum), station: St. Mary Major; Council of Ephesus
440–461	Leo the Great.
Mid-5th century	all tituli of the Lenten stational system have been constructed; Ash Wednesday in place
452	Attila the Hun ravages Northern Italy; Leo intercedes and persuades the Huns to withdraw
455	Rome pillaged for 14 days by the Vandals under Genseric despite intercession of Leo; as the power of the emperors decreases, the power of the popes increases
475	Roman Empire falls
Late 5th century	Quinquagesima added to calendar
Late 5th century	earliest Sacramentaries

475-526	Ostrogothic King Theodoric; disputes with Rome over antipope Laurentius; Rome constantly under threat of pillage; drastic population decrease in Rome; Church's wealth greatly diminished
Early 6th century	scrutinies moved to weekdays and increased to seven in number
526–536	Gothic tyranny reigns in Rome
536	Eastern Roman troops oust Goths from Rome, then are beseiged by Goths under Vitiges, who cuts aqueducts; Pope Sylverius plots with Goths, is caught, and sent into exile in Asia Minor
544	Totila attacks Rome and takes it in 546; Pope Vigilius flees and is taken to Constantinople
6th century	third Christmas Mass added, Mass at Dawn, station: St. Anastasia
6th century	Veronese Sacramentary, compiled from various libelli; various parts are from the early fifth century
Mid-6th century	Sexagesima added to calendar
568	Italy invaded by Lombards under Alboin
Late 6th century	Advent added to Church calendar; its appearance at the beginning of the liturgical year is found first in chant books at a time when Sacramentaries and Lectionaries still begin with the Vigil of Christmas. These chant books, however, date from the late eighth century[7]
Late 6th century	Septuagesima added to calendar
590–604	Gregory the Great
Early 7th century	Old Gelasian Sacramentary, a layered document containing some parts that date to the early sixth century
Early 7th century	full stational system in place
7th century	Liber diurnus mentions national "scholae" for pilgrims in Rome
680s	Arab incursions interfere with Mediterranean trade
692–731	Ordo I
Late 8th century	first antiphoners and graduals
846	Arabs sack Rome and plunder the tombs of Saints Peter and Paul
9th and 10th centuries	power struggles by leading Roman families over papacy
ca. 900	first extant musical notation for Mass proper

otherwise they would not have been indicated.[9] The Philocalian calendar and the *Liber Pontificalis* indicate that the Roman Church may have begun to organize a formal stational system by the mid-third century with the establishment of 25 tituli for the administration of Baptism and Penance.

A letter of Pope Innocent I to Decentius, Bishop of Gubbio (Umbria), in 417 states:

> Concerning the fermentum [Eucharist], which we send to the titular churches on Sundays, it is needless for you to ask, for all of our churches are set up within the city. As to the presbyters who are not able to join with us [in the main Eucharist] on Sundays because of the people they serve, these receive the fermentum made by us from the acolytes, so they may not judge themselves separated from our communion, especially on Sundays. This practice ought not be observed in the outlying churches nor in the cemeterial churches, for we have assigned presbyters there who have the right to confect the sacrament, which in the first place should not be carried too far.[10]

The content of this letter could have one of two meanings: that the papal liturgy was the main liturgy and consecrated hosts were carried to other Roman churches, or that the hosts were confected at a central location and distributed to outlying parishes where they were consecrated. Both would have served the purpose of unifying the Roman Church.

The homilies of Gregory the Great often list the churches where he spoke, but it is not clear whether the same church was used on the same day the following year. In any case, since there are substantial differences between the churches listed in the homilies and later stational lists, we have to conclude that the stational system was not rigid at the time of Gregory and that different churches would be chosen as stations for the same liturgical day in different years.

The Comes of Wuerzburg contains an epistolary (a Lectionary with first readings) and also has the earliest stational list. The date of authorship of this list is definitely before 687; Morin dates it to the mid to late sixth century, but the early seventh century is more likely, since Gregory the Great himself did not adhere to this stational list.[11] The evangelary of Wuerzburg of the mid- to late seventh century contains a larger stational list and shows a rapid expansion of the stational system.

The earliest Sacramentaries date from the beginning of the sixth century. Before that date, the prayers had been organized in libelli, which are leaflets containing the prayers and texts for particular feasts. The earliest extant Sacramentary is found in Verona ms. 85, known as the Leonine Sacramentary, but more correctly from the reign of Vigilius (537–555). This Sacramentary mentions several stations. The Old Gelasian Sacramentary is found in a Frankish copy of around 750, the Codex Vaticanus Reginensis latinus 316. While it contains some Gallican elements, the original document is clearly Roman and contains parts that range from the early sixth to the early seventh century. The earliest stratum of the so-called Gregorian Sacramentary stems from the time of Honorius (625–638), but elements of it could be older. It contains an Ordo Missae (Qualiter Missa Romana Caelebratur) with an entrance rite made up of introit/kyrie/gloria. A later form, copied around 811–812 and found in Ms. Cambrai 164, reflects the "Hadrianum" that was sent to Charlemagne 785–786.

The Ordines Romani, liturgical directives for papal stational Masses, are extant only in copies made on Frankish soil. They are divided into groups A and B, the former reflecting Roman usage, and the latter being heavily Gallicanized. All ordines derive from Ordo I (692–731). This ordo divides the city into seven regions. The clergy and the deacons of each region are assigned to one particular day of the week. If a stational liturgy falls on that day, the clergy and deacons of that region are required to assist at the papal celebration that day by participating in the stational liturgy.

The earliest antiphoners, as found in Hesbert's *Antiphonale Missarum Sextuplex*, indicate stational churches in the heading for each liturgical day.

The Stational Mass–History

The term "statio" means "standing," "place of standing," or "military guard post." It is first mentioned in the second century Greek "Shepherd" by Hermas, where the term is used in relation to fasting. Tertullian, at the beginning of the third century, likens the keeping of the statio (fast) to military guard duty. The relationship between statio and fasting remained until the sixth century.

Tertullian also called the place where Stoics and Academicians met a statio, and Cyprian of Carthage, 50 years later, used the term to denote an ecclesiastical non-liturgical assembly. In fourth-century Rome, the supporters of the antipope Ursinus (against Damasus) met in liturgical assemblies called stationes in the Basilica Julia (Sta. Maria in Trastevere). When statio was used to mean fast, it was linked with prayer, as it had been done in the Jewish usage, where fast days were accompanied by processions and prayer services in town squares. The Christian Church in Jerusalem in the fourth century fasted on Wednesdays and Fridays; on those days there were also liturgical services in specific churches. Baldovin conjectures that the term statio evolved from fasting to assemblies on fast days to ecclesiastical assemblies to the place denoting liturgical celebrations.

At the end of the second century, there were between nine and 40 Christian communities of different ethnic and cultural backgrounds in Rome. The Eucharist was used as a unifying factor by sending hosts (fermentum) from the papal service to the outlying communities (tituli). The pope was also not tied to one particular titulus but moved from community to community to celebrate the Eucharist. By the third century, the calendar included commemorations of martyr feasts in the cemeteries, which the pope visited on the martyrs' anniversaries. The next statio was announced at the end of the liturgy to let people know at which titulus or cemetery the next papal Eucharist was to take place. This movement not only served as a further unifying factor for the Christian community, but it was also necessary in times of persecution. By the late fifth century, the stational practice had achieved a definite organization, as is already evident from documents of the time of Leo the Great (440–461). Hilarius (461–468) gifted the tituli with liturgical vessels for stational services.

The stational system evolved side by side with the development of the feasts, especially in regard to a full-blown Lent. The earliest stational list of the mid-fifth century includes Ash Wednesday. Wednesdays and Fridays had been known as fast days from an early time, and Mondays, Tuesdays, and Saturdays were added as liturgical days in Lent in the late fifth century. Therefore, a fully developed Lenten stational system was possible only after the middle of the fifth century (Septuagesima was added in the late sixth century). The most important and the oldest feasts tended to be celebrated in the most important churches, and the feasts drawing the largest number of congregants were assigned to the largest basilicas. By this time, the Lenten stational churches had been constructed. St. Vitale was the last titulus built (401–417), and the last church on the early list is St. Stefano Rotondo (468–483). The Lateran basilica was somewhat of a failure; it did not become an urban or ecclesiastical center until the nineteenth century. Many of the areas containing tituli were no longer populated after the fifth century, but these churches still maintained their status as venerable places of Christian worship.

The Lenten organization of the stational system is its most remarkable aspect. Most major basilicas are listed in the earliest list, and this is the only period in which some stations appear. It seems that the development of liturgical texts and the stational system are concurrent. Both of them developed after Ash Wednesday had been fixed as the beginning of Lent. Two of the most venerable tituli, St. Sabina and Ss. Giovanni e Paolo were used on Wednesday and Friday of that week. Also, Psalms 1–26 were sung as Lenten weekday communions in a numerically ascending way, beginning with Ash Wednesday, excepting Thursdays, which did not become liturgical until 731. In an effort to keep the stational liturgies moving about the city, the distribution of tituli in the Lenten arrangement avoids repeating the same ecclesiastical region on consecutive days.

At this point, I need to go back to the numerical sequence of the Lenten weekday communions, since they are of profound importance to our subject. There are five instances where that sequence is broken and a Gospel antiphon is substituted in place of the psalm that should be there. All of these antiphons are from the Gospel of the day, and three deserve special mention: the woman at the well (Third Friday), the man born blind (Fourth Wednesday), and the raising of Lazarus (Fourth Friday). To a liturgically astute reader these will jump out as the Gospels for the scrutinies. What about the other two: the prodigal son (Second Saturday) and the woman caught in adultery (Third Saturday)? The answer for all of this is rather complex. The scrutinies were celebrated on the Third, Fourth, and Fifth Sundays of Lent from the late fourth century on, and our contemporary way of celebrating the Rite of Christian Initiation of Adults restored that original arrangement. Christianity became the state religion in 379. We may assume that a large proportion of the population was still pagan, and adult Baptisms were common. Converts went through a process of public scrutiny to prepare for Baptism at Easter, and the Sundays of Lent were best suited for this. As a matter of fact, it was the process of baptismal preparation that helped shape the whole season of Lent. As the number of converts dropped and infant Baptisms became the norm, the scrutinies were moved to Lenten weekdays at some point in the early sixth century. This practice is documented in the Old Gelasian Sacramentary and Ordo XI, but we must assume that it had existed for some time before that. I believe that the prayers, readings, and any assigned chants were all moved at the same time. It would have been difficult, for example, to move only the communion chant and not the introit, because that would have required a tremendous amount of copying by hand. However, it would have been quite simple to move the corresponding libelli from one location of the collection to another.

Before reading Table 1.2, the reader should be reminded that the more historical Roman/Gallican numbering of psalms is applied in the first half of this book, whereas the more practical Hebrew numbering is employed in the second half.

What about the two Gospel communions that do not seem to belong? Some experts have claimed that the existence of five Gospel communions speaks against the claim that they have anything to do with the scrutinies, since there should only be three.[12] However, when the scrutinies were moved to weekdays, their number was actually increased to seven.[13] It could be that these two, the prodigal son and the woman caught in adultery, were two of the additional four scrutiny Gospels. Because of the obvious penitential character of those texts, it could also be possible that they were associated with preparations for the rite of penance, which at that time was also a public process, administered on Holy Thursday. The other two scrutinies were celebrated on the First Monday (enrollment) and Holy Saturday morning (final preparation), making the total number seven.

In examining the melodies of the Lenten weekday communions, Brad Maiani discovered that there was a tendency among the earlier ones to be of a simpler, more homogeneous type, which he calls the core group.[14] The communions assigned to later Lenten weekdays belong more to the exceptional group, where the melodies tend to be more complex and transmission between different documents is not as consistent as is the case with the core communions. He offers the possibility that the core communions were part of an original ad hoc set to be chosen from for the Lenten weekdays, much as was the case with the post-Pentecostal chants. The exceptional communions, he claims, might have been added later to fill the missing dates once Ash Wednesday was set. It is thus possible that the core communions antedate the assignment of Ash Wednesday as the start of Lent, and that the exceptional communions were added after Ash Wednesday was established in order to complete the set of 26.

When looking at the stations for some of the days in question, we find more coincidences. For the Third Friday, St. Lorenzo in Lucina is the station. The Gospel is the woman at the well, and the church is located over the site of an old well. On the Fourth Wednesday, the station is St. Paul, named after the saint who gained sight through faith. The Gospel is about the man born blind, regaining his sight through faith. St. Eusebia is the station for the Fourth Friday. Located on the site of an ancient necropolis, it is the perfect place for the Gospel of the raising of Lazarus. On the Third Saturday, the Gospel is about the woman caught in adultery; the station is St. Susanna, and the epistle is the story of Susanna. These are clear indications that some stations were chosen to make the readings come alive.

There are other signs that stations were carefully selected to bring out a particular theme. Sta. Croce was the station on Good Friday. On Septua-, Sexa-, and Quinquagesima, the stations of St. Lorenzo, St. Paul, and St. Peter circumscribe the city, symbolizing a protective ring at a time when this was badly needed. These Sundays were added in the fifth and sixth centuries, which were characterized by invasions, epidemics, and floods. The introit for Septuagesima, thought to be added by Saint Gregory I, sums up the theme of that time:

> Groans of death surround me; anguish of hell encircles me. And in my tribulation I called upon the Lord, and from his holy temple he heard my voice.[15]

During Easter week, St. Peter is the station on Monday, the Gospel is about Peter, and the epistle is one of his speeches.

Table 1.2 Lenten Weekday Communions

	Original series	Gospel series	Thursday series (post 731)
Ash Wednesday	Psalm 1:1–3 Qui meditabitur		
Thursday			Psalm 50:21 Acceptabis
Friday	Psalm 2:11–12 Servite		
First Week			
Monday	Psalm 3:5–7 Voce mea		
Tuesday	Psalm 4:2 Cum invocarem		
Wednesday	Psalm 5:2–4 Intellege		
Thursday			John 6:52 Panis quem
Friday	Psalm 6:11 Erubescant		
Saturday	Psalm 7:2 Domine Deus		
Second Week			
Monday	Psalm 8:2 Domine Dominus		
Tuesday	Psalm 9:2–3 Narrabo domnia		
Wednesday	Psalm 10:7 Iustus Dominus		
Thursday			John 6:5–7 Qui manducat
Friday	Psalm 11:8 Tu Domine		
Saturday	(Psalm 12 missing)	Luke 15:32 Oportet te	
Third Week			
Monday	Psalm 13:7 Quis dabit		
Tuesday	Psalm 14:1–2 Dominus quis		
Wednesday	Psalm 15:11 Notas mihi		

Table 1.2 *continued*

	Original series	Gospel series	Thursday series
Thursday			Psalm 118:4–5 Tu mandasti
Friday	(Psalm 16 missing)	John 4:13–14 Qui biberit	
Saturday	(Psalm 17 missing)	John 8:10–11 Nemo te	
Fourth Week			
Monday	Psalm 18:13–14 Ab occultis		
Tuesday	Psalm 19:6 Laetabimur		
Wednesday	(Psalm 20 missing)	John 9:6–38 Lutum fecit	
Thursday			Psalm 70:16–18 Domine memorabor
Friday	(Psalm 21 missing)	John 11:33–44 Videns Dominus	
Saturday	Psalm 22:1–2 Dominus regit		
Fifth Week			
Monday	Psalm 23:10 Dominus virtutum		
Tuesday	Psalm 24:22 Redime me		
Wednesday	Psalm 25:6–7 Lavabo		
Thursday			Psalm 118:49–50 Memento
Friday	Psalm 26:12 Ne tradideris		

On Tuesday at St. Paul, the epistle begins "In diebus illis surgens Paulus" (Acts 13:16). And on Thursday at Ss. Apostoli, formerly the basilica of Ss. Philip and James, Acts 8:26–40 tells how Philip meets the Ethiopian Eunuch. The choice of stations for Ember Days is also consistent with this pattern.

The stations for Christmas developed in stages, as the various liturgies were added. The first and only original Mass (today's Mass of the Day) was at St. Peter's. After the Council of Ephesus (437), a second Mass "ad galli cantum" was added (today's Midnight Mass), the station being St. Mary Major. And in the sixth century a third liturgy was celebrated at dawn at St. Anastasia.

Chapter 2

The Form of the Introit

OVERALL STRUCTURE

As far as texts are concerned, there is no difference in poetic form
between the Mass proper found in Old Roman and Gregorian sources.
However, the musical differences apparent between Gregorian
sources, starting in the ninth century, and the Old Roman, beginning
in the eleventh, have led to many divergent theories that will most
likely never be proven beyond the shadow of a doubt. One theory
claims that the Frankish cantors did not have the capability to copy
the cantus romanus (original chant) exactly, and that the differences
produced what we now know as Gregorian chant, in other words,
that the Old Roman melodies are actually closer to the original cantus
romanus than the Gregorian. By another theory the chant was copied
more or less exactly, but over the centuries both repertoires under-
went more changes, often leading to substantial musical differences.
Others claim that Rome might have had two styles, that one of
these was transferred to the Franks, which is now the Gregorian, and
that the other repertoire survived in Rome, which is now known as
the Old Roman chant. All of these theories have their strong and
weak points, but the true nature of the cantus romanus will probably
never be known. All we have is the texts of the Mass propers and
several documents that describe the form of these compositions, so
we will concentrate on these.

     The introit and communion chants belong to the category of
antiphonal Mass chants.[1] At one point, the psalmic parts of the Mass
consisted of entire psalms. Remnants of this can be found in the tracts,
the forerunners of which were chanted "in directum" or all the way
through by a solo voice. Early descriptions categorize these psalms with
the readings of the Mass, but it is clear that they possessed a musical

character. The melodies themselves, however, must have been much simpler than the present tracts, and, as they grew in elaboration and complexity, their extended length necessitated truncation to just a few verses of the psalm. Other psalms were chanted by a soloist with a congregational or, later, choral response; these responsorial chants include the forerunners of the gradual and the alleluia. Again, we must assume that the melodies of the refrains of the graduals were much simpler when they were sung by congregations, and that they grew in complexity as the performance was transferred to the schola. The verses of the graduals and alleluias also grew in length and elaboration. The verses of the tracts and graduals witness to a substantial amount of formulaic writing, both in Old Roman and Gregorian melodies, alluding to structured embellishment, possibly through improvisation. A third way of chanting the psalms is represented by the offertories, which resemble the form of the Great Responsories of the Office of Matins. And, finally, we arrive at our present matter of discussion, the antiphonal chants.

This, of course, is a tremendous oversimplification, but it helps to categorize the various types of chant, whose development undoubtedly overlapped to some degree. Just to mention one area of complexity: the communion melodies behave in very different ways. What Maiani calls the core communions and the exceptional communions would actually resemble in style the introits. The responsory communions, however, are more complex, and even their origin set them apart from the entire remainder of the repertoire of the Mass proper, being duplicates of responsories of Matins as well as two office antiphons.[2]

In its earliest documented form in Ordo Romanus Primus (692–731), the introit consisted of an antiphon, an entire psalm or greater portion thereof, the Gloria Patri (doxology), and a repeat of the antiphon. As such, it mirrored antiphonal psalmody as found in the Liturgy of the Hours. In this ordo, the pope arrives at the stational church and is ushered into the sacrarium for some preliminary matters. When everything is ready, he gives a signal to the "quartus scholae," the fourth in charge of the choir or somewhat of an underling, who proceeds to the schola cantorum, assembled in two sets of two rows facing each other on the sanctuary steps, boys in front, men in the back. The cantor intones the antiphon, the schola completes it and then proceeds with the psalm verses. The document does not say that the antiphon is repeated at any time before the very end of the composition; the psalm verses were thus chanted back to back, possibly in an antiphonal style, with the two sides of the choir alternating. When the pope passes through the schola, he gives a signal to the "prior scholae." After finishing that particular verse, the schola continues with the doxology and repeats the antiphon. While there is no directive for chanting the whole psalm, since the psalm is cut whenever the pope gives the signal, we can assume that at some earlier point that might have been the case.

There is no indication at all that introits were ever sung responsorially before the nineteenth century. None of the Ordines Romani or later Pontificals supports that theory. The confusion seems to stem from a misinterpretation of Ordo XV, a highly gallicanized version of Ordo I. This Ordo contains the most explicit description of the introit, but this has to be taken in context. In this description, only the first verse of the psalm is sung after the antiphon, the antiphon is repeated, followed by the first half of the Gloria Patri, another antiphon, the second half of the Gloria Patri, the antiphon again, and then one or several "versus ad repetendum," finishing with the antiphon. This composition bears little resemblance to that described in Ordo I. Vogel asserts that the author of Ordo XV was someone who had an admiration for the Roman rite but who was unfamiliar with it.[3] The versus ad repetendum, which will be discussed below, seems to be a Frankish invention. In the *Antiphonale Missarum Sextuplex*, a collection of the six earliest extant antiphoners, the versus ad repetendum is used extensively in the introits of Compiegne and Senlis, and quite often this will be the second verse of the psalm (this is the case, for example, in all the Christmas liturgies). This leads me to conclude that in those cathedrals only the first verse had been chanted before the doxology, which would concur with the description of the introit in Ordo XV. The two cities are North of Paris, about 20 miles apart, and would have been in the same sphere of influence. It is thus possible that Ordo XV or a similar document was written for use in that geographical area and that it had no influence at all in other parts of the realm. In my opinion, scholars have placed much more importance on that document than it deserves.

The medieval usage of the word "antiphona" could mean either "antiphon" or "alternating liturgical chant."[4] In its earliest usage, this alternation would have been between soloists, singing the verses, and choir, singing a refrain. However, later forms included compositions like the introit, where the psalm verses would be alternated by two choirs. In fourth-century Syria, psalms were sung by two choirs antiphonally, and the Gloria Patri was also added, sung by all.[5] Antiphonal singing apparently came from the East to the West. In 382, Ambrose became familiar with antiphonal singing through the influence of Eastern, Syrian, and Greek bishops and their liturgical practices during a council convened by Pope Damasus (366–384). By 386 antiphonal singing was instituted in Milan. Augustine, who was in Milan at the time and was baptized there in 387, brought antiphonal singing to Hippo.[6] Augustine's writings mention antiphons, psalms, and hymns in Milan, but the meaning of the early antiphons is unclear, except that they were characterized by spirited congregational singing. Isidore of Seville (560–633) is more specific, as he indicates that the antiphons were chanted by two choirs alternately,[7] "in antiphonis autem versibus alternant chori."[8]

The documented structure of the introit, as found in the ordines Romani and pontificals, paints a varied picture. Because of the complexities involved, I have placed the texts relating to introits of all ordines and pontificals in an appendix, but I would like to summarize two different forms here, as found in Ordos I (Roman) and XV (Gallicanized).

Ordo I	*Ordo XV*
Antiphon	Antiphon
Psalm verse 1	Psalm verse 1
verse 2	Antiphon
verse 3	Gloria Patri, first half
etc.	Antiphon
last verse (signal from pope)	Gloria Patri, second half
Gloria Patri	Antiphon
Antiphon	Versus ad repetendum (one or several)
	Antiphon

Note that there is no repetition of the antiphon between psalm verses in either example.

We can imagine that there must have been regional differences in the number of psalm verses, when the antiphon was repeated, and whether a versus ad repetendum was used.

Antiphon

Of all the chants of the proper of the Mass, introit and communion antiphons are unique in that they are musically very homogeneous.[9] They tend to be syllabic or neumatic, with only occasional melismas, and they are of similar lengths throughout the church year. Also, whereas other genres use only a few of the church modes, introits and communions use all eight.

About a third of the 145 introits are non-psalmic. The texts assigned to the feasts of the Lord are usually specific to the theme, whereas others tend to be more general and uphold a seasonal idea. This is in stark contrast to communion texts, which are much more specific throughout the Church year. This makes sense. Why would one sing an introit on a particular theme before that theme has been proclaimed in the readings? The communions, however, take advantage of their position after the readings and continue the specific thought, usually by invoking a central sentence from one of the readings. On a metaphysical level, we partake of the word by listening to the readings, and we partake of the Word in the Eucharist.

The psalmic texts in the Gregorian repertoire are generally divided into two translations: the Roman psalter for the antiphons and the Gallican psalter for the verses (Old Roman chant uses the Roman psalter for both) (a more complete description of these psalters is given in the discussion on biblical texts in chapter 4). Originally, the Roman psalter was used throughout, but when the chant was adopted in the Frankish kingdom, the Gallican psalter was used for the verses, since this was the psalter that had been committed to memory by the Franks sometime before the Carolingian reforms. The antiphons were musically more elaborate than the simple psalm tones, and thus the text could not be changed. The verses, however, sung in Rome to simple psalm tones, were more adaptable to the psalter that was in use in Gaul at the time. In a way, the cantors learning the cantus romanus took a shortcut; rather than relearning the whole book of Psalms and adopting the Roman psalter throughout, they applied the psalter that was already memorized, the Gallican psalter, to those parts of the compositions that were more adaptable. But even among the antiphons, there are some textual deviations from the Roman psalter. This has led some scholars to believe that there was a certain amount of freedom on the part of the singers "composing" the chant to adjust the text according to what would fit best.[10] However, on closer examination, most of these textual deviations can be traced back to Old Latin psalters, of which there were many, making these texts very old indeed.

The non-psalmic texts are a different matter altogether. They are from other biblical sources (and one non-biblical), sometimes spliced freely together from several verses of two different books. There is a tendency for the texts assigned to older feasts to be influenced by Old Latin texts and for later feasts to exhibit adherence to the Vulgate.

PSALM

Originally, the psalms attached to the introits were sung in their entirety. The abbreviations "Ps" or "PSL" in the earliest sources attest to this, in distinction to "V" for "versus," which means "verse of the Bible,"[11] and which terminology was used in the responsorial chants of the Mass. Over the centuries, as the music became more elaborate and processions became shorter, the psalm was truncated more and more, until only one verse was left. In this context it should be pointed out that the aisles of early Roman basilicas were rather long compared to those in most Frankish Romanesque churches, and processions in the Frankish empire, where Gregorian chant as we know it was formed, were considerably shorter than in Rome. Sicardus of Cremona says that Gregory the Great composed both antiphons and tropes to be sung in modulations (it is unclear what he meant by that) instead of entire psalms. "Therefore one should sing—together with the Gloria Patri—the first verse of the psalm which pertains most to the actual feast and which was formerly performed in its entirety."[12] Besides the historical inaccuracy about Gregory the Great as a composer of chant, characteristic of much medieval scholarship, we see that the psalm is already truncated to one verse, whereas formerly it had been performed in its entirety.

But it is clear that, in the original form of the introit, a major portion of the thematic context of the introit chant lay on the psalm. In today's usage of only one verse, that connection often fails.[13] There is, however, an effort to restore psalmody within the introit composition.[14]

Psalm verses were sung to any of eight tones, found in the ninth century in theoretical writings and before the year 1000 in tonaries. An incomplete tonal list of Mass chants from Saint Riquier may even date back to the closing years of the eighth century.[15] This does not mean that psalm tones did not exist before then; they were just not written down, since music notation had not yet been devised. Introit psalm tones in Rome were identical to the office psalm tones, whereas in the Frankish Empire the more elaborate canticle tones were applied.[16] The psalm tones found in our Solesmes editions are standardized forms of numerous different tones used in the Middle Ages.

GLORIA PATRI

The psalm verses were followed by the Gloria Patri, the Trinitarian formula used in so many of our prayers and so characteristic of office psalmody. This prayer was a result of the Council of Nicaea in 325, which concerned itself with the theology of the Trinity. The *Admonitio generalis* 70 of Charlemagne, 789, states "that the Gloria Patri should be sung among [by?] all with highest honor."[17] This could mean that it was to be sung by everybody, by both choirs, or in all churches. However, no Carolingian Ordo mentions the song of the people. More credible is the Capitula of Herard of Tours, 858, that "the Gloria Patri, as well as the Sanctus and the Creed and the Kyrie should be sung by all in a reverent manner."[18]

The use of the doxology, however, does not seem to have been uniform outside of Rome. Amalar of Metz (early ninth century) claims in "De ordine Antiphonis" that the Gloria Patri had only recently been introduced into antiphonal singing. This concurs with his description (see below, monastic) of office psalmody, where the Gloria Patri is obviously missing. However, he is clearly talking about office psalmody, and the use of the doxology in the introit, if we take into account Charlemagne's earlier decree, would have been different.

The later Roman practice is exemplified by San Pietro F. 22 (thirteenth-century Roman chant book), which indicates Gloria Patri in Advent I, and euouae (the vowels of "seculorum amen," the finishing vowels of the doxology; this is called the "differentia") for all other antiphons, to pinpoint the psalm tone of that particular mode.

Versus ad Repetendum

An apparently Frankish contribution to the introit chant was the versus ad repetendum. Versus ad repetendum are selected psalm verses (note that the word "versus" has the same form in the singular and plural and could therefore mean one verse or multiple verses) added after the singing of the doxology, followed by another repeat of the introit antiphon. Frankish and German chant books often show agreement on the choice of versus ad repetendum, but the many occasions where they do not agree leads to the conclusion that this was not a Roman trait but a local Gallican characteristic.[19] Two of the six antiphoners in the *Antiphonale Missarum Sextuplex*, Senlis, and Compiegne make copious use of the versus ad repetendum, whereas the other four make no or only sporadic mention (one of them, Monza, is actually a gradual, containing only the chants connected with the liturgy of the word). But even within the antiphoners of Senlis and Compiegne the choices for versus ad repetendum are not always in agreement (for example, on Septuagesima Sunday), leading to the conclusion that these were added after the transfer of these texts from Rome.

The purpose of the versus ad repetendum might have been one of these two:
- to cover an extended liturgical action, where the bishop's ascension of the altar steps was already tied into the doxology, and more music was needed to cover the rest of the entrance rite;
- to cover an extended liturgical action, when only one verse of the psalm had been completed before the doxology, as in Ordo XV.

Aurelian of Reome reports: "The Office of Mass, on the other hand, consists of antiphons called introits, so named because they are sung as people enter the basilica. The singing of the introit is prolonged . . . ."[20] This apparently refers to the versus ad repetendum.

In many ordines, the doxology is begun after a signal by the pope to the choir director, when the former ascends the altar steps.

Thus, if additional actions take place in the entrance rite, one or more additional verses would be necessary. There could even be a beautiful theological explanation for the use of the versus ad repetendum, worthy of an Amalarian discourse of symphonic proportions, as the entrance into the sanctuary is highlighted with praises of the Trinity, followed by specific verses of the psalm linked thematically to the season or feast.

The practice of the versus ad repetendum could also have found its origin in a misreading of Ordo I and its mention of "versu" for the final antiphon. In that connection we can also add a possibly mistaken placement of an antiphon between the two halves of the Gloria Patri, when Ordo I is misread toward the end of paragraph 8.[21]

In any case, the practice of adding versus ad repetendum seems to have been a common practice in Frankish and German sources, especially in the ninth century, taken to Italy during the Ottonian reform and dying out by the thirteenth century, as documented by ordines, pontificals, and chant books of the time. Chant books of the eighth through the thirteenth century show this pattern:

France and Germany
- Rheinau (Sextuplex), late eighth century: no versus ad repetendum
- Mont-Blandin (Sextuplex), around 800: few versus ad repetendum
- Compiegne (Sextuplex), ninth century: versus ad repetendum on major feasts
- Senlis (Sextuplex), ninth century: versus ad repetendum throughout
- Saint Gall 359, Cantatorium of the ninth century: frequent use of versus ad repetendum
- Laon 239, Antiphonale of the ninth to tenth century: only a handful of versus ad repetendum
- Corbie (Sextuplex), around 900: No versus ad repetendum
- Chartres 47, Antiphonale of the tenth century: versus ad repetendum for the first two Sundays of Advent only
- Saint Gall 339, Antiphonale of the tenth century: no versus ad repetendum
- Einsiedeln 121, Antiphonale of the tenth to eleventh century: only one versus ad repetendum, Easter
- Verdun 759 (thirteenth century): no versus ad repetendum

Italy
- Sta. Cecilia in Trastevere: Graduale of 1071: indicates versus ad repetendum throughout
- Lateran Vat. Lat. 5319 (twelfth to thirteenth century): occasional versus ad repetendum
- San Pietro F. 22 (thirteenth century): does not indicate any versus ad repetendum

This pattern, which is the same in the ordines and pontificals, would confirm that the use of versus ad repetendum peaked in France and Germany in the ninth century, that its admission into Italy would have coincided with the introduction of the Romano-German Pontifical in the tenth and eleventh centuries,[22] and that the practice there died out by the thirteenth century. However, we must be careful about making such assumptions, since many cathedrals that indicated no versus ad repetendum might have had versicularies that were used to indicate additional verses in separate books.

Tropes, florid passages on prosaic texts, were sometimes used to introduce the introit from before 850. Tropes are not mentioned at all in the ordines or pontificals and will not be discussed here.

An important facet of monastic psalmody, and thus also of the introit, is antiphonal singing. It is often difficult to ascertain exactly what each generation meant by the term antiphonal. It is hardly possible that the earliest examples would have resembled a performance practice as described by Amalar of Metz,[23] and particular practices differed greatly from one region to another.

Chapter 3

Monasticism and the Creation of the Introit

The most determinant factor in the spread of psalmody in the fourth and fifth centuries was the establishment of monastic communities. The recitation of the psalter became a daily practice for monks, and schemes developed by which the whole psalter was to be recited in a certain period of time, the standard being one week. The psalter was memorized not only by monks, but also by any educated person, since the study of the psalter was thought essential to the study of Latin. But what influence did the monastic movement exert on church music in Rome?

Monasteries were best suited to develop and maintain liturgical singing during the trying times of the fifth and sixth centuries.[1] It is difficult to tell, however, whether monasticism exerted a direct influence on the creation of the Mass proper, or whether the Mass proper influenced the creation of office music. Certainly the clue that the Roman Mass proper is based on psalmody should at the very least be an indication of a close link. In all likelihood, the two elements went hand-in-hand and developed side by side. Roman monasticism is little understood today because of the lack of documentary evidence.[2] We do know, however, that in Rome every basilica had its own monastic community, at one point numbering as many as 41, but that the distinction between the secular and monastic office was already blurred from the fifth century onward.[3]

It is important to understand that the recitation of the daily office had very little to do with the Mass. Monastic communities were founded for daily prayer, but monks attended weekly and feast day

Masses with the rest of the people. "Those brought up on the
heady Benedictine-revival literature of the liturgical movement will
recall references to the daily conventual Mass as 'the summit of the
divine office.' This view owes more to 19th century romanticism
than to reality. Daily Eucharist has nothing whatever to do with the
daily office."[4]

While daily Mass was already in place in Milan, Aquileia, Spain,
and North Africa by 400, this practice does not appear in Rome until
much later. The Mass, therefore, played no part in the daily prayer
of monks. Their daily routines were separated from the laity and clergy,
and many communities did not admit priests. The pre-Benedictine
Rule of the Master mentions that the lay abbot was to distribute daily
communion, but this was done at a communion service with pre-
consecrated hosts. The daily conventual Mass in Benedictine or other
Western monasteries does not appear until the Carolingian period.

Several fifth-century popes concerned themselves with the
establishment of monastic communities in Rome for the purpose
of singing chant. Sixtus (432–440) founded a monastery at the cata-
combs for singing chant, Leo the Great (440–461) established near
St. Peter's Basilica a monastic community for the observance of
the canonical hours, and Saint Hilary (461–468) founded two monasteries for the care of chant.[5]

Let us see in which way the monastic practice might be
reflected in the introits.

Musical Form

The earliest documented introits, as described by Ordo I around 700
(see appendix, Ordines Romani), consist of an antiphon, a psalm sung
to a psalm tone, the Gloria Patri, and a repeat of the antiphon. In this
way, it is a direct copy of the antiphonal form of office psalmody as
found to this day.

Amalar of Metz, in his "Liber officialis" (823), describes the
performance of monastic psalmody during vespers. We need to note
the absence of the Gloria Patri in the following paragraph, which has

been discussed already. Considering that by that time Charlemagne had already issued a decree regarding the Gloria Patri, we must assume that Amalar is referring only to office psalmody and that Charlemagne meant the Gloria Patri as sung during Mass.

> II. Liber officialis: De off. vespert: de quinque ei psalm. et ant.
>
> 10. Antiphona dicitur vox reciproca. Antiphona inchoatur ab uno unius cori, et ad eius symphoniam psalmus cantatur per duos coros; ipsa enim, id est antiphona, coniunguntur simul duo cori. Quanto enim melior est anima corpore, tanto melior est cantus animae quam corporis. Igitur intendendum est quae sit antiphona animae. Videtur nobis virtus dilectionis esse quae coniungit opera duorum fratrum simul.
>
> 11. Psalmi ad opera referuntur, antiphona ad illam dilectionem, qua uniusque fratri suo porrigit suum opus. Verbi gratia, unus legit et discit doctrinam in scola, alter seminat in campo; tempore fructus doctor seminanti porrigit doctrinam, sator doctori panem. Duobus coris alternatur antiphona, quoniam non potest minus esse caritas quam inter duos. Hanc vicissitudinem caritatis significant cantores, qui alternatim ex ultraque parte antiphonas levant.[6]

While the language is rather convoluted and full of theological hyperbole, and it is clear that a liturgical description is not the main purpose, we can nevertheless get a glimpse of the performance practice. However, we should point out that there have been as many interpretations of this text as there have been people attempting the translation:[7]

> The antiphon [in early medieval Latin, antiphon could also mean "an alternated liturgical chant"] is said with reciprocal voice [alternated]. The antiphon is begun by a member of one choir, and to his tune [or mode] the psalm is sung by [or between] two choirs. To it [read "ipsi . . . antiphonae"] are joined two choirs together [in other words, one singer intones, both choirs sing the psalm, possibly in alternation, followed by the repetition of the antiphon by both choirs] . . . . The antiphon is alternated between the two choirs . . . . The singers who lift up the antiphon alternately from each side symbolize this exchange of love [the next antiphon is intoned by a member of the other choir, and so on for the next of the five psalms].

Thus the scheme of this performance, divided between two facing choirs of singers, would be as shown in Table 3.1.

Table 3.1 Scheme of the Performance of the Introit

Left Side of the Choir	Right Side of the Choir
antiphon #1 (solo intones)	
	psalm #1, v. 1
psalm #1, v. 2	
	psalm #1, v. 3
psalm #1, v. 4	
etc.	
antiphon #1 (sung by both choirs)	
	antiphon #2 (solo intones)
psalm #2, v. 1	
	psalm #2, v. 2
etc. for all five psalms of vespers	

Except for the absence of the Gloria Patri, which in the case of Amalar has been discussed already, the form is identical to the introit described in Ordo I.

The earliest antiphoners do not contain music. Notation of music became part of Frankish/Gregorian antiphoners in the ninth century and of Old Roman antiphoners in the eleventh century. The Frankish sources indicate canticle tones for the psalm verses, whereas the Roman books give monastic psalm tones. If we assume that the Roman form might have been closer to the original chants at the time of transferal to the Frankish empire, this would indicate another instance where the musical use of psalmody in the monastery and in the stational church would have been identical. But then why would the Franks adopt the canticle tones? Considering that the antiphoners compiled right after the Carolingian reform did not contain musical notation, we really do not know what kind of tones were transferred. However, since the Northern canticle tones were used with the Gallican psalter and the Roman monastic psalm tones with the Roman, this could indicate that Rome had always used the monastic psalm tones with the introit psalm.

Musical Composition

The introit antiphons are very similar to the office antiphons, in that they are very compact and more neumatic and syllabic than melismatic. Medieval music theorists (for example, Aurelian of Reome, Hucbald, Guido, and John) all treat introit and communion antiphons with antiphons in general, that is, with the office antiphons. It should, however, be indicated that these are the versions of the Roman chants as found in the Gregorian repertoire, which may have been somewhat altered by their transmission to Frankish cantors.

The communion antiphons are of similar musical content to the introit antiphons, although the choice of texts is somewhat different. It is generally agreed that, because of this close similarity between introits and communions in regard to music and form, the two bodies of music would have been composed during roughly the same time period. Communions in some Frankish sources also indicated a versus ad repetendum. Practical experience has taught me the value of this invention. As part of our weekly Gregorian chant Mass, our schola sings the communion chant during the distribution of communion. In some instances the antiphon, assigned psalm verses, Gloria Patri, and the repeat of the antiphon are not enough to cover the distribution. At that point the schola will add several additional verses and conclude with the antiphon toward the end of communion, thus extending the composition to cover the action.

Choral Performance

We know from the form of the introit as described in Ordo I that it was a choral or schola chant, unlike the gradual, which contained solo verses. The term choral in the monastic tradition indicates the whole community, whereas the same word in Ordo I denotes a select group of "clerici." Let us examine the development of choral singing in both traditions.

For early monastic psalmody, solo singing was the rule.[8] Over the centuries, however, it became preferable and necessary for monastic communities to perform their office chorally. By the sixth century it was probably the preferred method of singing the psalms. Cassian mentions solo singing of the psalm, with everyone responding in the

Gloria Patri.[9] The Rule of the Master (520) indicates that solo singing is still the case and also mentions antiphons.[10] The Rule of Saint Benedict prescribes solo singing of psalms "in directum" (all the way through without refrains) for small communities, but for larger ones, in order to give each monk a chance at participating in singing the psalms, a communal refrain is added and sung at certain points within the psalm. And in the late sixth-century Rule of Paul and Stephen we encounter choral singing where a senior member begins and others come in on the second or third syllable.[11] In Vienne and Lyon, around 600, the cathedral office contained antiphonal psalms which were alternated between two choirs.[12] However, we have to assume that whenever a particular practice is mentioned in the documents, it would have been fairly well established already. As monastic organizations grew and established larger communities, solo singing became less practical, and choral singing became a necessity.

The musical forms of the Mass proper contain parallel forms in the monastic office. The tracts are examples of direct psalmody, the graduals responsorial, and the introits and communions antiphonal. Should we expect these forms to have been composed concurrently with the monastic parallel?

The tracts and graduals in Italian sources are in separate chant books, indicating that they were performed by a medium other than the schola cantorum. They are part of the "cantor chant" repertoire, which would have been sung by a soloist. The Gregorian usage, of course, blurred that line by lumping tracts and graduals with the other chants in the same books, which means that they were sung by a combination of schola and cantors in Carolingian churches.

Some say that the communion chants were in place in responsorial form from the earliest times. However, the sources that mention responsorial performance of Psalm 33 ("O taste and see") and others as part of the communion repertoire are all from the East, where the limited number of communion psalms actually became a part of the ordinary of the Mass. We have no indication what the practice was in Rome. In fact, among the 150 or so communions, Psalm 33 appears only once.

Numerical Sequencing

At first glance, the numerically ascending sequence of introit psalms on the Sundays after Pentecost appears to mirror the numerical programming often found in the office. In my doctoral dissertation, I hypothesized that the numerically ascending post-Pentecostal introits are an indicator that the readings for those Masses had not been firmly established, and that a monastic sense of programming was at work here, in a sense related to a "lectio continua." There is, however, another important significance that becomes clear only after examining the other genres of the Mass proper. See Table 3.2.

The numbering of Sundays indicated in the following table mirrors that of a Frankish simplification of the Roman system. The 23 formularies are run through, and then the twenty-third is repeated as many times as necessary to arrive at Advent. The Roman system divided this sequence into Pentecost (4 Sundays, 1–4), Apostles (near June 29, the feast of Saints Peter and Paul, 5 Sundays, 5, 6, 8–10 [7 was vacat, meaning the pope did not celebrate Mass that Sunday]), Lawrence (around August 10, the feast of Saint Lawrence, 6 Sundays, 11–16), and Angel (around September 15, the feast of Saints Cornelius and Cyprian, later changed to September 29, feast of the Archangel Michael, 7 Sundays, 17–23), whereby the needed repetition was made at the end of the Pentecost mini-season leading up to Apostles and at the end of Angel leading up to Advent.[13]

The numerical assignment of psalmic introit texts in this season is substantially different from that of the Lenten weekday communions, which run numerically without skips from 1 to 26. There are many reasons why this series might be so. I tend to believe that it indicates a rather early composition of texts. The Old Gelasian Sacramentary gives for the post-Epiphany and post-Pentecostal seasons a set of generic prayers, to be chosen at will; Mass texts were not assigned for those Sundays. If introits existed then, they would have been lumped together in a generic pool. The incomplete arrangement seen above supports the theory that these introits were once in a list of generic chants to be chosen ad hoc for the particular Sundays. While the Lenten weekday communions were assigned to fit the 26 weekdays, these introits were chosen from throughout the psalter, as though somebody had taken the psalter and marked several

Table 3.2 Post-Pentecostal Mass Propers

Sunday	Introit	Grad.	Alt. Gr.	Offert.	Comm.
1 PeI	Ps 12	Ps 40	Ps 6	Ps 5	Ps 9
2 PeII	Ps 17	Ps 119	Ps 8	Ps 6	Ps 12
3 PeIII	Ps 24	Ps 54	Ps 9	Ps 9	Ps 16
4 PeIV	Ps 26	Ps 78	Ps 9	Ps 12	Ps 17
5 ApI	Ps 26	Ps 83	Ps 18	Ps 15	Ps 26
6 ApII	Ps 27	Ps 89	Ps 26	Ps 16	Ps 26
7 [vac]	Ps 46	Ps 33	Ps 33	Dan	Ps 30
8 ApIII	Ps 47	Ps 43	Ps 43	Ps 17	Ps 33
9 ApIV	Ps 53	Ps 70	Ps 44	Ps 18	Mt
10 ApV	Ps 54	Ps 8	Ps 71	Ps 24	Ps 50
11 LaI	Ps 67	Ps 16	Ps 82	Ps 29	Prv
12 LaII	Ps 69	Ps 27	Ps 83	Ex	Ps 103
13 LaIII	Ps 73	Ps 33	Ps 89	Ps 30	Wis
14 LaIV	Ps 83	Ps 73	Ps 101	Ps 33	Jn
15 LaV	Ps 85	Ps 117	Ps 101	Ps 39	Jn
16 LaVI	Ps 85	Ps 117	Ps 106	Ps 39	Ps 70
17 AnI	Ps 118	Ps 101	Ps 117	Dn	Ps 75
18 AnII	Sir	Ps 112	Ps 121	Ex	Ps 95
19 AnIII	Ps 36,77	Ps 121	Ps 140	Ps 137	Ps 118
20 AnIV	Dn	Ps 144	Ps 142	Ps 136	Ps 118
21 AnV	Est	Ps 89	Ps 89	Jb	Ps 118
22 AnVI	Ps 129	Ps 132	Ps 132	Ps 129	Lk
23 AnVII	Jer	Ps 101	Ps 101	Est	Mk

selections, and another person at a later date decided to copy the selections out in the order in which he found the markings.

There is another striking numerical series that occurs during the post-Pentecostal season. The Mont-Blandin antiphoner in the *Antiphonal Missarum Sextuplex* indicates primary graduals and "item resp. grad.," in other words an alternate set of graduals for all Sundays except five. The Rheinau antiphoner contains only these alternates, but a complete set. On those same five Sundays, the Rheinau graduals are the same as the first set in the Mont-Blandin source, which points

to the conclusion that on those Sundays the primary gradual and the
alternate were the same, so there was no need for the scribe of the
Mont-Blandin document to notate them again. We now know that
there were two lists of graduals that were transferred to the Franks,
reflecting these two sets. But there is something else that is striking in
this series.

    The alternate list of graduals of the Mont-Blandin series in
the above table clearly shows numerical sequencing from Sundays 1
through 20 after Pentecost. This seems to indicate that these alternates
were also originally from an ad hoc series, and that a second series
was made at a later time, possibly when texts and readings were firmly
assigned to those Sundays. But why make a second series of graduals
and not proceed thus with the introits? The reason has to do with the
placement of these chants within the Mass. The introit, being placed
at the beginning of the Mass, is specific to the readings only on certain
specific feasts where the daily theme would be known in advance. The
introits during the seasons apply a general seasonal theme, since it
would not make much sense to sing about a particular reading before
that reading is proclaimed. The graduals, however, are intimately
connected with the readings; as a matter of fact, they are readings in
themselves, although proclaimed in a musical form. Therefore, when
readings were firmly assigned to the post-Pentecostal season, it was
necessary to establish a new series of graduals to go along with those
readings. Somehow the first series (called here the alternate) survived,
because, luckily for us, the pertinent documents had not been
destroyed and were used in the transmission of chants to the Franks.

    Other numerical sequences in the same post-Pentecostal
season apply to offertories and communions as well. Offertories use
Psalms 5, 6, 9, 12, 15, 16, 17, 18, 24, 29, Exodus 32, Psalms 30, 33, 39,
and 39 to the end of Lawrence (Roman series) or the sixteenth Sunday
(Frankish series). The communions run through the psalter with other
biblical references interspersed from the beginning to the Twenty-
third Sunday, with one notable exception, Lawrence 2 or the Eleventh
Sunday, the same Sunday, by the way, on which we find the offertory from Exodus. It does appear, however, that the communion list
had been adjusted, since the psalmic sequence is broken up significantly
by non-psalmic antiphons. As we have seen in our discussion of the

Lenten weekday communions, the relationship between communion texts and the readings was very important to early liturgists.

Another interesting fact in the communion series is the Roman Pentecost mini-season, the first four Sundays after Pentecost. Its communions are "Narrabo omnia" (Psalm 9), "Cantabo Domino" (Psalm 12), "Ego clamavi" (Psalm 16), and "Domine firmamentum" (Psalm 17). The first one is the duplicate of a Lenten weekday communion, and the other three are some of those same psalms that were replaced by Gospel antiphons when the scrutinies were moved to weekdays. None of these four belong into Maiani's core group, indicating that the exclusive communions were in place before the scrutinies were moved to Lenten weekdays in the late sixth century and these same psalms were moved to the post-Pentecostal season. Leaving out these four chants, we observe that the Lenten weekday communions run from Psalm 1 through 26, and the post-Pentecostal series from 26 to 118 (with an out-of-sequence Psalm 103 on Lawrence II), which might be an indication of a more comprehensive design.

I have already mentioned that Psalm 33 ("O taste and see" or "Gustate et videte") was mentioned in Eastern documents as a frequent communion psalm but appears in Roman sources only once. It appears in this very post-Pentecostal set. If we eliminate the four Lenten communions at the beginning of the list and the out-of-sequence Psalm 103, only eight psalms are left to be distributed between 23 to 26 Sundays. If it was part of an ad hoc group, Psalm 33, being one of them, would have received more opportunity for performance than just once.

I tried comparing all four numerical sequences to see whether there was an overall design. The curious thing about introits, offertories, and communions is that they use an incomplete series, almost as if the choice of texts was made by looking at the psalter, marking appropriate texts as they came up, and then stopping when a certain number of requisite texts had been achieved. The introits run from the beginning to Psalm 85, the offertories only to Psalm 39, and communions to Psalm 118. The only comprehensive series is found in the graduals.

There is remarkably little duplication of psalms; five psalms are used in two genres, and four are used in three. There is even less duplication in antiphon or respond texts. Only two texts use the same psalm and verse: "Protector noster" (Psalm 83) appears as an introit and a gradual, but the second half of the text differs; and "Unam petii" (Psalm 26) belongs to a communion and a gradual, but here the communion antiphon adds more text than is assigned to the gradual. Since we are dealing with two different translations, the gradual list must have been created at a different time from the other three. Also, greater care was taken in the gradual list to cover the whole psalter, since the gradual was considered a reading. The next most complete set, the communions, should not surprise us; we have already noted the closeness of communion texts to the readings.

The numerical sequencing seen in the introit, the gradual, the offertory, and the communion in the post-Pentecostal season helps us date these texts, and clearly the non-numerical chants in that season belong to a later time period. The alleluias were transmitted to the Franks in the only remaining ad hoc list for this season; they do not appear as firm assignments until much later in the Roman antiphoners Vat. lat. 5319 and San Pietro F. 22.

It seems, then, that the numerical programming found in the post-Pentecostal introits has no connection to a monastic "lectio continua," or a system by which the 150 psalms are chanted in a particular order every week, but is rather an indication of an ad hoc list of chants which later became standardized. Any notion that the retention of this sequence after the assignment of other Mass texts shows monastic programming can be put to rest by considering the graduals, which changed from a numerical order to an order specific for the particular readings, and the communion list, which interjected strategic non-psalmic antiphons into an otherwise numerical sequence. The most logical reason for the proliferation of numerical sequences (rather than a random order) in these ad hoc repertoires is the way these texts would have been indicated in the earliest times: in the form of margin notes in psalters, placing them automatically in numerical order. The incomplete use of the psalter in introits and offertories and to a lesser extent in the communions supports this hypothesis.

REPERTORIAL DISCONTINUITY TO OFFICE CHANTS

There is hardly any repertorial continuity between the introit and the office antiphon texts. The initial thought would point against monastic influence. However, quite the opposite could be true: the antiphons of the monastic office in Rome and the introit antiphons could have been composed at the same time to complement each other. We know that certain antiphons were written for certain offices, so we should expect to find a distinct corpus of antiphon texts for the introits. In regard to the communions, it must be mentioned that several communions of the Easter season are derived from the Gospels, but never the Gospel of the day. They are, instead, textual duplicates of three antiphons and seven responsories from the offices of Ascension and Pentecost,[14] indicating that the composers were very familiar with the office. But in regard to the whole repertoire of Gregorian chant this is a very minuscule proportion. The repertorial discontinuity and avoidance of textual duplication of the introits, as compared with the chants of the divine office, would seem to indicate that the development of the two repertoires of Mass and office were closely related.

Possible Link to a Specific Office

The liturgies we celebrate during Holy Week are very ancient indeed, the Easter Vigil being the oldest. This liturgy contains several characteristics of interest to our discussion:
• The priest enters in silence.
• The Mass actually begins with the Gloria. The Service of Light and the readings with their canticles and prayers were originally all pre-Mass activities having to do with the pre-baptismal vigil.
• The alleluia is actually a gradual. It was common from the earliest mention of graduals in the Easter season to choose psalms that contain the word "Alleluia." Hence the use of two alleluias in the liturgies of the Easter season; one is technically the gradual, the other the alleluia proper, although the forms are now the same. During the Easter Vigil, however, the alleluia is placed between the epistle and the Gospel, the original place for the gradual. There is no second alleluia. This only alleluia, moreover, bears no musical similarity to other alleluia compositions. It is connected with Psalm 117 (118), and modern Lectionaries add several verses of that psalm to accord with the original intent. The Easter Vigil alleluia is therefore nothing more than a gradual with an alleluia refrain. Most scholars believe that this melody is very ancient, possibly as old as the Vigil itself. The Easter

Vigil, therefore, contains a gradual but no alleluia, which was added to the Mass proper in general much later.

The second point here is central. The Introit/Kyrie couplet did not exist at the time the Easter Vigil liturgy was fully developed. In later sources, however, we find the triplet Introit/Kyrie/Gloria to begin Mass on other days. Where did the introit and Kyrie come from? Because the introit resembles monastic psalmody, might this couplet have been inspired by a monastic office?

This highly speculative hypothesis relies on the form of some minor offices that were often celebrated before the capitular Mass. The sources do not permit us to establish this with certainty for Rome between the fourth and the seventh century, but it seems to have been the practice elsewhere. Although much later in Milan, the twelfth-century Beroldus documents the singing of a psalm with antiphon at the end of the office, as the procession enters the stational church, presumably followed by the ingressa. There is also documentary evidence that the community Mass of the ninth and tenth centuries at ecclesiastical centers was generally celebrated after the office of terce.[15] In some places, this is still the case today. We can assume that this practice existed long before the ninth century in some form. Two essential elements of the minor offices were an antiphonal psalm and a threefold Kyrie. Because the Kyrie's entrance into the liturgy is shrouded in as much mystery as the introit's, I would like to offer the possibility that the use of an antiphon with psalm and Gloria Patri, followed directly by a Kyrie, received its inspiration (not its repertoire) from a minor office being celebrated before the principal Mass.

Conclusions

The evidence of the musical performance of the introit and the development of the texts indicates many similarities to monastic antiphonal psalmody. Later evidence, although not from Rome, shows a direct connection with this type of monastic psalmody and the beginning of the stational Mass. Even if we cannot conclude that the Roman introit grew out of the monastic tradition, we can at the very least infer that the introit and monastic antiphonal psalmody developed side by side.

Chapter 4

The Origin of the Introit

The *Antiphonale Missarum Sextuplex* contains the oldest chant books and thereby the earliest documented Roman chant texts available. We know for a fact (discussed below) that these Italian and Frankish books contain the original Roman texts. Before the main corpus of these introit texts could have been composed, three requirements would have had to be fulfilled:
• an effort to order the Mass texts according to the liturgical year
• a choir capable of performing and composing the introit chants
• a need to elaborate the entrance rite with song

The effort to order the Mass texts came in the form of early Sacramentaries and Lectionaries. The Sacramentaries, or collections of Mass prayers, were used in some form from the late fourth through the thirteenth century, when they were replaced by the Missal.[1] They took on their official form in the mid-ninth century as authentic Carolingian service books.

By the end of the fourth century, Sacramentaries per se did not exist in complete book form, but rather in the form of official compilations and collections of prayer formularies. These were promulgated at the instigation of local councils and synods: the council of Hippo of 393, for example, decreed that all prayers be addressed to the Father; Fulgentius of Ruspe (468–533) describes doxological formulas; and the second council of Mileve, 416, forbade all unapproved prayer texts. Prayer texts for particular feasts were collected in "libelli," and collections of these were called "libelli missarum" or "liber sacramentorum." From the fifth century on, the compilation of Sacramentaries was a regular duty of local bishops. In Rome around 500—where the liturgical year would have already included most of the stational Masses, including Christmas, Christmas season,

Epiphany, a full Lent without Thursdays (the scrutinies would be celebrated on the Third, Fourth, and Fifth Sundays), Easter, Easter season, Pentecost, and a variety of other temporal and sanctoral feasts—the liturgical texts were read from libelli, which were most likely kept in central locations. It would have been quite easy to move feasts around in such a system, as we have already seen when the scrutinies were moved to weekdays at some point in the late sixth century.

In Rome, the *Liber pontificalis* reports of Pope Gelasius I (492–496) that he "fecit sacramentorum praefationes et orationes cauto sermone." Although no such service book has come down from Roman sources earlier than the sixth century, we can find traces of authentic collections of liturgical formularies at Rome well before Gelasius.

It is generally believed that the earliest Sacramentaries were compiled in the late fifth century, about 50 years before the first documented existence. Even when Sacramentaries were compiled, Mass formularies were very localized with no intended uniformity. The earliest extant "Libelli missarum" is found in the Codex LXXXV of Verona, also called the Veronese or Leonine Sacramentary. But this compilation dates from 537–555 and consists of a random collection of Masses. The so-called Old Gelasian Sacramentary survives only in a Frankish manuscript of around 750 and draws upon a series of Lateran libelli of the sixth and early seventh century.

The Easter Vigil was celebrated by Christian communities from the earliest times. In Rome there was always a strong connection between baptism and the Easter Vigil. The catechumens would spend the night listening to readings and prayers, and at daybreak they would be baptized and join the rest of the community for the Eucharist. While the earliest reports of this vigil and service are very sketchy, some readings seem to have been very central to the celebration of the vigil of readings, but there is no evidence that a particular choice or order of readings was followed year by year in the early Church. They were, however, set both in Rome and Jerusalem by the fourth century. Then, as the liturgical year expanded, so did the need for uniformity of readings for assigned feasts, which in the early centuries were very small in number.

Before Lectionaries, readings were indicated directly in Bibles or Bible fragments in the form of margin notes. As a matter of fact, the earliest surviving Lectionaries are nothing more than indices for

Bibles, giving the beginnings and endings of the readings and possibly Eusebian numbers, which were a standardized system of running one sequence of numbers through a whole book of the New Testament. The forerunners of the earliest Lectionaries existed as early as the fifth century, and the earliest extant examples are from the end of the fifth century. The earliest extant Roman Lectionaries contain sections composed around 600.

Economy of material and manpower is apparent in the development of Sacramentaries and Lectionaries. Manuscripts had to be copied by hand on cowhide. It is estimated that about 100 cattle would have had to relinquish their hides for the production of one complete Bible. When changes were made, existing material was reused wherever possible, and only the minimum necessary was actually written or copied. Changing a translation, as for example from Old Latin to the Vulgate, would have been a very slow process, since the production of new materials would have taken decades, and people would have been reluctant to part with their precious old books.

With prayers and readings already discussed, the only other element is music. The earliest antiphoners date from the late eighth century but show a mature development. In the absence of earlier evidence, we can only conjecture about earlier books. The extent to which chant books or chant libelli were produced at an early time depends on the nature and development of these texts themselves. If Mass chants were originally non-variable, there would have been no need for chant books to tie into the liturgical year. However, the texts that appear in the eighth-century books exhibit the same variable character as the prayers and the readings. Moreover, the numerical sequencing of ad hoc groups of chants in the Lenten and post-Pentecostal seasons is an early sign pointing to a preference for variable chants. In addition, the chant texts for the oldest feasts utilize Old Latin sources of before 500. We must thus assume that the beginnings of the compilation of chant texts coincided with the standardization of prayers and readings.

A choir capable of performing and composing the introit chants would probably have been found in an ecclesiastical or a monastic community. During the first few centuries after the Edict of Milan, each basilica in Rome had its own monastic community but a very small number of clerics.[2] The ecclesiastical community was not a practical forum for the development of these chants. The line between ecclesiastic and monastic was already blurred, however, so that the function of the monastic community spilled over into the realm of the ecclesiatic quite easily. This, in turn, developed over time into the breeding ground for the Roman schola cantorum. In medieval usage, the word "schola" did not necessarily imply a school. The official definition was a building that housed a company, association, or body.[3] This could include craft guilds, a bishop's retinue of ecclesiastics, a body of priests attached to a cathedral, a dormitory, or especially in Rome, a colony of aliens established as a corporation (scole peregrinorum). It was an official title with rights and responsibilities. The usage of the term schola cantorum, therefore, implies a community, living together and attached to the papal court, whose purpose was to apply and perfect the art of liturgical singing. It was precisely this schola cantorum that was responsible for transmitting the cantus romanus to the Franks in the eighth century.

The need to elaborate the entrance rite was apparent immediately after the Edict of Milan of 313. Christian worship moved from the house church into large basilicas and immediately became more formal. Christianity was now a visible institution of public character. In early Christian worship there was no need for an entrance rite. The presbyter was most likely already present in the room and would begin the liturgy with the greeting. In Constantinian and post-Constantinian times, however, the pope or bishop or priest needed to enter the basilica, creating the need for a procession. Exactly when music became part of this rite and what the nature of that music was is pure conjecture. We do know, however, that while Milan, Gaul, Constantinople, and Jerusalem opted for non-variable or limited-variable entrance chants, Rome eventually adopted a variable style of introit, indicating that outside influences had little to do with its creation.

The introit was the last part of the Mass proper to be added. While the present communion antiphons, which share many musical characteristics with the introit antiphons, might have been composed at about the same time, singing a psalm at communion had been a part of Christian worship since the earliest times.

The later fourth-century Mass psalmody is lector chant. The tracts attest to this and might be seen as older than the other parts of the Mass proper. The responsorial form of the graduals suggests solo performance of the verses with congregational refrains, at least if we are to believe that these compositions were originally much simpler. However, by the end of the seventh century, the introits and communions show that they were composed in an environment that favored choral performance,[4] since they reflect the same choral character that was described later in the monastic tradition. "Introits and communions consistently maintain the two essential traits of uniqueness and liturgical appropriateness throughout the entire church year, while graduals, offertories . . . do not."[5] This would seem to indicate that introits and communions were the last musical pieces to be added to the Mass chant repertoire.

McKinnon suggests that the seeming incompleteness and frequent borrowings in the cycle of graduals is a sign that the composers could not deal with the size of the overall project of compiling the Mass proper.[6] I would rather see it as an indication that the graduals were originally composed at a time when the stational system, with its assigned Mass texts, was not completely structured, and that the seeming completeness of the introit cycle points to a later date. Regarding the development of the gradual, sources of around 400 (albeit non-Roman) attest to spirited congregational participation in the psalm between the readings, which is hardly possible with the chants of the first notated books. Therefore, I am speculating that graduals did have direct simpler antecedents, which were later elaborated by cantorial embellishment.

Ordo I shows a mature form of the introit and a highly developed hierarchical schola cantorum. The introduction of the introit must have occurred some time before Ordo I. The absence of clear documentary evidence makes it difficult to pinpoint the exact decade, or even the century, of the introit's birth. It seems that every authority has his own opinions on the matter. Alberto Turco places the origin of the introit in the period between 492 and 525 (time of Gelasius I and after).[7] Ekenberg hypothesizes that the introit became part of the Roman Mass in the sixth century.[8] McKinnon's whole premise behind *The Advent Project* is the creation of the entire Roman Mass Proper in the later seventh century. I tend to agree with Turco's dating for reasons that will be explained later in this chapter, with the possibility of some introit texts dating even further back into the fifth century.

During the late fifth and the early sixth centuries, there were several popes who concerned themselves with a "yearly cycle" of chants, an ordering of chants according to the liturgical year. The *Liber pontificalis* reports that yearly chant was published by Gelasius (492–496), Symmacus (498–514), John I (523–526), and Boniface II (530–532). In addition it is said of Hormisdas (514–523) that he brought the clergy together to teach them the psalms.[9] It is not clear which chants were ordered in these "yearly cycles" or what type of psalmody was taught. But we can be sure that the process of compiling the cantus romanus began at an early time, even though these chants would change considerably over centuries of oral tradition. The mature Gregorian repertoire, as passed down in the *Antiphonale Missarum Sextuplex,* reflects the liturgical calendars of Gregory II (725–731) and Gregory III (731–741).[10]

ENTRANCE CHANTS IN NON-ROMAN RITES

Rome did not exist in a vacuum. Through various councils and synods, the papal court became familiar with the practices of other Christian rites, as was already shown to be the case with Saint Ambrose, who instituted singing at the entrance after attending a council in which he witnessed this practice by Eastern clerics. Undoubtedly, ecclesiastical authorities in Rome would have been exposed to the practice of singing an opening chant in several of the other rites.

At the emperor's court in Constantinople, during the fifth and early sixth century, the choir was a compulsory part of the Byzantine liturgy. At the beginning of the service, there were three antiphons (Trisagion). Later, three psalms were added, chosen according to the day and interspersed with refrains, which were also changeable.[11] The Gallican rite began with the antiphona ad praelegendum with psalm verses; the Old Spanish rite with the praelegendum; and the Milanese Rite with the ingressa, which did not involve psalmody.[12]

Rome was always slow to adopt new traditions. The evidence of entrance chants in other parts of the Christian world and the complete silence from Rome would seem to indicate that this practice was begun somewhat later. Whether there was any direct inspiration from one of the other rites is debatable. There is no repertorial continuity between the Roman introit and entrance chants of other traditions, and, moreover, the form itself is unique amongst entrance chants. Therefore, any outside influence could not have gone far beyond inspiration. As we will see, however, the advent of the introit for stational Masses is contemporaneous with the institution of entrance chants in other rites.

THE USE OF PSALMODY IN SYNAGOGUE AND EARLY CHRISTIAN WORSHIP

The book of Psalms is at the heart of the introits. About two-thirds of the 145 introit antiphons are psalmic, as are all verses. Moreover, while contemporary practice has greatly reduced the use of the psalms in the context of the introit, originally a whole psalm, or a substantial portion thereof, would have been chanted.

Many people believe that the roots of present day Christian worship lie in the synagogue service of the early apostolic times, and that early Christian communities adopted the practice of psalm singing from the synagogue. "Music historians are virtually unanimous in attributing the source of early Christian psalmody to the synagogue." "The so-called Liturgy of the Word that preceded the Eucharist appears to have been modelled after the scripture-centered order of synagogue worship. And when one observes that the principal vehicle of early Christian chant was the Old Testament Book of Psalms, it seems a natural assumption that the singing of those psalms was a practice borrowed from the synagogue."[13] "Until recently it has been assumed that the Jewish Book of Psalms constituted a chief source of texts for singing in the early church, and that continuity must have existed between Jewish and early Christian worship. This view is no longer accepted."[14]

The Talmud describes temple music and its proper psalms.[15] The Hebrew word for synagogue is *beth ha-knesset,* or "house of assembly"; in Greek synagogue means "a coming together." Synagogues were meeting places used not exclusively for religious services. The synagogue service consisted of readings from the Torah (Pentatuch) and translation, followed by a sermon, and shema and tefillah (confession of faith and benedictions). Prayer is never mentioned in connection with the synagogue, as it is with the temple.[16] However, many functions of temple worship were taken over by the synagogue after the destruction of the temple in 70 AD, but "psalm singing . . . was one of the last elements of temple worship to be taken up in the synagogue."[17] It is absent from the documents until the sixth century AD.

The question of prayer provides the only proper context for the question of psalmody.[18] Contrary to Dix, there is no documentary evidence of psalmody in the synagogue service before the destruction of the temple in 70 AD, and even then it took almost five centuries for the psalms to appear in any regularized way.[19] The exception is the Hallel (Psalms 113–118), which is mentioned in the context of private and public recitation on feast days (for example, at the end of the Passover meal), and it could have been used in synagogues as well.[20] The passage in Matthew 26:30 is often considered a reference to the Hallel, "after the psalms had been sung, they left for the Mount of Olives."[21]

The Mishnah (redacted 200 AD) and the Jerusalem and Babylonian Talmuds (redacted 400–500 AD) make no mention of psalms in the synagogue service. Even the eighth-century Sopherim expresses scruples about the use of psalms in the synagogue because of the association with temple sacrifice.[22]

The common evening meal was the principal venue of Christian psalmody in the first three centuries.[23] Psalm 33 is often mentioned in Eastern sources as a communion hymn because of verse 8: "Taste and see the goodness of the Lord." But references to song are more common after the end of Christian persecutions.

In the fourth and fifth centuries, there was a great wave of enthusiasm for the Old Testament psalms. There had been nothing like it before or after in Christianity or Judaism. Basil, John Chrysostom, Jerome, Augustine, Ambrose, and Niceta all wrote commentaries on the psalms. There is considerable evidence of psalms within the liturgy of the word in the late fourth and early fifth centuries. This seems to have been regularized to some degree by Pope Celestine.[24] Moreover, because of the increased size of the assembly and consequently the need for a more regular and formal structure during the course of the fourth century after the Edict of Milan, the psalms were no longer freely chosen and sung by individual members of the community, but were now fixed and performed by an officially appointed cantor.[25]

Among ordinary people, however, the knowledge of psalms must have been rather modest. Saint John Chrysostom complains,

"Most of you know filthy songs, but who would be able to recite just one single psalm?" He suggested knowing the morning and evening psalms (62, 140) by heart. Caesarius of Arles (sixth century) suggested Psalm 50 (Miserere) and 90 (Qui habitat).[26]

One aspect responsible for the rapid spread of psalm singing was the establishment of monastic communities, beginning in the fourth century. "Virtually all the outstanding ecclesiastical leaders of the later 4th century lived as monks at some point in their careers."[27] They would have been used to reciting the psalter on a daily basis. Lauds and Vespers were soon celebrated in ecclesiastical centers as a "cathedral office." Urban monastic communities added their own offices (Terce, Sext, None). For Rome, the difference between the cathedral and the monastic office was inconsequential when the delineation between the clerical and monastic elements became sufficiently blurred.

"Students of early Christian chant are increasingly of the opinion that, until the later 4th century, psalms figured in the Christian liturgy as readings rather than set musical pieces."[28] These readings, however, would most likely have involved simple recitation tones out of which grew the psalm tones. As a matter of fact, there is evidence that even the readings and the Gospels were proclaimed to simple musical formulae.

The report about Pope Celestine I (d. 432) in the *Liber pontificalis*, regarding the institution of a cycle of psalms taken from the 150 psalms before the "sacrificium," must be mentioned in any discussion of early psalmody: "He instituted that David's 150 psalms be sung before the sacrificium in alternation from [by?] all, which heretofore had not been done, only the reading of the letter of blessed Paul and the holy gospel."[29]

There is no doubt that Celestine refers to singing ("psalli") and not reciting the psalms. Moreover, the words "antephanatim ex omnibus," which incidentally does not appear in the earliest edition of the book, can have different meanings: sung in an alternating fashion by all present, sung in an alternating fashion from all psalms, or chosen selectively from all of them.[30]

The most important question in this passage, however, is whether it refers to the introit or some other part of the Mass. Jungmann, on the basis of this quote about Celestine in the

Liber pontificalis, claims that at the time of the origin of this level of the *Liber pontificalis*, before the middle of the sixth century, the practice of singing the psalmic introit had already been practiced for a long time.[31] More skeptical is Leitner, who questions whether Pope Celestine's quote in the Liber pontificalis, which assigns 150 psalms to the feasts at the beginning of the Eucharist, had anything to do with the introduction of the introit.[32] Peter Jeffery argues in favor of the institution of variable gradual psalmody by Pope Celestine.

The term "sacrificium" in the fourth and fifth centuries sometimes meant the second half of the worship service, following the homily. A psalm sung "ante sacrificium" could therefore refer to the entrance, the readings, or the offertory. The term "psalli" might not apply to tracts and graduals, since they were considered part of the readings. Undoubtedly, experts will continue to debate this issue for a long time. We must consider, however, that this official standardization by Celestine might have been a common practice before 432.

What the *Liber pontificalis* attributes to Celestine, then, is the singing of either the gradual psalms or tracts, selected from the 150 psalms, or the offertory psalmody, or the introit psalmody.

THE SCHOLA CANTORUM

In his *Advent Project*, McKinnon places the creation of the introits within the parameter of the schola cantorum. He argues that the establishment of such an elite group of singers could only have occurred during times of peace, prosperity, and spiritual welfare, and that the sixth century would not have been a good time for such an establishment. He argues further that the schola cantorum, within the span of a generation, compiled existing chants and then added its own compositions to complete the yearly cycle. One consideration, however, which makes this hypothesis difficult to accept, is that there is too much evidence pointing to whole segments of the repertoire already being in place before the mid-seventh century, at least as far as texts is concerned. The question is, however, whether the schola cantorum, per se, was responsible for the introits, or whether the schola cantorum grew out of another antecedent under which the bulk of the chant material was developed and transmitted to future singers. Without a doubt, the foundation and maintenance of a choral

440–461	Leo the Great
Mid-fifth century	all tituli of the Lenten stational system have been constructed; Ash Wednesday in place
452	Attila the Hun ravages Northern Italy; Leo intercedes and persuades the Huns to withdraw
455	Rome pillaged for 14 days by the Vandals under Genseric, despite intercession of Leo; as the power of the emperors decreases, the power of the popes increases
475	Roman Empire falls
Late fifth century	Quinquagesima added to calendar
475–526	Ostrogothic King Theodoric; disputes with Rome over antipope Laurentius; Rome constantly under threat of pillage; drastic population decrease in Rome; Church's wealth greatly diminished
Early sixth century	scrutinies moved to weekdays and increased to seven in number
526–536	Gothic tyranny reigns in Rome
536	Eastern Roman troops oust Goths from Rome, then are beseiged by Goths under Vitiges, who cuts aqueducts; Pope Sylverius plots with Goths, is caught, and sent into exile in Asia Minor
544	Totila attacks Rome and takes it in 546; Pope Vigilius flees and is taken to Constantinople
Sixth century	third Christmas Mass added, Mass at Dawn, station: St. Anastasia
Mid-sixth century	Sexagesima added to calendar
568	Italy invaded by Lombards under Alboin
Late sixth century	Advent added to Church calendar; its appearance at the beginning of the liturgical year is found first in chant books at a time when Sacramentaries and Lectionaries still begin with the Vigil of Christmas; these chant books, however, date from the late eighth century
Late sixth century	Septuagesima added to calendar
590–604	Gregory the Great

institution in the fifth or sixth century would have been extremely difficult during several decades of those centuries. However, there were several windows of opportunity. We also have to keep in mind that there were other liturgical developments that took place in the Church at that time (work on the Sacramentary and Lectionary, establishment of the Advent season, continued construction of churches), and advances that had been made previously were not undone. In addition, during those troubled times, we must seek liturgical and musical innovation and maintenance in the monasteries, not necessarily at the papal court. Let us look closer at the timeline on page 52.

Alberto Turco's proposed dates for the composition of the introit (492–525) fall into the reign of the Ostrogothic kings. While Rome was constantly under the threat of pillage, the population of the city decreased dramatically, and the church's wealth was diminishing, the reign of Theodoric was relatively enlightened. And although Goths were Arian Christians, they did respect the bishop of Rome. The turbulent time between 526 and 568, however, was not good, and the last 30 or so years before Gregory the Great were characterized by ecclesiastical decadence as reflected in papacies that were bought and sold. And yet, during the late sixth century, Advent was finalized at four weeks.

Gregory the Great, a Benedictine abbot, sought to reform the decadent ecclesiastical situation. Having made conciliatory overtures toward the Lombards, he could devote himself to matters of the Church. He imposed strict and severe superintendence and issued the equivalent of a monastic rule in his "Rules for the Pastoral Office." During his papacy, the sphere of influence of the Roman Church greatly increased by sending missionaries to England and winning Spain back from Arianism. He also placed many monks into high adminis-trative positions, for which he was greatly resented by the Roman clergy. Gregory's own otherwise prolific writings do not mention music, yet John the Deacon says in the ninth century that Gregory the Great established the Schola Cantorum. In light of recent scholarship, it is questionable how much credence we can give John the Deacon. The first hints of the schola appear in the *Liber pontificalis* of the late seventh century with Leo II, Benedict II, and Sergius I.[33] Given the fact that the Advent introits have a newer text than others (to be discussed later), the bulk of the other repertoire must have been composed somewhat earlier than Gregory.

There is a remarkable homogeneity among the introit anti-phons. These were entirely new compositions showing a deliberate thematic program. At first glance, it would seem that these were written over no more than a generation or two. However, there is considerable evidence (again to be cited later in this chapter) that the compilation of these chants and texts occurred in stages over a longer period of time.[34]

The influx of pilgrims to Rome in the seventh century provided additional revenue that would have made the maintenance and development of a non-monastic schola cantorum possible. The *Liber diurnus,* toward the end of the seventh century, mentions an ordo cantorum that sang at papal Masses. The Vita of Pope Sergius I (687–701) in the *Liber pontificalis* mentions a schola cantorum. He was taken into the clergy in the reign of Pope Adeodatus II (672–676). The entry reads: "He was studious and capable in the ministry of singing and handed over to the prior cantorum for teaching."[35] This seems to indicate that the schola was well established by 675. McKinnon places the time of its creation between Gregory the Great and Adeodatus (602–672).[36] However, as argued before, it is likely that a monastic antecedent of the schola existed already before the sixth century, which gradually became more clerical as the line between ecclesiatic and monastic began to blur. The issue of the origin of the schola cantorum is shrouded in complexity, especially in regard to the basilical monastic system. While the founding of the schola cantorum as an ecclesiastical group of singers devoted to the composition and maintenance of chant by one particular pope is possible, we must assume that the monastic influence on its creation must have been substantial.

In the ninth century, the schola cantorum was a choir school for boys, where the students ate and slept. Boys of good voice were found in other schools and brought to the schola cantorum. The sons of commoners then became chamber servants (cubicularii), while the sons of noble descent did not.

Ordo XXXVI, Saint Gall, around 897, says the following:[37]

> At first, boys of good voice are found in whatever school, taken from there, and nourished in the schola cantorum, and after that they are made chamber-servants. If they, however, are boys of noble descent, they are nourished steadfastly in the bedchamber.

DEVELOPMENT OF BIBLICAL TEXTS

We have already examined the development of the Sacramentary and the Lectionary. The development of biblical language itself, however, is much more complex. Greek was the language of the Church until around 200 in North Africa and 250 in Rome, when it was replaced by Latin. "Old Latin" versions of various parts of the Bible appeared from the second century, done in various locations by various translators. However, no complete Old Latin Bibles exist. These translations were intended for the ill-educated and called "Vulgate," but not in the present sense of the term. The term "Vulgate," as applied to the present Latin bible, did not come into use until the sixteenth century. For this work, when we use the term "Vulgate," it will refer to the present Latin Bible.

From the examination of various chant texts, we see that different Old Latin versions were used at different times. Compare, for example, Christmas Dawn (Lux fulgebit hodie super nos: quia natus est nobis Dominus et vocabitur Admirabilis, Deus, Princeps pacis, Pater futuri saeculi, cuius regni non erit finis) with Christmas Day (Puer natus est nobis, et filius datus est nobis: cuius imperium super humerum eius: et vocabitur nomen eius, magni consilii Angelus). Christmas Day was celebrated in Rome already in 336 (although this text might have been added much later), and Christmas Dawn was added in the sixth century. Both texts use part of the same quote, but not only is the Latin translation different, the Septuagint bases from which the translations were made differ as well.

The one person most responsible for the present-day Vulgate was Saint Jerome. He translated the Old Testament directly from Hebrew, for which he was severely criticized by his contemporaries. Most scholars and clerics preferred translations from the Septuagint (Greek), since the Christian Church found its root in Greek Jewry. Even Gregory the Great, who was an ardent defender of Jerome's work, frequently quoted Old Latin texts in his sermons where he could have used Jerome's translations.

The deuterocanonical books of the Old Testament (Wisdom, Sirach, Baruch, and 1 and 2 Maccabees) were not translated by Jerome and appear in the Vulgate essentially in one of the Old Latin forms. Of the New Testament books in the Vulgate, all have an

Old Latin base and were revised against the original Greek. Jerome revised the Gospels, but it is not known who revised the other New Testament books. We have no conclusive evidence that he translated the Acts of the Apostles, the epistles, and Revelation, but it is clear that the versions in the Vulgate are not Old Latin.[38]

As far as Jerome's work is concerned, the chronological order is as follows:

- 383 Revision of the Gospels
- after 386 Gallican Psalter, on the basis of the Septuagint of the Hexapla
- 390–405 translations from Hebrew: books of Samuel and Kings, Hebrew psalter, the prophets, Job, Ezra, Nehemiah, Chronicles, Proverbs, Ecclesiastes, the Song of Songs, the Pentatuch, Joshua, Judges, Ruth, Esther, and probably toward the end of that period Tobit and Judith

Of the books of the New Testament that are not Jerome's, the first trace of the Vulgate texts appears in the writings of Pelagius and his circle at the beginning of the fifth century. The earliest trace of the Old Testament books of the Vulgate that are not Jerome's appears in the oldest complete Latin Bible, the Codex Amiatinus, written in Northumbria soon after 700,[39] but the origin of those texts is thought to be much older.

Many manuscripts of the various books of the Bible continued to be copied, and the texts were continually revised. The most important revision occurred under Alcuin of York at Charlemagne's court. This became the basis for the Paris Bible of the thirteenth century, which in turn was used as the base for the first printed Bible. Then there were only a few changes until the first official Roman edition of 1592 under Clement VIII. It is important to note that the Vulgate did not become the official norm for the Catholic Church until 1592.

Because the psalter is at the heart of the chant repertoire, we need to examine this subject in more detail:

Roman Psalter: Pope Damasus asked Saint Jerome to edit a correction of the Old Latin version of the Gospels against the Greek. In his preface ("Novum opus"), Saint Jerome talks about a correction of the Old Latin psalter texts; this correction is thought to be the

Roman psalter, composed about 384, while Saint Jerome was in Rome.
Still used in St. Peter's Basilica in Rome, it was used elsewhere in
Italy until replaced by the Gallican psalter under Pius V (1566–1572),
and it is the basis for chants sung at Mass in Gregorian and Old
Roman chant. It should be pointed out that Jerome's authorship of the
Roman psalter is disputed. He prefaced the Gallican and the Hebrew
psalters, but we do not have a preface to the Roman psalter. Some
authorities (for example, Dom DeBruyne) claim that Jerome used the
Roman psalter, which in fact might be an Old Latin version, to create
his first edition, which is now lost.

   Gallican Psalter: Saint Jerome found in the library of Caesarea
in Palestine Origen's *Hexapla,* which contained a psalter in six columns.
The fifth column was Origen's own edition of the Septuagint version with splits and asterisks to mark redundancies and deficiencies in
the Septuagint as compared to the Hebrew. Jerome used this version
to make his own translation into Latin. The Gallican psalter was
used North of the Alps and replaced the Hebrew version (see below)
when the Vulgate Bible was assembled under Alcuin, hence the
name Gallican.[40]

   Hebrew Psalter: This was a new translation by Saint Jerome
about 400 from original Hebrew sources. Used in Spain, it did not
make it into the Vulgate, because the Gallican psalter was more
popular North of the Alps.[41]

   Alcuin of York came to the Frankish empire in 793 and died
there in 804. At Charlemagne's instruction, he assembled Vulgate
Bible fragments into one Bible. The question arose about which psalter
to incorporate. Technically, the rest of the Old Testament books
surrounding it were from Jerome's Hebrew translation, and all other
Vulgate Bibles contained the Hebrew psalter. However, Alcuin and
his advisers decided to include the Gallican psalter instead because of
its popularity and usage in the Frankish empire. As abbott of Tours,
Alcuin oversaw the production of many Bibles and was responsible for
the spread of the Gallican psalter within the Vulgate Bible.[42]

   Jerome's translations, especially those of Old Testament texts,
were not accepted as the norm at first; it is only in the 6th century
that we see a preference for the Vulgate. In any case, we cannot talk
about official Latin translations until 1592. We therefore have to
be very careful about the term "textual adjustment" in relation to chant

texts, since the norm during the time of creation of the chant repertoire could have been a host of different translations.

We know that the psalter was memorized by anyone having a monastic education. It was the basis of the study of grammar. By the time Bibles came North of the Alps in a significant way, the Gallican psalter was more current, and this became the accepted version in Gaul. The fact that the Gallican psalter was not used in Italy would give credence against Jerome's authorship of the Roman Psalter, allegedly composed just eight years before the Gallican. Instead it is much more likely that the Roman psalter is actually one of the Old Latin versions, which was already so entrenched in the minds of the ecclesiastical community that they preferred this version to Jerome's first version and the Gallican psalter when they appeared. The Hebrew psalter, and indeed Jerome's other Old Testament translations from the original Hebrew, was not really accepted by the ecclesiastical authorities at first. Even Saint Augustine expressed scruples about using anything but Septuagint derivatives. Aside from its acceptance in Spain, the Hebrew psalter is therefore only of literary importance. However, Jerome's other Old Testament translations from the Hebrew Bible grew in importance and acceptance over the next few centuries, especially in Italy.

In the late sixth and the early seventh centuries, there were strong endorsements of the Vulgate version of the Bible from Saint Isidore of Seville and Pope Saint Gregory. It spread further into England, Germany, and Gaul during the eighth century, partly due to English and Irish missionary activity. Supremacy of the Vulgate was seen as early as the sixth century, and documents of the eighth century show that it was firmly established.

Psalmic Mass antiphon texts throughout their history have used the Roman psalter as a textual source, pointing to Roman origin. As expected for Rome, the Graduale of Sta. Cecilia in Trastevere[43] uses mostly the Roman psalter for both the antiphons and the psalm verses. The antiphoners found in Hesbert's *Antiphonale Missarum Sextuplex*, however, being of Frankish origin, use the Gallican psalter for the psalm verses while adhering to the Roman psalter for the antiphons, which is also expected.

Dom Gribomont's statistics about the usage of Old Latin and Vulgate texts over the centuries[44] elucidates the use of these translations:

fourth century	3 OL	
fifth century	26 OL	5 V
sixth century	15 OL	24 V
seventh century	11 OL	37 V
	(7 Italian)	(16 Italian, 7 English)
eighth century	15 OL	142 V (14 Italian, 41 English, 22 English missions in Germany)

The later Old Latin versions are mainly psalters (Roman psalter). Through the sixth century, most sources listed are Italian. This statistic shows that the Vulgate was preferred in Italy in the sixth century. We also learn that most of the seven Old Latin Italian sources in the seventh century were psalters, so the number of Old Latin non-psalmic sources must be three or less. However, there are 16 Italian Vulgate sources, and most of those would not be psalters, since neither the Gallican nor the Hebrew psalter were used in Italy at that time.

On the basis of this statistic, we can assume that the year 550 might have been a turning point from a preference of Old Latin to Vulgate. This, however, is somewhat of an oversimplification, since some books of the Vulgate (for example, the Gospels) would have been the standard already in the late fifth century.

THE QUESTION OF LANGUAGE

What can be deduced from a study of the introit texts? What would we expect to find? Firstly, we would expect to find the Gallican psalter in the use of the Gregorian chant psalm verse texts, and that is indeed the case. We would also expect to find the Roman psalter used for the psalmic antiphons because of their Roman origin, and that is for the most part also true. There are, however, some exceptions from the Roman psalter that point to Old Latin sources. But what about the non-psalmic texts? Can we make any assumptions about them?

The forerunners of the earliest Lectionaries existed as early as the fifth century, and the earliest extant examples are from the end of the fifth century, albeit not from Rome.[45] Some of these are Vulgate and some a mixture of Old Latin and Vulgate. The language practice in Rome, however, is represented by the following Gospel Lectionaries:[46]
- Paris BN (Biblioteque Nationale) na 1203, Roman, 781, Vulgate
- Rome (Vatican Library) Pal lat 46, ca. 800, Vulgate

- Rome (Vatican Library) Reg lat 8, end of seventh century, Vulgate
- Rome (Vatican Library) Vat lat 5465, ca. 800, Vulgate
- Rome (Vatican Library) Vat 7016, ca. 800, Vulgate
- Trier Stadtbibliotek 22, Roman, ca. 800, Vulgate
- Wuerzburg Universitaetsbibliothek Mp. th. fol. 62, Roman, seventh centurt, Vulgate
- Wuerzburg Universitaetsbibliothek Mp. th. fol. 68, Roman/ Neapolitan, seventh/eighth centuries, Vulgate

The Vulgate translation is thus firmly established in liturgical texts in Rome by the seventh century. Let us examine the earliest Lectionary.[47] The Gospel list is from Wuerzburg 62 above, but the Lectionary also contains an epistle list, which dates from around 600. This Lectionary uses the Vulgate with minor alterations to accommodate passages being taken out of context.

I believe that Gregory the Great is the pivotal personality in the use of the Vulgate. As mentioned above, he was a great advocate of Jerome's translations but continued to quote Old Latin texts as well. The Vulgate would therefore be the standard in Rome after Gregory, and the Wuerzburg Lectionary seems to support that notion.

Even though the Vulgate Bible as a whole seems to be the norm in Rome after about 600, we must assume that some books of Vulgate translation (for example, the Gospels) would have been used earlier. To try to trace this history is a very involved matter that we cannot discuss in this confined space. What I mean to show in the following pages is not so much an exact history of the introit texts but a general tendency for Old Latin translations to be assigned to older feasts.

If the introit antiphons originated in the late seventh century, as McKinnon claims, we would expect to find that most non-psalmic antiphons use the Vulgate Bible. However, as we shall see, the Vulgate Bible was used only for a few non-psalmic antiphons which were clearly composed during or after this period, and the remainder seems to indicate Old Latin sources,[48] making it much more likely that the composition of the introits of older feasts took place in the sixth or even the later fifth century. This would coincide with the earliest time when Sacramentaries (libelli) and Lectionaries were being assembled.

At first we must establish the seventh-century Roman Lectionary text as the Vulgate. It should be pointed out that this Lectionary contains only beginnings and endings of passages. As such it is only a directory. But it contains enough of the text to draw some conclusions. The major differences that occur in the epistle cycle, which is the older of the two cycles in the *Comes Romanus Wirziburgensis,* relate to adjustments of the passages when they are taken out of context. For example, "Domini nostri" is added to "Jesu Christi" to end the passage at the Christmas Vigil. The word "enim," which appears in the Vulgate's parallel passages on several occasions, is omitted in the epistle incipit, and the Vulgate's "quod" is often changed to "quia," one of the frequent Vulgate alternates. In the Gospels, there are frequent additions to the Vulgate texts to make them stand on their own. These include the words "In illo tempore," "Iesus," and "Dixit Iesus discipulis suis." There is also the occasional omission of the word "autem" in the opening passage. All in all, these changes occur in a manner that makes the chosen texts an independent entity to be read at Mass. The final passages listed in the epistle and Gospel cycles show hardly any deviation from the Vulgate.

In the following analysis of non-psalmic introit texts, we will follow the rubrical assignments as indicated in the *Antiphonale Missarum Sextuplex* rather than the modern assignments, since we are dealing with the history of chant. For Old Latin sources, we will follow the Vetus Latina as published by the Beuron Institute, the standard for this type of text. Their fairly comprehensive research includes not only biblical fragments but also quotes of biblical texts in patristic and other Latin sources, as well as chant texts. Since chant texts are included in the Vetus Latina, we have to exclude those sources from our research and consider only the other sources. However, the fact that the Beuron Institute sees fit to include chant material among Old Latin sources speaks in favor of my hypothesis that the older texts are of Old Latin origin. Also, only Italian sources and those in Rome's sphere of influence are considered here; this mainly includes Italian and North African sources. The printed version of the *Vetus Latina* is incomplete. Many biblical books are not yet covered, and there is no timeline as to when this immense work will be finished. However, the index cards of the verses of the incomplete sections are available online at www.brepolis.net, and I included these in this analysis. The index cards, together with the published books, gave me a comprehensive look of available Old Latin biblical texts. For the Vulgate, I chose the Stuttgart edition, which for this purpose is the most scholarly edition, indicating variations in the text whenever they occurred.

It must be mentioned that the *Vetus Latina* does not cover all Old Latin biblical sources ever written. Naturally, many were lost or destroyed or reused as binding material for newer books. When a particular introit text appears to be a duplicate or a close associate of a verse from an Old Latin source, it does not automatically mean that the text is derived from that source. What I mean to show by this analysis is merely that the earlier non-psalmic introit texts were influenced by the language of Old Latin biblical fragments.

The abbreviations citing the sources in the following analysis indicate an author and the work where a particular passage may be found. The authors' abbreviated names are explained here; however, because of space limitations, the listed works appear only in their abbreviated citation. Interested readers may find the complete listing by consulting the Vetus Latina printed or online version.

The following Old Latin sources were found to agree with certain introits in the following analysis, and I am using here the abbreviations as found in the *Vetus Latina*.

A-SS	Actavel Passiones vel Vita Sanctorum
AM	Ambrose, Bishop of Milan (d. 397)
A-SS	Actavel Passiones vel Vita Sanctorum
AM	Ambrose, Bishop of Milan (d. 397)
AM-A	Ambrosius Autpertus, Abbot of San Vincenzo al Volturno, Northern Italy, (d. 784)
AN-s-Bou	Anonymous, Omelia de oratione dominica, North African, fifth century
AN-s-Le	Anonymous, Homiliary, North African, fifth century
AN-sy	Anonymous, Commentarius in Symbolum Nicaenum, Northern Italy, after 350
AN-Ver-hae	Anonymous, Contra hereticos, aggresively Arian, fifth century?
AN-Ver-s	Anonymous, Sermones 15, Arian author, North Africa, fifth century
ANT-M	Antiphonale Mozarabicum
AP-E Jac	Apocrypha Evangelia, second-century Greek, translated into Latin fourth century

AR	Arnobius the Younger, African monk in Rome (d. after 455)
ARN	Arnobius Rhetor, North African, early fourth century
AU	Augustine, Bishop of Hippo (d. 430)
PS-AU hyp	Pseudo Augustine, North African, first half of fifth century
PS-AU s	Cai Pseudo Augustine
PS-AU s	Mai Pseudo Augustine
Brev. Goth.	Breviarium Gothicum
CAr	Flavius Magnus Aurelius Cassiodorus Senator (d. 583), until 538 at the court of Ravenna, 540 to Constantinople, 554 returned to Vivavium, Italy
CHRO	Chromantius, Bishop of Aquileia, Northern Italy (388–407)
CO-Brac	Concilia Baracarensis, Braga
CY-op	Thascius Caecilius Cyprianus, Bishop of Carthage, North Africa (d. 258)
DION-E	Diunysius Exiguus, Scytian monk in Rome (d. 545)
EP-Sc-ct	Epiphanius Scholasticus, Friend of Cassiodorus CAr (sixth century)
FAC	Facundus, Bishop of Hermiane, North Africa (d. after 571)
FEL-M	Felix, who disputed with AU on 7 and 12 Dec 404, North African
FIL	Filastrius, Bishop of Brescia (d. before 396)
FU	Fulgentius, Bishop of Ruspe, North Africa (d. 527)
PS-FU s	Pseudo Fulgentius, North African fifth/sixth centuries
GAU	Gaudentius, Bishop of Brescia (d. 410)
HI	Jerome (b. 347, d. 420)
PS-HI	Pseudo-Jerome
INS	same as Pseudo Damasus, fourth-century Roman
LEO	Pope Leo the Great (440–461)
PS-LEO s	Pseudo-Leo, Sermones of later date
LEX	Vis Leges Visigothorum fifth century
LUC	Lucifer, Bishop of Cagliari, Sardinia (d. 370)
M-R	Missale Romanum
MAR-M	Marius Mercator, North African (d. after 451)
NIC	Nicetas, Bishop of Remesiana, Dacia, Balkans (d. 414)

OPT	Optatus, Bishop of Mileve, North Africa (d. before 400)
PET-C	Petrus Chrysologus, Bishop of Ravenna (d. ca. 450)
PRIS	Priscillianus, Bishop of Avila, Spain (d. 385)
QU	Quodvultdeus, Bishop of Carthage (437–439), 439 to Kampania, never returned to North Africa, d. 453
RES-R	Responsoriale Romanum
RUF	Rufinus of Aquileia, Presbyter, Northern Italy (d. 411); all works and translations were done after his return to the West in 397
RUS	Rusticus, Roman deacon (d. after 565)
PS-SIX I	Pseudo Sixtus I, early second-century Roman
VER	Verecundus, Bishop of Junica, Tunisia (d. 552 in Chalcedon)
VIG-P	Pope Vigilius (537–555)
VIG-T	Vigilius, Bishop of Thapsus, North Africa (d. after 484)
PS-VIG	Pseudo Vigilius of Thapsus, fourth-century North African
VINC	Vincentius of Lerins, island off Southern Gallican coast (d. 445–450)

Codex Parisiensis
Codex Vercellensis
Codex Veronensis
Comes Wirziburgensis

Analysis of Texts, Temporale

Dom V ante Nat Dni (R only) Jeremiah 29:11, 12, 14
Dicit Dominus, ego cogito cogitationes pacis, et non afflictionis: invocabitis me, et ego exaudiam vos. (14) Et reducam captivitatem vestram de cunctis locis.
Vulgate: Ego enim scio . . . ait Dominus, cogitationes pacis et non adflictionis . . . et invocabitis me . . . et exaudiam vos.
Analysis: Except for the difference between "scio" and "cogito," the introit is very close to the Vulgate.
　　Dom II Adv Isaiah 30:19, 27, 30
Populus Sion, ecce Dominus veniet ad salvandas gentes: et auditam faciet Dominus gloriam vocis suae, in laetitia cordis vestri.

Vulgate: (19) Populus enim Sion, (27) ecce nomen Domini venit, (30) et auditam faciet Dominus gloriam vocis suae . . .

Analysis: An example where the text was significantly altered while splicing together three verses. However, the vocabulary is compatible.

 Dom III Adv Philippians 4:4−6

Gaudete in Domino semper: iterum dico, gaudete: modestia vestra nota sit omnibus hominibus: Dominus prope est. Nihil soliciti sitis: sed in omni oratione petitiones vestrae innotescant apud Deum.

Vulgate: Gaudete in Domino semper: iterum dico gaudete. Modestia vestra nota sit omnibus hominibus: Dominus prope est. Nihil soliciti sitis: sed in omni oratione . . . petitiones vestrae innotescant apud Deum.

Analysis: An exact duplicate of the Vulgate.

 Feria IV Q T Adv Isaiah 45:8

Rorate caeli desuper, et nubes pluant iustum: aperiatur terra, et germinet Salvatorem.

Vulgate: Rorate caeli desuper, et nubes pluant iustum: aperiatur terra, et germinet salvatorem.

Analysis: An exact duplicate.

 Vig Nat Dni cf. Exodus 16:6, 7; Isaiah 35:4

Hodie scietis quia veniet Dominus, et salvabit nos: et mane videbitis gloriam eius.

Vulgate: (6) Vespere scietis quod Dominus eduxerit vos de terra Aegypti, (7) et mane videbitis gloriam Domini. (4) Deus ipse veniet et salvabit nos.

Vetus Latina: 16:7−Brev. Goth. (664A)

Analysis: The fact that these remote passages were spliced together into one coherent sentence shows a theological understanding of the material at hand. There is always the possibility that the introit compilers were well versed in scripture, but they could also have borrowed material from the Church fathers. In any case, the vocabulary appears to be fairly close the vulgate translation.

 Nat Dni 2 Isaiah 9:2, 6; Luke 1:33

(2) Lux fulgebit hodie super nos: quia natus est nobis Dominus (6) et vocabitur Admirabilis, Deus, Princeps pacis, Pater futuri saeculi, (33) cuius regni non erit finis.

Vulgate: Lux orta est eis . . . et vocabitur nomen eius, Admirabilis, consiliarius, Deus fortis, Pater futuri saeculi, princeps pacis . . . Et regni eius non erit finis.

Vetus Latina: (2) identical in AM and AP-E; (6) identical in PS-AU s Cai 1,15 (33) identical in AU Jud 3 / AU Ps 88 s 28,4 / CAr Ps 44,3 / CAr Ps 145,10 / CO-Brac 3 / GAU serm 20 / LEX Vis / RUS CO 2,3 / VIG-P cap 6.

Analysis: Compare the titles with Christmas Day. There were two different Septuagint versions of this text, and Christmas Dawn used one translation, while Christmas Day used the other. Two different versions of the OL were used for these Masses. The introit text appears to be identical to sources beginning with the early fifth century in Northern Italy and North Africa. The feast was not added until the sixth century.

   Nat Dni 3 Isaiah 9:6

Puer natus est nobis, et filius datus est nobis: cuius imperium super humerum eius: et vocabitur nomen eius, magni consilii Angelus.

Vulgate: Parvulus enim natum est nobis, et filius datus est nobis, et factus est principatus super humerum eius: et vocabitur nomen eius, Admirabilis, consiliarius, Deus fortis, Pater futuri saeculi, princeps pacis.

Vetus Latina: idential in AM. The words "puer" and "imperium" are also found in PS-FU s1 / PS-FU s61 / LEO s59. The words "magni consilii Angelus" are found in PS-FU s8 1/2 and LEO, as well as the "Decretum Gelasii" of the late fifth century.

Analysis: The introit text appears at the end of the fourth century in Ambrose, and the vocabulary is consistent with North African and Roman sources of the fifth century. It appears that this text is the older usage of the two (Christmas Dawn and Christmas Day). The feast was celebrated in Rome in 336.

   Dom I post Nat Dni Wisdom 18:14–15

Dum medium silentium teneret omnia, et nox in suo cursu medium iter haberet, omnipotens sermo tuus, Domine, de caelis a regalibus sedibus venit.

Vulgate: Cum enim quietum silentium contineret omnia, et nox in suo cursu medium iter haberet, omnipotens sermo tuus de caelo a regalibus sedibus . . . posilivit.

Vetus Latina: "Dum medium" and "teneret" are found in a Vulgate variant, and the words "Domine," "caeli," and "venit" are found in LUC and PS-AU.

Analysis: The Vulgate text of the book of Wisdom is an Old Latin version. Some of the vocabulary variants are found in Sardinian and North African sources of the fourth century.

Epiphania cf. Malachi 3:1; 1 Chronicles 29:12

Ecce advenit dominator Dominus: et regnum in manu eius, et potestas, et imperium.

Vulgate: Ecce . . . venit . . . Dominator . . . Dominus . . . tu dominaris omnium, in manu tua virtus et potentia . . . et imperium . . .

Vetus Latina: "Ecce venit Dominus omnipotens" in CHRO lap12 / RUF sy32 / AM Ps 36,26,1. "Ecce veniet Dominus exercitum" in GI exc 89.

Analysis: The Vetus Latina shows that there were several variants of this text. Although the introit text itself could not be found, it is possible that this passage belonged to a fragment that is lost. However, it is more likely that the introit is based on a commentary on a biblical passage by a Church father. As mentioned already, the biblical references attached to this text were added by scholars at a much later time, and it is highly unlikely that the compiler of the introit text would have spliced together these two passages into one coherent sentence.

Dom I p Epiph cf Daniel 7:9, 10, 13, 14; Isaiah 6:1–3

In excelso throno vidi sedere virum, quem adorat multitudo angelorum, psallentes in unum: ecce eius imperii nomen est in aeternum.

Vulgate: (9) Aspiciebam donec throni positi sunt et antiquus dierum sedit . . . (10) . . . milia milium ministrabant ei . . . (14) et dedit ei potestatem et honorem et regnum. (1–3) . . . vidi Dominum sedentem super solium excelsum . . . seraphim stabant super illud . . . et clamabant alter ad alterum et dicebant: sanctus, sanctus, sanctus Dominus exercituum.

Vetus Latina: Isaiah 6: North African and European sources begin: "Vidi Dominum sedentem super throno excelsum."

Analysis: See above under Epiphany.

Fer IV Cin Wisdom 11:24–25, 27

Misereris omnium, Domine, et nihil odisti eorum quae fecisti, dissimulans peccata hominum propter paenitentiam, et parcens illis: quia tu es Dominus Deus noster.

Vulgate: Misereris omnium, quia omnia potes, et dissimulans peccata hominum propter paenitentiam . . . parcis autem omnibus: quoniam tua sunt Domine, qui amas animas.

Vetus Latina: "Misereris omnium, et nihil odisti eorum quae fecisti, dissimulans peccata hominum propter paenitentiam, parces autem omnibus, quia . . ." "Eorum," "parces," and "quia" are Vulgate variants.

Analysis: It must be kept in mind that the book of Wisdom in the Vulgate is an Old Latin version.

Dom IV Quad Isaiah 66:10–11

Laetare Ierusalem: et conventum facite omnes qui diligitis eam: gaudete cum laetitia, qui in tristitia fuistis: ut exsultetis, et satiemini ab uberibus consolationis vestrae.

Vulgate: Laetamini cum Ierusalem, et exsultate in ea omnes qui diligitis eam: gaudete cum ea gaudio universi, qui lugetis super eam. Ut sugatis, et repleamini ab ubere consolationis eius . . .

Vetus Latina: The introit text can be pieced together from various Old Latin sources, but not one single source.

Analysis: The fact that several Old Latin sources support smaller elements of the introit text, we might assume the possibility of one single source, now lost, which contained all of those elements.

Fer IV Hebd IV Quad Ezekiel 36:23–26

Dum sanctificatus fuero in vobis, congregabo vos de universis terris: et effundam super vos aquam mundam, et mundabimini ab omnibus inquinamentis vestris: et dabo vobis spiritum novum.

Vulgate: Et sanctificabo nomen meum magnum . . . congregabo vos de universis terris . . . et effundam super vos aquam mundam et mundabimini ab omnibus inquinamentis vestris . . . et dabo vobis cor novum.

Vetus Latina: Identical in the Missale Ambrosianum.

Analysis: Except for the opening words, the text from "congregabo" to the end is almost the same as the Vulgate. The change to "spiritum novum" could have been made to make the antiphon more appropriate for the feast.

Sab Hebd IV Quad Isaiah 55:1

Sitientes venite ad aquas, dicit Dominus: et qui non habetis pretium, venite, bibite cum laetitia.

Vulgate: . . . Sitientes venite ad aquas, et qui non habetis argentum, properate, emite et comedite . . .

Vetus Latina: "habetis" HI Is / AM-A / INS 784; "pretium" AM ep7; "venite" AM-sp; "bibite" AM inst / CY

Analysis: This text seems to be influenced by North Italian translations of the late fourth/early fifth century.

Fer V Hebd V Quad cf. Daniel 3:31, 29, 30, 43, 42

(31) Omnia quae fecisti nobis, Domine, in vero iudicio fecisti, (29) quia peccavimus tibi, (30) et mandatis tuis non obedivimus: (43) sed da gloriam nomini tuo, (42) et fac nobiscum secundum multitudinem misericordiae tuae.

Vulgate: (31) Omnia ergo quae induxisti nobis . . . nobis vero iudicio fecisti, (29) peccavimus enim . . . (30) et praecepta tua non audivimus . . . (43) . . . et da gloriam nomini tuo, (42) sed fac nobiscum iuxta mansuetudinem tuam.

Vetus Latina: "Omnia quaecumque nobis fecisti, in vero iudicio fecisti . . ." Cod. Paris. (345) / VER cant 4. "Omnia quaecumque fecisti nobis in vero iudicio fecisti . . ." FU ep 7,22

Analysis: Except for a few sources of the sixth century, where verse 31 seems to have compatible vocabulary between the Old Latin and the introit, the rest of the text is inconclusive. However, the introit is certainly not based on the Vulgate version.

Fer IV Maj Hebd Philippians 2:10, 8, 11

(10) In nomine Domini omne genu flectatur, caelestium, terrestrium et infernorum: (8) quia Dominus factus obediens usque ad mortem, mortem autem crucis: (11) ideo Dominus Iesus Christus in gloria est Dei Patris.

Vulgate: (10) Ut in nomine Iesu omne genu flectatur, caelestium, terrestrium et infernorum: (8) humiliavit semet ipsum factus oboediens usque ad mortem, mortem autem crucis: (11) . . . quia Dominus Iesus Christus in gloria est Dei Patris.

Vetus Latina: (10) DION-E Proc 17 / PS-HI bre 121 + 62,12 + 131,28 / LEO eo 35 + 124 + 165 / MAR-M 29 / PET-C ep / RUF Jdc 2,3 + Rm 3,3 / PS-SIX I / VIG-T Eut 3,9 / PS-VIG tri 12,9 + Var 1,2; (8) PS-HI / LEO ep 124 + 165 / RUF fi 46 / VIG-T Ar 1,11 / PS-VIG tri 3,3 + Var 1,3.

Analysis: The introit appears to follow the usage of Pseudo-Jerome, Leo, Rufinus, Vigilius of Thapsus, and Pseudo-Vigilius, reflecting the practice of Rome and North Africa in the fifth century.

Fer V in Caena Dni Galatians 6:14

Nos autem gloriari oportet, in cruce Domini nostri Iesu Christi: in quo est salus, vita, et resurrectio nostra: per quem salvati, et liberati sumus.

Vulgate: Mihi autem absit gloriari, nisi in cruce Domini nostri Iesu Christi, per quem mihi mundus crucifixus est, et ego mundo.

Vetus Latina: While "nos autem gloriari oportet" does not appear in the VL, there are several other versions: "gloriemur ergo et nos in cruce Domini Iesu Christi" (AU sfrg), "non ergo gloriemur cruce Christi" (HIL syn85), "gloriemur in cruce" (Brev. Goth.), "gloriantes in cruce" (GAU 3,7 / PRIS can34), "gloriemur ergo in cruce Domini" (Nic fic7). RES-R has both "nos autem gloriari oportet in cruce . . ." and "absit nobis gloriari, nisi . . ." RUF, LEO, AU, and AM use the Vulgate version.

Analysis: Although the introit text could not be found verbatim, enough variants are represented in the Vetus Latina to indicate that the introit might be an Old Latin form of Galatians 6:14.

Fer II Pasch Exodus 13:5, 9

Introduxit vos Dominus in terram fluentem lac et mel, alleluia: (9b) et ut lex Domini sempter sit in ore vestro, alleluia, alleluia.

Vulgate: (5) . . . introduxerit te Dominus in terram . . . fluentem lacte et melle, (9b) et ut lex Domini semper in ore tuo.

Vetus Latina: Very close to Vulgate, but differences in verse 5: "introduxit," "lac," and "mel"; Vulgate omits "sit."

Analysis: Second person changed to plural, since the introits prefer the plural form of address. Otherwise, the introit is very close to the Vulgate.

Fer III Pasch Sirach 15:3, 4

(3) Aqua sapientiae potavit eos, alleluia: firmabitur in illis, et non flectatur, alleluia: (4) et exaltabit eos in aeternum, alleluia, alleluia.

Vulgate: Aqua sapientiae . . . potavit illum: firmabitur in illo et non flectetur: (4) et exaltabit illum apud proximos suos.

Vetus Latina: text can be spliced together as "aqua sapientiae potavit eum, firmabitur in illo et non flectetur, et exaltabit eum apud proximos suos."

Analysis: Except for the ending, the introit is very close to the Vulgate. Again, the second person is changed to plural, since the introits prefer the plural form of address. It must be kept in mind, however, that the Vulgate form of Sirach is an Old Latin version.

Fer IV Pasch Matthew 25:34

Venite benedicti Patris mei, percipite regnum, alleluia; quod vobis paratum est ab origine mundi, alleluia, alleluia.

Vulgate: Venite benedicti Patris mei, possidete paratum vobis regnum a constitutione mundi.

Vetus Latina: AN-s-Bou 1 / An-s-Le 8 / An-sy / An-Ver-hae 3/4 / AR Ps 102 / AU Jo 14,8,25 + 1 Jo 3,11 + Pet 2, 54 ` Ps 35,5,22 + Ps 48s,4,6,3 + Ps 49,11,48 + Ps 52,4,18 + Ps 63,19,4 + Ps 64,2,21 + Ps 79,13,43 + Ps 85,21,24 + Ps 90s1,10,19 + Ps 95,15,26 + Ps 98,8,8 + Ps 111,5,5 + Ps 113s1,9,9 + Ps 120,11,21 + Ps 121,9,52 + Ps 129,10,23 + Ps 141,4,18 + Ps 145,20,2 + s37,39 + s58,3 + s86,4 + s328 + s389,5 + s-dni 2,38 + s-DOL 22,6 + s-lam 18,3 + s-MOR 13,5 / PS-AU hyp 1,4 + hyp 6,8 / Brev. Goth. 86 / CAr Ps 9,9 + Ps 91,14 + Ps 118,112 / CY op 23 + or 13 + te 2,30 + te 3,1 + ze 15 / EP-Sc-ct / FEL-M / FIL 137,8 / FU Thr 3,4,1 / JUS U5 + 195 / LUC par / OPT Par 5,7 / PET-C s 9,5 + s 41,4 + s 70 / QU pro 4,30 / RUF Jos 8,5. Besides "ab origine," AU also uses "ab initio."

Analysis: The introit reflects Old Latin usage as found in North Africa from the third through sixth century, in North Italy from the fourth through sixth century, and in Rome in the fourth and fifth century.

Fer V Pasch Wisdom 10:20, 21

Victricem manum tuam, Domine, laudaverunt pariter, alleluia: quia sapientia aperuit os mutum, et linguas infantium fecit disertas, alleluia, alleluia.

Vulgate: Vitricem manum tuam laudaverunt pariter: quoniam sapientia aperuit os mutorum, et linguas infantium fecit dissertas.

Vetus Latina:

Analysis: introit very close to Vulgate, which is an Old Latin form.

Oct Pasch 1 Peter 2:2

Quasimodo geniti infantes rationabiles, sine dolo lac concupiscite . . .

Vulgate: Sicut modo geniti infantes, rationabile, sine dolo lac concupiscite . . .

Vetus Latina: Identical in PS-AU s Cai I,35,1 / PS-LEO s14,2 / RUF Rm3,2.

Analysis: The typical and well-known beginning "quasimodo" is found only in Old Latin versions of early fifth-century North Africa and Rome.

Dom V post Pasch Isaiah 48:20

Vocem iucunditatis annuntiate, et audiatur: nuntiate usque ad extremum terrae: liberavit Dominus populum suum.

Vulgate: In voce exsultationis annuntiate: auditum facite hoc, et efferte illud usque ad extrema terrae . . . Redemit Dominus servum suum Iacob.

Vetus Latina: The whole text of the antiphon is verbatim version L, but the sources for this version are ANT-M and M-R.

Analysis: Inconclusive, since the Vetus Latina version is based on chant texts.

Ascens Dni Acts 1:11

Viri Galiaei, quid admiramini aspicientes in caelum? Quemadmodum vidistis eum ascendentem in caelum, ita veniet.

Vulgate: Viri Galiaei, quid statis aspicientes in caelum? Hic Iesus, qui assumptus est a vobis in caelum, sic veniet quemadmodum vidistis eum euntem in caelum.

Vetus Latina: "Viri Galilaei, quid admiramini? Hic Iesus . . ." (CAr Ps 46,6). "Viri Galiaei, quid admiramini aspicientes in caelum? Ita veniet, alleluia" (VINC Aug8). Both AU and LEO use "quid statis" among many different variations of this text.

Analysis: A North Italian source of the fifth century and a Mediterranean French source of the sixth-century use the vocabulary found in the introit.

Dom Pent Wisdom 1:7

Spiritus Domini replevit orbem terrarum: et hoc quod continet omnia, scientiam habet vocis.

Vulgate: Spiritus Domini replevit orbem terrarum . . . et hoc, quod continet omnia, scientia habet vocis.

Vetus Latina:

Analysis: Almost an exact duplicate of the Vulgate, but the book of Wisdom in the Vulgate is an Old Latin text.

Fer III Pen 4 Ezra 2:36, 37

Accipite iucunditatem gloriae vestrae, alleluia: gratias agentes Deo, alleluia: qui vos ad caelestia regna vocavit, alleluia, alleluia, alleluia.

Vulgate: Accipite iucunditatem gloriae vestrae . . . gratias agentes ei qui vos ad caelestia regna vocavit.

Vetus Latina:

Analysis: The introit uses the same language as the Vulgate. Four Ezra is not a canonical book; it was appended to the end of the Clementine Bible and is of Old Latin origin.

Sab Pent Romans 5:5

Caritas Dei diffusa est in cordibus nostris: per inhabitantem Spiritum eius in nobis.

Vulgate: Caritas Dei diffusa est in cordibus nostris per Spiritum sanctum, qui datus est nobis.

Vetus Latina: In AU, all quotes accord with the Vulgate's "per Spiritum sanctum," except for one mention of "per euntem Spiritum sanctum."

Analysis: Inconclusive, but even among the texts of Augustine, there are variations.

De Trinitate (S only) Tobit 12:6

Benedicta sit sancta Trinitas, atque indivisa Unitas: confitebimur ei, quia fecit nobiscum misericordiam suam.

Vulgate: Benedicite Deum caeli, et coram omnibus viventibus confitemini ei, quia fecit vobiscum misericordiam suam.

Vetus Latina:

Analysis: Here is an example where a typically Christian motif is superimposed on an Old Testament text. However, the second half, aside from the change in person, is the same as the Vulgate. This was originally a Frankish feast.

Dom XVIII p Pent Sirach 36:18, 19

Da pacem, Domine, sustinentibus te, ut prophetae tui fideles inveniantur: exaudi preces servi tui, et plebis tuae Israel.

Vulgate: Da mercedem sustinentibus te, ut prophetae tui fideles inveniantur: et exaudi orationes servorum tuorum (19) . . . de populo tuo.

Vetus Latina:

Analysis: No match to either Vetus Latina or the Vulgate, but Sirach is in the Vulgate in an Old Latin form.

Dom XXI p Pent Esther 13:9, 10, 11

(9) In voluntate tua, Domine, universa sunt posita, et non est qui posit resistere voluntati tuae: (10) tu enim fecisti omnia, caelum et terram, et universa quae caeli ambitu continentur: (11) Dominus universorum tu es.

Vulgate: In dicione enim tua cuncta sunt posita, et non est qui posit tuae resistere voluntati: tu fecisti caelum et terram et quidquid caeli ambitu continetur: Dominus omnium es.

Vetus Latina: (9) CAr Ps 103,27, no other match available.

Analysis: The only match for one of the verses is North Italian, sixth century.

Dom XXIII p Pent Jeremiah 29:11–12, 14

Dicit Dominus: Ego cogito cogitationes pacis, et non afflictionis: invocabitis me, et ego exaudiam vos: et reducam captivitatem vestram de cunctis locis.

Vulgate: Ego scio cogitationes . . . pacis, et non afflictionis . . . Invocabitis me . . . et ego exaudiam vos . . . Et reducam captivitatem vestram . . . de . . . cunctis locis.

Vetus Latina:

Analysis: Except for the change of "scio" to "cogito," the rest of the text appears to be Vulgate.

Christ the King Revelation 5:12; 1:6

Dignus est Agnus, qui occisus est, accipere virtutem, et divinitatem, et sapientiam, et fortitudinem, et honorem. Ipsi gloria et imperium in saecula saeculorum.

Vulgate: Dignus est Agnus, qui occisus est, accipere virtutem, et divinitatem, et sapientiam, et fortitudinem, et honorem . . . ipsi gloria, et imperium in saecula saeculorum.

Vetus Latina:

Analysis: The introit text is identical to the Vulgate, which should not surprise us, since the feast of Christ the King is a fairly recent addition to the calendar; this introit does not appear in the *Antiphonale Sextuplex* and seems to have been specifically written for this feast.

Analysis of Texts, Sanctorale

S. Ioannis Ev 2 Sirach 15:5

In medio ecclesiae aperuit os eius: et implevit eum Dominus spiritu sapientiae, et intellectus: stolam gloriae induit eum.

Vulgate: In medio ecclesiae aperiet os eius: et adimplebit illum spiritu sapientiae et intellectus et stolam gloriae vestiet illum.

Vetus Latina: Identical in codex Veronensis LXXXVIII, also Comes Wirziburgensis f.62 (=q.32).

Analysis: Keeping in mind that the Vulgate's Sirach translation is Old Latin, the introit and the Vulgate are very close.

S. Marcelli Sirach 45:30

Statuit ei Dominus testamentum pacis, et principem fecit eum: ut sit illi sacerdotii dignitas in aeternum.

Vulgate: Statuit ad illum testamentum pacis, principem sanctorum et gentis suae: ut sit illi in sacertotium sui dignitas in aeternum.

Vetus Latina:

Analysis: Keeping in mind that the Vulgate's Sirach translation is Old Latin, the introit and the Vulgate are very close.

     S. Gregorii Daniel 3:84, 87

Sacerdotes Dei, benedicite Dominum: sancti et humiles corde, laudate Deum.

Vulgate: (84) Benedicite sacerdotes Domini Domino: (87) . . . sancti et humiles corde . . . laudate et superexaltate eum.

Vetus Latina:

Analysis: No match was found, but the vocabulary is consistent with the Vulgate.

     Ss. Philippi et Iacobi Neh. vel 2 Ezra 9:27

Exclamaverunt ad te, Domine, in tempore afflictionis suae, et tu de caelo exaudisti eos, alleluia, alleluia.

Vulgate: In tempore tribulationis suae clamaverunt ad te, et tu de caelo audisti.

Vetus Latina:

Analysis: Inconclusive, but there are enough differences between the introit and the Vulgate to point to Old Latin influence.

     Dedic. S. Mariae ad Martyres Genesis 28:17, 22

Terribilis est locus iste: hic domus Dei est, et porta caeli: (22) et vocabitur aula Dei.

Vulgate: Terribilis inquit est locus iste . . . hic . . . domus Dei et porta caeli: et . . . vocabitur Domus Dei.

Vetus Latina: (17) HI q 43,30; (22) HI Pel 3,8

Analysis: The text of the introit is very close to the Vulgate, but also reflects the Old Latin usage of St. Jerome. Since the Vulgate version of Genesis is the work of Jerome, the difference at the end ("aula" for "domus") could be explained in that Jerome incorporated in Pel 3,8 either somebody else's translation or an earlier version of his own, before he actually translated Genesis from the Hebrew. This would place the text into the Old Latin Roman repertoire of the late fourth century.

     Ss. Primi et Feliciani Sirach 44:15, 14

(15) Sapientiam sanctorum narrent populi, et laudes eorum nuntiet ecclesia: (14) nomina autem eorum vivent in saeculum saeculi.

Vulgate: Sapientiam ipsorum narrent populi, laudem eorum nuntiet ecclesia: nomen eorum vivet in generationes et generationes.

Vetus Latina:
Analysis: Keeping in mind that the Vulgate's Sirach translation is Old Latin, the introit and the Vulgate are very close.

   Vig S. Ioannis Bapt Luke 1:13, 15, 14

(13) Ne timeas Zacharia, exaudita est oratio tua: et Elisabeth uxor tua pariet tibi filium, et vocabis nomen eius Ioannem: (15) et erit magnus coram Domino: et Spiritu Sancto replebitur adhuc ex utero matris suae: (14) et multi in nativitate eius gaudebunt.

Vulgate: Ne timeas Zacharia . . . exaudita est deprecatio tua: et uxor tua Elisabeth pariet tibi filium, et vocabis nomen eius Ioannem: erit enim magnus coram Domino . . . et Spiritu Sancto replebitur adhuc ex utero matris suae: et multi in nativitate eius gaudebunt.

Vetus Latina: (13) AP-E Jac 4, 13 / PS-FU s 53 / PET-C s 91; (15) AP-E Mar 3,3 / AU Ev 2,17 / PS-FU s 53 / PS-HI ep 50,4 / PET-C s 91; (14) AM / AN Ver s 9,5 / AR exp Lc 1 / PS-FU s 53 / PET-C s 88 + s 91

Analysis: There is agreement in all three verses among PS-FU s (fifth-/ sixth-century North African) and PET-C (fifth-century Ravenna).

   S. Ioannis Bapt 2 Isaiah 49:1, 2

(1) De ventre matris meae vocavit me Dominus nomine meo: (2) et posuit os meum ut gladium acutum: sub tegumento manus suae protexit me, posuit me quasi sagitam electam.

Vulgate: Dominus ab utero vocavit me: de ventre matris meae recordatus est nominis mei: et posuit os meum quasi gladium acutum: in umbra manus suae protexit me, et posuit me sicut sagittam electam.

Vetus Latina: (1) A-SS / Brev. Goth. / HI; (2) Am ep 39,10. Overall, A-SS, AM, AM-A, CHRO, and Brev. Goth. are very close.

Analysis: The introit text is very close to North Italian translations of the late fourth century.

   Vig S. Petri John 21:18, 19

(18) Dicit Dominus Petro: Cum esses iunior, cingebas te, et ambulabas ubi volebas: cum autem senueris, extendes manus tuas, et alius te cinget, et ducet quo tu non vis: (19) hoc autem dixit, significans qua morte clarificaturus esset Deum.

Vulgate: Amen Amen dico tibi: cum esses iunior, cingebas te, et ambulabas ubi volebas: cum autem senueris, extendes manus tuas, et alius te cinget, et ducet quo tu non vis: hoc autem dixit, significans qua morte clarificaturus esset Deum.

Vetus Latina: Except for the beginning form of address, the introit is like the Vulgate. However, several Old Latin texts are also identical to the Vulgate: AU Jo 123,4 / FAC def 3,3 / FU Thr 3,24,6, all of them African, fifth and sixth centuries.

Analysis: The fact that a text is identical to the Vulgate does not necessarily rule out Old Latin influence, as is shown here. We know that Jerome made his adaptations of the four Gospels rather hastily from Old Latin texts, and much of that substance was transferred into the new revisions as found in the Vulgate. Could be Vulgate or Old Latin.

> *S. Petri* Acts 12:11

Nunc scio vere, quia misit Dominus Angelum suum: et eripuit me de manu Herodis, et de expectatione plebis Iudaeorum.

Vulgate: Nunc scio vere, quia misit Dominus angelum suum: et eripuit me de manu Herodis, et de omni expectatione plebis Iudaeorum.

Vetus Latina: The introit is exactly like the Vulgate, but also identical to AM Ps 36,60,3.

Analysis: The fact that Ambrose used this text already in the late fourth century, before the Vulgate's Acts translation had been made, points to Old Latin usage; therefore, the text could be either Vulgate or Old Latin.

> *S. Pauli* 2 Timothy 1:12

Scio cui credidi, et certus sum, quia potens est depositum meum servare in illum diem.

Vulgate: Scio enim cui credidi, et certus sum, quia potens est depositum meum servare in illum diem.

Vetus Latina: the introit and the Vulgate are the same, but this translation is also found in CAr 2 Tm 1,12.

Analysis: Cassiodorus uses this text in the sixth century, pointing to Old Latin usage. Incidentally, Augustine argues in AU gest 35 in favor of the term "commendatum" instead of "depositum," which is found in the "codices."[49] This indicates that the Latin bible at Augustine's disposal used the terminology as found in the introit, but which he thought was defective. Inconclusive.

> *Ss. Processi et Martiniani* Wisdom 3:8

Iudicant sancti gentes, et dominator populis: regnabit Dominus illorum in perpetuum.

Vulgate: Iudicabunt nationes, et dominabuntur populis: et regnabit Dominus illorum in perpetuum.

Vetus Latina:

Analysis: The vocabulary is compatible, but we must keep in mind that the Vulgate's book of Wisdom is an Old Latin version.

　　S. Clementis Isaiah 59:21; 56:7

(21) Dicit Dominus: Sermones meos quos dedi in os tuum, non deficient de ore tuo: adest enim nomen tuum, (7) et munera tua accepta erunt super altare meum.

Vulgate: Dicit Dominus . . . Verba mea quae posui in ore tuo non recedent de ore tuo: holocausta eorum et victimae eorum placebunt mihi super altari meo.

Vetus Latina: the only close translation is in M-R.

Analysis: Inconclusive, since M-R is a chant text.

　　Vig S. Andreae Matthew 4:18, 19

(18) Dominus secus mare Galiaeae vidit duos fratres, Petrum et Andream: (19) et vocavit eos: venite post me: faciam vos fieri piscatores hominum.

Vulgate: Ambulans autem iuxta mare Galiaeae vidit duos fraters . . . Petrum et Andream: (19) et ait illis: venite post me, et faciam vos fieri piscatores hominum.

Vetus Latina: codex Vercellensis; (18) PS-AU spe 5 / CHRO Mt 16,1; (19) AU Jo 7,9,11 / CHRO Mt 16,1 / PET-C s 47,3.

Analysis: Chromantius (late fourth, early fifth centuries, Northern Italian) coincides with both verses.

　　There are three multiple assignments of texts in the sanctorale cycle: the feast of Processus and Martinianus shares its introit with the fourth-century feast of Prothus and Jacinthus. The introit for Primus and Felicianus is also used for three other feasts of early origin. Finally, the only problematic assignment belongs to the introit of Saint Gregory, a seventh-century feast; this text is also used for four early feasts.

　　The books of Wisdom, Sirach, and 4 Ezra are represented in the Vulgate in an Old Latin version. Jerome chose not to translate these books, because he did not believe they should be included in the canon. Considering that seven of 32 temporal introits and four of 14 sanctoral introits are from those books, a substantial set by any standard, we must assume that Rome continued to believe very strongly in the canonical value of those texts, showing for post-Jeromian feasts a rejection of Jerome's work. Another striking characteristic in the choice of texts is the number of introits from the books of Wisdom,

Sirach, and Isaiah, 21 out of the total of 46; these three books happen to be adjacent in the arrangement of the Bible.

In the following table I am taking the liberty of grouping the deuterocanonical books with Old Latin texts if they belong to feasts of early origin, even when they are close to the Vulgate, since even the Vulgate version is Old Latin. For later feasts, whenever the introit texts from those books coincide with the Vulgate, I will group them with other Vulgate texts.

The change from Old Latin to the Vulgate in Rome occurred at some point during the sixth century, with the Vulgate firmly established after Gregory the Great. Let us examine the above results, taking the hypothetical year 550 as a dividing line. See Tables 4.1 and 4.2.

Temporale
Pre 550: 15 Old Latin texts, 5 Vulgate texts, 2 inconclusive
Post 550: 2 Old Latin text, 6 Vulgate texts, 2 inconclusive
Sanctorale
Pre 550: 6 Old Latin, 0 Vulgate, 5 inconclusive
Post 550: 0 Old Latin, 1 Vulgate, 1 inconclusive

In percentages, 64 to 85 percent of introits assigned to pre-550 feasts are Old Latin, and 58 to 83 percent of introits assigned to post-550 feasts are Vulgate. Leaving out the deuterocanonical texts does not change this statistic appreciably. It should be mentioned again that the year 550 is a very hypothetical dividing point for this study. It is clear that some books of the Vulgate Bible (for example, the Gospels) entered standard usage somewhat earlier. However, the evidence cited here suggests a tendency that the non-psalmic introits assigned to feasts before 550 adhere to Old Latin texts, whereas the later feasts prefer the Vulgate. We can therefore deduce that the origin of the introit belongs to the time period before 550.

Conclusions

Structural, formal, and textual evidence seems to suggest that the introit developed side by side with monastic antiphonal psalmody. The form, as described in Ordo I, is identical to that type of composition, and the musical structure and style of the introit compositions in both the Gregorian and the Old Roman idiom is similar to office antiphons.

An examination of introit texts reveals chronological layering. Feasts that entered the stational system at an early stage exhibit a

Table 4.1 Summary, Temporale

Liturgical Day	Year of Origin	Book of Bible	Introit Text Analysis
Dom V ante Nat Dni (R)	late 6th c.	Jer	close to Vulgate
Dom II Adv	late 6th c.	Is	vocabulary compatible with Vulgate
Dom III Adv	late 6th c.	Phil	Vulgate
Feria IV Q T Adv	3rd c.	Is	Vulgate
Vig Nat Dni	4th c.	cf Ex/Is	splice, but vocab. compatible with Vulgate
Nat Dni 2	early 6th c.	Is/Lk	5th c. N. Italian/N.African
Nat Dni 3	336	Is	N. It. (4th c.), Roman/ N.African (5th c.)
Dom I p Nat Dni	5th c.	Wis	Sardinian/N. Afr. (4th c.)
Epiph	late 4th c.	cf. Mal/1 Chron	splice, unsure
Dom I p Epiph	late 6th c.	cf. Dan/Is	splice, unsure
Feria IV Cin	mid-5th c.	Wis	unsure, not Vulgate (OL)
Dom IV Quad	late 4th c.	Is	Old Latin likely
Feria IV Hebd IV Quad	late 4th c.	Ezek	close to Vulgate
Sab Hebd IV Quad	late 4th c.	Is	influenced by N. It. (late 4th, early 5th c.)
Feria V Hebd V Quad	after 730	cf. Dan	unsure, but not Vulgate
Feria IV Maj Hebd	late 4th c.	Phil	Rom./N. Afr. (5th c.)
Feria V in Caena Dom	4th c.	Gal	Probably OL
Feria II Pasch	4th c.	Ex	close to Vulgate
Feria III Pasch	4th c.	Sir	close to Vul (OL)
Feria IV Pasch	4th c.	Mt	N. Afr (3–6th c.), N. It. (4–6th c.), Rom. (4–5th c.)
Feria V Pasch	4th c.	Wis	close to Vul (OL)
Oct Pasch	4th c.	1 Pet	Rom/N.Afr (early 5th c.)
Dom V p Pasch	4th c.	Is	unsure, but not Vulgate
Ascens Dni	4th c.	Acts	vocab. compatible with N.It (5th c.)
Dom Pent	1st c.	Wis	close to Vul (OL)
Feria III Pent	early 6th c.	4 Ezr	Vulgate (OL)
Sab Pent	4th c.	Rom	close to Vulgate
De Trinitate (S)	7th c.	Tob	close to Vulgate
Dom XVIII p Pent	late 6th c.	Sir	unsure, but not Vulgate (OL)
Dom XXI p Pent	late 6th c.	Esth	close to N.It. (6th c.)
Dom XXVIII p Pent	late 6th c.	Jer	close to Vulgate
Christ the King	modern	Rev	Vulgate

Table 4.2 Summary, Sanctorale

Liturgical Day	Year of Origin	Book of Bible	Introit Text Analysis
S. Ioannis Ev 2	4th c.	Sir	close to Vul (OL)
S. Marcelli	6th c.	Sir	close to Vul (OL)
S. Gregorii/others	7th c./5th c.	Dan	vocab. close to Vulgate
Ss. Philippi et Iacobi	563	Neh	unsure, not Vulgate
Dedic S. Mariae	after 608	Gen	Rom (late 4th c.), also Vulg?
Ss. Primi et Feliciani/ others	4th c.?	Sir	close to Vul (OL)
Vig S. Ioannis Bapt	5th c.[50]	Lk	N.Afr. (~500), N.It. (5th c.)
S. Ioannis Bapt	5th c.	Is	close to N. It. (late 4th c.)
Vig S. Petri	258[51]	Jn	close to Vulgate, also N. Afr. (5 – 6th c.); unsure
S. Petri	258	Acts	Vulgate, also N. It (late 4th c.); unsure
S. Pauli	258	2 Tim	Vulgate, also N. It. (6th c.); unsure
Ss. Processi et Martiniani/ Proth-Jac.	4th c.	Wis	vocab. close to Vulgate (OL)
S. Clementis	4th c.	Is	unsure, but not Vulgate
Vig S. Andreae	6th c.?	Mt	N. It. (~400)

tendency to adhere to Old Latin translations of non-psalmic texts of the Bible, whereas newer feasts use the Vulgate. The completeness of the introit cycle also points to a time when most of the stational system had been in place. This all indicates that the earliest layer of introit texts was created before the mid-sixth century.

The post-Pentecostal numerical sequencing, which is discussed at length above and which also extends into other chant genres, is a sign of an ad hoc series of chants, compatible with ad hoc liturgical texts assigned to the whole season by the Old Gelasian Sacramentary. If we are to believe that communions were composed concurrently with the introits, we can enter into speculation about the Lenten weekday communions and their numerical sequence, which is broken when the scrutinies are moved to Lenten weekdays in the late sixth century, and we again arrive at a time before the mid-sixth century as a plausible origin.

Chapter 5

The Carolingian Reform

Historical Background

The dissemination of the Roman repertoire of chant North of the Alps and its eventual (albeit in a somewhat changed form) almost universal use in the Latin Church is due in large part to the efforts of Pepin III and his son, Charlemagne. The Old Gelasian Sacramentary was already widely circulated in the Frankish Empire before Pepin III (751–768). It was the principal agent of Romanization before the royal initiatives. As in Rome, this liturgy coexisted in Gaul with other liturgical usages.[1] Ordines Romani also circulated in Gaul (Tours, Corbie, Besançon region) before Pepin.[2]

There were two stages of Romanization:[3]
• private initiatives before Pepin by monks, priests, and bishops without coordination
• coordinated efforts by the Frankish monarchy.

The Venerable Bede reports that Bishop Benedict of York obtained permission from Pope Agatho (678–681) to bring to England John, abbot and archcantor from Rome, to teach Roman chant and liturgy.[4] Egbert of York (732–766) alludes to several antiphoners in York modeled after the Roman example.[5] The popes of that time did not promote this Romanization, and councils and synods did not address the subject.[6] Besides these and other isolated instances, the main initiative for a coordinated effort lay solely with the Frankish monarchy.

Charlemagne expanded and consolidated Romanization, but the coordinated effort seems to have begun with Pope Stephen's visit to the Frankish Empire under Pepin III, Charlemagne's father. The Roman chant repertoire was transmitted across the Alps for the first time in a significant way by members of Pope Stephen's clerical

entourage in the winter of 753/754.[7] Carolingian sources describe
Pope Stephen's visit as the occasion when Pepin decided to adopt the
"cantus romanus." At least that is what the official record says. Actually,
Bishop Chrodegang had been sent to Rome in 753 to invite Pope
Stephen to come North, and probably accompanied him on his return
trip. He thus had the opportunity to observe the pope's liturgical
practices and probably convinced Pepin to adopt them. It is unlikely
that Pepin himself would have thought of using the liturgy as a
politically unifying tool, as many experts claim. The impetus for
adopting the "cantus romanus" must have been foremost ecclesiastical
interest. Chrodegang himself, in his "Regula canonicorum," invokes
the example of Rome on three different occasions.[8]

     The cantus romanus was recreated by the cantors of Metz,
who in turn were reorganized into a schola cantorum by Bishop
Chrodegang as early as 754/755.[9] Roman unnotated antiphoners were
used in the oral transmission of chant. Since antiphoners differed
in minor ways, some cathedrals in the Frankish sphere of influence
received slightly different books, as is evidenced when comparing the
gradual lists of the Rheinau and Mont-Blandin antiphoners to those
of Monza, Compiegne, Corbie, and Senlis. The musical practice,
however, seems to have spread from Metz, since there is a great similarity between the Gregorian repertoires of various geographical
regions in the Frankish kingdom as compared to the Old Roman
notated sources.

     Pope Paul I (757–767) and Pope Hadrian I (772–795) sent
cantors to the Frankish Empire under Pepin and Charlemagne "for
the concord of the apostolic see and peaceful harmony of the holy
Church of God."[10] Bishop Chrodegang's successor, Bishop Angilram
(768-791), declared that the Roman Mass proper was sung by
the canons of Metz, and he lists particular chants that are the same
in Frankish and Roman sources.[11] In addition, after the Carolingian
reforms of the eighth century, clerics performed increasingly a full
cycle of the office after the Roman or monastic pattern.[12]

     Why was the Romanization of Gaul so successful?
- There was a general admiration of Rome and its liturgy, as reflected
  in the reports of pilgrims.
- By Romanizing, the monarchy could unify the kingdom and
  establish unity with Rome.

- Romanization quelled whatever Byzantine influence may have remained in Gaul.[13]

There followed a period of great interest in copying all aspects of the Roman liturgy. Cantors of the Roman schola were sent to ecclesiastical centers, where they taught their chant by rote (musical notation would not be invented for quite some time) to Frankish singers. This did not always give the desired result. The cantors often had a condescending attitude toward their Frankish students and accused them of being incapable of good musicianship. On the other hand there was also some resistance on the part of the Frankish singers.[14] For one part, they insisted on retaining the Gallican psalter for the psalm verses, which had already been committed to memory, rather than learning the Roman psalter which the cantors used. For another, it is likely that the Frankish scholae cantorum adjusted the newly taught Roman chants to their Frankish style of singing.

The system of eight modes, completely unknown in Rome at the time of Ordo I, was borrowed by the Carolingians from Byzantium (Octoechos). Certain changes to the Roman chant were necessary to adapt it to this system.[15] The Franks seem to have learned the chant repertoire from Rome without reference to any modal system, since the Old Roman chant shows no modal classification (of course, this assumes that the Old Roman chant is in some ways related to the cantus romanus). "Tonaries, like much intellectual writing of the time, are evidence of the intellectual curiosity of the Carolingian musicians, having newly mastered an immense repertoire of liturgical music, aware both of some aspects of sophisticated Byzantine practice and of the classical theoretical knowledge transmitted by Boethius, and eager to understand, analyze, and classify their own music. A didactic purpose is also present, for several theorists speak of their wish to rectify corrupt practices."[16]

Oral transmission sometimes led to an antiphon beginning in one mode, moving through another, and ending in a third. That practice could be different in the neighboring cathedral; when comparing documents, we sometimes find the same chant in two different modes.[17] Even the written text was not without errors, as manuscripts were copied by hand and passed on to other locations for more copying.

The center of Carolingian liturgical activity and dissemination was Metz, but, even there, errors, discrepancies, and divergences from the Roman model were found. In the early ninth century, Amalar of Metz describes how he discovered discrepancies among different antiphoners in the region, and how he was sent to Rome to ask Pope Gregory for an authentic antiphoner. The pontiff answered that he did not have any to spare, since the last spare had been taken by Wala (Walafrid Strabo, who in about 840 wrote "De ecclesiam rerum exordiis et incrementis") to the Frankish Empire. So Amalar compared his own antiphoner to the Roman, found that many antiphons not only differed in text but also in number, and marked on the margins where the two concurred and where they differed.[18]

As late as the mid-twelfth century, the Cistercians tried to adopt the musical practice of Metz, thought to be the leading exponent of Roman chant, and thought to have the authentic Roman antiphoner. However, they found the practice and the documents to be unsuitable and corrupt and took upon themselves a complete re-editing of the chants for their community.[19]

The cantus romanus, imposed on Frankish and also Italian Churches, mixed differently and developed into Gregorian Chant North of the Alps and Old Roman Chant, which is first found in musical notation in thirteenth-century Roman chant books,[20] in Rome itself.

The earliest eighth- and ninth-century graduals and antiphonaries, found in Hesbert's *Antiphonale Missarum Sextuplex,* are remarkably uniform throughout. The gradual of Monza (M) contains only solo chants, whereas the five antiphoners (Rheinau (R), Mont-Blandin (B), Compiegne (C), Corbie (K), and Senlis (S) contain the whole proper, texts only. In a discussion of the introits, we can therefore leave out the gradual of Monza. Four of the antiphoners, R, B, C, and K, contain the entire text of the introit antiphons and the incipit of the psalms, whereas S contains only incipts throughout. The latter could be the sign of a directorium, pointing the reader to another document, which we do not have, or it could have assumed that the antiphons were memorized and could be recalled once the reader saw the incipit. In all five cases, however, we must assume that the psalter itself was memorized, and that therefore only the incipit of the first verse of the psalm was necessary.

The indications of the Roman stational churches in the headings of Sundays and feasts (for example, "VIII Kalendas Januarias / in Die Natalis Domini / Statio ad Sanctum Petrum," "Dominica in

Palmis / Statio at Lateranis," or "Dominica Sancta / Statio ad Sanctam Mariam") make it clear that we are dealing with copies of original Roman documents, and that the Roman liturgy was held in high esteem. Any reference to Roman origin was thought to indicate authenticity and compliance with the wish for uniformity.

Roman liturgical documents—Sacramentaries, Lectionaries, antiphoners, ordines, and so on—were meticulously copied and applied. Over the years, however, some local customs took a foothold in the recensions, as we will see in our discussion of the Ordines Romani in the appendix, while holding on to Roman wording to establish authority. For example, the Old Gelasian Sacramentary reflects the use of the titular churches in Rome between 628 and 715 and was probably copied around 750. The Frankish or eighth-century Gelasian Sacramentary exhibits some characteristics that point to Gallican input. The Gallicanization of Ordo I was necessary to a point, since the document is sometimes tied to a particular church, and also to avoid offending local usages that were close to people's hearts.[21]

The Gregorian Sacramentary, compiled probably under Pope Honorius (625–638), circulated in York, Aachen, and Salzburg. Another eighth-century copy was sent to Charlemagne by Hadrian I (772–795) between 784 and 791. A ninth-century copy of this document still exists. There are also four eighth-century Gallican Sacramentaries that contain a small amount of Roman material.

We have to assume that the earliest graduals would have come North at about the same time as other liturgical books. The earliest extant example of this is in the form of chant text incipits copied into a fifth-century Gallican Lectionary (Wolfenbuettel).[22]

There is plenty of evidence that the Franks did not simply reproduce the Roman liturgy and its music exactly, but that liturgical modifications were made to accommodate local requirements.[23] However, whereas the Frankish leaders were concerned with uniformity within the liturgical rites, the same cannot be said about the popes. While there was general uniformity North of the Alps, Rome was surrounded by different rites, the major ones being the Beneventan and the Ambrosian, and there was no attempt by Rome to coerce the surrounding areas into compliance with Roman liturgical practices. That coercion came later from the North.

With the restoration of the Empire in the establishment
of the Holy Roman Empire in 962, travel and exchange of information
back and forth across the Alps increased considerably. Emperor Otto
I, who made numerous visits to Rome, showed a great deal of concern
about the liturgical state in Rome, which had declined somewhat
after Charlemagne, and brought the Romano-German Pontifical with
his entourage of bishops and abbots to the Holy City. This pontifical
became very popular and was later even called a "Roman" document.
The "Ottonization" of the Roman liturgy was sealed by a series of
German popes between 1046 and 1073.[24] This led to some practices
being transmitted South of the Alps, like the versus ad repetendum,
which was just diminishing in importance in France and Germany,
and which was introduced into the Roman performance of the introit
at that time, to last for another two centuries.

MEDIEVAL THEOLOGY OF THE INTROIT

Medieval theologians, liturgists, and scholars approach the subject
of the introit from two different viewpoints, the practical and
the theological. Hrabanus Maurus, in his De institutione clericorum
of about 820, writes: "The introit has the purpose of preparing the
congregation for the following Eucharistic celebration."[25]

For ninth- through twelfth-century theologians, the introit
and its tropes articulated the prefiguration of Christ in the Old
Testament and presented the priest as Christ coming into the world.
Most introit antiphons and psalm verses represent the Hebrew
tradition. Singers represent the people welcoming Christ as prophets,
patriarchs, apostles, and angels, predicting and announcing the theme
of the feast.[26]

Chapter 6

The Thematic Use of the Introit

Originally, the introit consisted of an antiphon, several verses of a psalm, the doxology, and a repetition of the antiphon. In later centuries, as processions became shorter and the compositions became more elaborate, the psalm was truncated to one verse. This lost much of the thematic connection to the readings of the day or the season, and the psalm itself diminished in importance. The current missal, for instance, gives only the antiphon text, completely disregarding the psalm verses.

In our discussion about the thematic usage of the introit within the context of the readings of the day, we will examine psalms as well as antiphons, since both applied to the thematic unity at the time the introits were written. But first we must establish the texts themselves.

The following list constitutes a comparison of historical usage of the introits for Sundays and major feasts of the Lord from Christmas through Pentecost. The listed introit and its psalm apply to all three usages. In this limited study, I only examined those days where the introit was consistent in all three traditions. Please excuse my labeling of feasts; since the early Medieval and Tridentine usage coincides in its labels, I opted to utilize that nomenclature, translating into English for the major feasts.

Vigil of Christmas

8th–10th c. Antiphoners: Introit: Hodie scietis, Exodus 16:6, 7; Isaiah 35:4 / Psalm: Domini est terra (24)
7th c. Roman Lectionary: Romans 1:1–6/Luke 2:1–14?
Tridentine Usage: Romans 1:1–6/Matthew 1:18–21
Vatican II Reform: Isaiah 62:1–5/Acts 13:16–17, 22–25/ Matthew 1:1–25

Midnight Mass

8th–10th c. Antiphoners: IN: Dominus dixit, Psalm 2:7/PS: Quare fremuerunt (2)
7th c. Roman Lectionary: Isaiah 9:2–7/Titus 2:11–15/Luke 2:1–14
Tridentine Usage: Titus 2:11–15/Luke 2:1–14
Vatican II Reform: Isaiah 9:1–3, 5–6/Titus 2:11–14/Luke 2:1–14

Christmas Dawn

8th–10th c. Antiphoners: IN: Lux fulgebit, Isaiah 9:2, 6; Luke 1:33/PS: Dominus regnavit (93)
7th c. Roman Lectionary: Titus 2:11–15/Luke 2:15–20
Tridentine Usage: Titus 3:4–7/Luke 2:15–20
Vatican II Reform: Isaiah 62:11–12/Titus 3:4–7/Luke 2:15–20

Christmas Day

8th–10th c. Antiphoners: IN: Puer natus est, Isaiah 9:6/PS: Cantate Domino (98)
7th c. Roman Lectionary: Isaiah 52:6–10/Hebrews 1:1–12/John 1:1–14
Tridentine Usage: Hebrews 1:1–12/John 1:1–14
Vatican II Reform: Isaiah 52:7–10/Hebrews 1:1–6/John 1:1–18

Sunday in the Octave of Christmas

8th–10th c. Antiphoners: IN: Dum medium, Wisdom 18:14–15/PS: Dominus regnavit (93)
7th c. Roman Lectionary: Galatians 4:1–7/Luke 2:21–32
Tridentine Usage: Galatians 4:1–7/Luke 2:33–40
Vatican II Reform: (Second Sunday after Christmas) Sirach 24:1–2, 12–16/Ephesians 1:3–6, 15–18/John 1:1–18

Epiphany

8th–10th c. Antiphoners: IN: Ecce advenit, Malachi 3:1; 1 Chronicles 29:12/PS: Deus iudicium (72)
7th c. Roman Lectionary: Isaiah 60:1–6/Titus 3:4–7/Matthew 2:1–12
Tridentine Usage: Isaiah 60:1–6/Matthew 2:1–12
Vatican II Reform: Isaiah 60:1–6/Ephesians 3:2–6/Matthew 2:1–12

Second Sunday after Epiphany

8th–10th c. Antiphoners: IN: Omnis terra, Psalm 66:5/PS: Iubilate
Deo (66)
7th c. Roman Lectionary: 1 Timothy 1:15–17/?
Tridentine Usage: Romans 12:6–16/John 2:1–11
Vatican II Reform: (Ordinary Time 2-A) Isaiah 49:3–6/1 Corinthians
1:1–3/John 1:29–34

Third Sunday after Epiphany

8th–10th c. Antiphoners: IN: Adorate Deum, Psalm 97:7, 8/PS:
Dominus regnavit (97)
7th c. Roman Lectionary: Hebrews 3:1–6/Matthew 8:1–13
Tridentine Usage: Romans 12:16–21/Matthew 8:1–13
Vatican II Reform: (Ordinary Time 3-C) Nehemiah 8:1–10/1
Corinthians 12:12–30/Luke 1:1–4; 4:14–20

Quinquagesima Sunday

8th–10th c. Antiphoners: IN: Esto mihi, Psalm 31:3–4/PS: In te
Domine (31)
7th c. Roman Lectionary: 1 Corinthians 13:1–13/Luke 18:31–43
Tridentine Usage: 1 Corinthians 13:1–13/Luke 18:31–43
Vatican II Reform: (Ordinary Time 6-A) Sirach 15:15–20/1
Corinthians 2:6–10/Matthew 5:17–37

Quadragesima Sunday

8th–10th c. Antiphoners: IN: Invocabit me, Psalm 91:15–16/PS:
Qui habitat (91)
7th c. Roman Lectionary: 2 Corinthians 6:1–10/Matthew 4:1–11
Tridentine Usage: 2 Corinthians 6:1–10/Matthew 4:1–11
Vatican II Reform: (Lent 1-A) Genesis 2:7–9; 3:1–7/Romans 5:12–19/
Matthew 4:1–11

Dominica 4ta in Quadragesima

8th–10th c. Antiphoners: IN: Laetare Ierusalem, Isaiah 66:10–11/PS:
Laetatus sum (122)
7th c. Roman Lectionary: Galatians 4:22–31/John 6:1–14

Tridentine Usage: Galatians 4:22–31/John 6:1–15
Vatican II Reform: (Lent 4-A) 1 Samuel 16:1, 6–7, 10–13/Ephesians 5:8–14/John 9:1–41

In Coena Domini

8th–10th c. Antiphoners: IN: Nos autem, Galatians 6:14/PS: Cantate Domino (98) or Deus misereatur (67)
7th c. Roman Lectionary: 1 Corinthians 11:20-32/(no Gospel assigned)
Tridentine Usage: 1 Corinthians 11:20–32/John 13:1–15
Vatican II Reform: Exodus 12:1–8, 11–14/1 Corinthains 11:23–26/John 13:1–15

Easter

8th–10th c. Antiphoners: IN: Resurrexi, Psalm 139:18, 5, 6/PS: Domine probasti (139)
7th c. Roman Lectionary: 1 Corinthians 5:7–8/Mark 16:1–7
Tridentine Usage: 1 Corinthians 5:7–8/Mark 16:1–7
Vatican II Reform: Acts 10:34, 37–43/1 Corinthians 5:6–8/John 20:20:1–9

First Sunday after Easter

8th–10th c. Antiphoners: IN: Quasimodo, 1 Peter 2:2/PS: Exsultate iusti (82)
7th c. Roman Lectionary: 1 John 5:4–10/John 20:24–31
Tridentine Usage: 1 John 5:4–10/John 20:19–31
Vatican II Reform: (Easter 2-B) Acts 4:32–35/1 John 5:1–6/John 20:19–31

Second Sunday after Easter

8th–10th c. Antiphoners: IN: Misericordia Dni., Psalm 33:5–6/PS: Exsultate iusti (82)
7th c. Roman Lectionary: 1 Peter 2:21–25/John 10:11–16
Tridentine Usage: 1 Peter 2:21–25/John 10:11–16
Vatican II Reform: (Easter 4-B) Acts 4:8–12/1 John 3:1–2/John 10:11–18

Third Sunday after Easter

8th–10th c. Antiphoners: IN: Iubilate Deo, Psalm 66:1–2/PS: Dicite Deo (66)
7th c. Roman Lectionary: 1 Peter 2:11–19/John 16:16–22
Tridentine Usage: 1 Peter 2:11–19/John 16:16–22
Vatican II Reform: (Easter 3-B) Acts 3:13–19/1 John 2:1–5/ Luke 21:1–19

Fourth Sunday after Easter

8th–10th c. Antiphoners: IN: Cantate Domino, Psalm 98:1/PS: Salvavit sibi (98)
7th c. Roman Lectionary: James 1:17–21/John 16:5–14
Tridentine Usage: James 1:17–21/John 16:5–14
Vatican II Reform: (Easter 5-B) Acts 9:26–31/1 John 3:18–24/ John 15:1–8

Fifth Sunday after Easter

8th–10th c. Antiphoners: IN: Vocem iucunditatis, Isaiah 48:20/ PS: Iubilate Deo (66)
7th c. Roman Lectionary: James 1:22–27/John 16:23–30
Tridentine Usage: James 1:22–27/John 16:23–30
Vatican II Reform: (Easter 6-B) Acts 10:25–26, 34–35, 44–48/1 John 4:7–10/John 15:9–17

Dominica infra Ascensionem

8th–10th c. Antiphoners: IN: Exaudi Domine, Psalm 27:7–9/PS: Dominus illuminatio (27)
7th c. Roman Lectionary: (Dom 6 post Pascha) 1 Peter 4:7–11/ John 15:26—16:4
Tridentine Usage: 1 Peter 4:7–11/John 15:26—16:4
Vatican II Reform: (Easter 7-A) Acts 1:12–14/1 Peter 4:13–16/ John 17:1–11

Ascension

8th–10th c. Antiphoners: IN: Viri Galiaei, Acts 1:11/PS: Omnes gentes (47)
7th c. Roman Lectionary: Acts 1:1–11/Mark 16:14–20

Tridentine Usage: Acts 1:1–11/Mark 16:14–20
Vatican II Reform: Acts 1:1–11/Ephesians 1:17–23/Mark 16:15–20

Vigil of Pentecost

8th–10th c. Antiphoners: IN: Letania et Gloria in excelsis
Gregorian Missal: IN: Dum sanctificatus, Ezekiel 36:23–26/PS:
Benedicam Dmnm (34)
7th c. Roman Lectionary: Acts 19:1–8/John 14:15–21
Tridentine Usage: Acts 19:1–8/John 14:15–21
Vatican II Reform: Genesis 11:1–9/Romans 8:22–27/John 7:37–39

Pentecost

8th–10th c. Antiphoners: IN: Spiritus Domini, Wisdom 1:7/PS:
Exsurgat Deus (68)
7th c. Roman Lectionary: Acts 2:1–11/John 14:23–31
Tridentine Usage: Acts 2:1–11/John 14:23–31
Vatican II Reform: Acts 2:1–11/1 Corinthians 12:3–7, 12–13/
John 20:19–23 (alt 14:15–16, 23–26)

We can make the following observations:
- In the major feasts of Christmas, Epiphany, Holy Thursday, Easter, Ascension, and Pentecost, there is general agreement of all three sources.
- There is general agreement on all Sundays between the earliest sources and the Tridentine usage.
- Considerable changes were made at Vatican II: the readings of the Christmas season were changed, the Sundays between Epiphany and Lent show no agreement at all to the earlier sources, the later Sundays in the Easter season differ, the three-year cycle obscures further the connection between the introits and the readings with which they were originally coupled, and the usage of the earlier cycle of readings within the three-year cycle is not consistent (that is, those readings do not all fall into the same year of the three-year cycle).

We will approach our discussion of the thematic connection according to these categories:

1. Sundays and feasts where there is overall agreement between all sources.

2. Other selected Sundays where we research the thematic connection in the earliest sources.

3. The same Sundays as in #2, where we research the thematic connection in the post–Vatican II source.

1. Sundays and feasts: Here I have chosen the Masses for Christmas.

Vigil of Christmas: Psalm 24 echoes the Advent theme, "Gates, lift high your heads, raise high the ancient gateways, and the king of glory shall enter!" (verses 7 and 9). While there is no direct textual connection to the readings, it does set the tone for the virgin birth of Matthew 1:18–21 and Luke 2:1–14. The Vatican II addition of the genealogy of Christ (Matthew 1:1–17) actually establishes the royal lineage of Christ, thus tying the introit psalm closer to the modern usage. The use of Isaiah 62:1–5 is also appropriate with Psalm 24; both announce the birth of a king, and Acts 13 harps on Christ's Davidic lineage. Thus the Vatican II readings have a closer connection to the introit psalm.

Midnight Mass: Again, there is no direct link between the psalm and the readings. Isaiah 9 announces the new king in the present tense, and the peace proclaimed in 9:5–6 is echoed in Luke 2:14. Psalm 2 is a complete antithesis of this idea: dominion comes by submission of the enemies. There is even more thematic conflict: Psalm 2 clearly gives the king dominion over the whole earth, whereas Isaiah's king comes to rule over the throne of David and his kingdom. By placing these texts side by side, we might infer that David's kingdom is the whole world.

Christmas at Dawn: Psalm 93 applies the kingship of God to Christ, predetermined since the beginning of time ("your throne is set form of old" [verse 2]). This is amplified in the antiphon text. In Isaiah 62:11, it is actually the ends of the earth that announce to Zion her salvation. Titus 2:11, found in the earliest Lectionary, picks up this universal theme, "God's grace has been revealed to save the whole human race," which is elaborated in Titus 3:4–7 of the Tridentine and Vatican II usages. Luke 2:15–20 is a continuation of the Christmas story, dealing with the adoration of the shepherds, who came at dawn.

Christmas Day: There are several parallels between Psalm 98 and Isaiah 52: both talk about God's holy arm (Psalm 98:1; Isaiah 52:10), and both reveal God's saving power to the whole world: "The whole wide world has seen the saving power of our God" (Psalm 98:3b), "all the ends of the earth have seen the salvation of our God" (Isaiah 52:10). Hebrews 1:3 places Christ's seat at the right hand of the divine majesty (see Psalm 98:1: "his saving power is in his right hand"). Hebrews 1:9 talks about Christ's "scepter of justice" (see Ps 98:9); unfortunately, this verse is left out of the Vatican II usage. The direct reference of the birth of Christ, theologized in the Gospel, is found in the introit antiphon (Isaiah 9:6).

2. *Other Selected Sundays* (earlier Lectionaries): Here I chose several Sundays where the readings were changed in contemporary usage; I will elaborate here on the original setting and discuss Vatican II usage in #3 below.

Sunday in the Octave of Christmas/Second Sunday after Christmas: The antiphon introduces Psalm 93 with these words: "While a profound silence enveloped all things, and night was in the midst of her course, your all-powerful Word, O Lord, leapt down from your royal throne" (Wisdom 18:14–15). The light of Christ coming down upon a dark world is echoed in the Nunc dimittis (Luke 2:29–32). The Tridentine continuation of this story loses some of the imagery of light. Galatians 4:5 make it clear that Christ was born a subject of the Law, to redeem the subjects of the Law. Psalm 93:5 says, "your decrees stand firm, unshakable." Thus the reading in Galatians applies the idea of the Law as sung at the beginning of Mass in the introit.

Third Sunday after Epiphany/Ordinary Time 3-C: Psalm 97 continues the Epiphany themes of light dawning for the upright (verse 11), and that "the heavens proclaim his saving justice, all nations see his glory" (verse 6). Hebrews 3:1–6 makes a comparison between Moses' trustworthiness within the household and Christ's trustworthiness over the household. Whereas Psalm 97:10 declares that God "loves those who hate evil, Romans 12 in the Tridentine usage goes a step further by explaining what it means to be upright: to forgive, to be at peace, and to master evil with good. The Gospel (Matthew 8:1–13) talks about healing and the power of faith in the healing of the centurion's servant. There is little direct connection between the introit text and the readings. However, the Epiphany theme inherent in the introit makes it appropriate for the season.

Dominica 4ta in Quadragesima/Lent 4-A: The joyful texts of Isaiah 66:10–11 gives us a break from the discipline of Lent on our pilgrimage of faith (Psalm 122 is a pilgrim psalm). Galatians 4:22–31 says that Abraham had two sons, one born of a slave girl "in the way of human nature," and one born of a freewoman through a promise. These two women "stand for the two covenants." Paul goes on to say that "we are the children not of the slave girl but of the freewoman." In the Gospel (John 6:1–14), Jesus performs the miracle of the multiplication of bread and fish. The introit text again seems to have more relevance to its placement within the season rather than specific readings.

Third Sunday after Easter/Easter 3-B: The introit sounds the spirit of the season in Psalm 66:6: "he changed the sea into dry land, they crossed the river on foot" echoes one of the Easter themes of the Exodus, which was read at the Easter Vigil, recalling God's salvation in the old covenant and linking it to Christ's salvation in the new. 1 Peter 2:11–19 exhorts the early Christians to live good moral lives and to respect worldly authority, so that others may come to believe. In John 16:16–22, Jesus explains to his disciples what he means by "in a short time you will no longer see me, and then a short time later you will see me again" (verse 16). This is a veiled reference to his approaching death and Resurrection. Again, the introit bears no direct connection to the readings but rather complements them in our understanding of the season.

3. Other Sundays (Vatican II usage):

Sunday in the Octave of Christmas/Second Sunday after Christmas: The antiphon introduces Psalm 93 with these words: "While a profound silence enveloped all things, and night was in the midst of her course, your all-powerful Word, O Lord, leapt down from your royal throne" (Wisdom 18:14–15). Sirach 24:1–2, 12–16 takes the voice of wisdom, who grows like the most delectable plants and spreads out like a vine; those who taste of her fruit will yearn for more. In his letter to the Ephesians (1:3–6, 15–18), Paul explains God's plan of salvation. The Gospel is the same as on Christmas Day. The Old Testament reading speaks of the Word of God, or his wisdom, present with God before the world began. The mission of this work is shown in the introit antiphon (see above), and in a cruder way in Psalm 93 (an early psalm). Thus, the antiphon and the psalm have a direct link to the Gospel reading.

Third Sunday after Epiphany/Ordinary Time 3-C: (Years A and B have a different assigned introit, so only Year C applies to our discussion.) Psalm 97 continues the Epiphany themes of light dawning for the upright (verse 11), and that "the heavens proclaim his saving justice, all nations see his glory" (verse 6). Nehemiah 8:1–10 describes how Ezra read from and explained the Law to the whole assembly, and how they "were in tears, as they listened to the Law." Paul draws a parallel between the parts of the body and the body of Christ (the Church) in 1 Corinthians 12:12–30. In the Gospel (Luke 4:14–20), Jesus reads Isaiah 61:1–2 ("The Spirit of the Lord is upon me . . .") from the scroll in the synagogue and then proclaims that the passage has been fulfilled. Both the reading from the Law by Ezra and the reading from Isaiah by Jesus have a link in the introit antiphon: "Zion has heard and is glad; the daughters of Judah have rejoiced" (Psalm 97:8).

Dominica 4ta in Quadragesima/Lent 4-A: The joyful text of Isaiah 66:10–11 gives us a break from the discipline of Lent on our pilgrimage of faith (Psalm 122 is a pilgrim psalm). First Samuel 16 talks about the choice and the anointing of David. Paul exhorts the Ephesians (5:8–14) to be children of the light. John 9 describes the miracle of the man born blind. Psalm 122 is a pilgrim's song in admiration of Jerusalem. This city is the goal of his journey, and the symbol of God's presence in the city is the throne of David. Thus, there is a slight connection between the first reading and the introit.

Third Sunday after Easter/Easter 3-B: The introit sounds the spirit of the season in Psalm 66:6: "he changed the sea into dry land, they crossed the river on foot" echoes one of the Easter themes of the Exodus, which was read at the Easter Vigil, recalling God's salvation in the old covenant and linking it to Christ's salvation in the new. In Acts 3:13–19, Peter explains to the people that it was the God of Abraham who cured the lame man, thus equating the God of the new covenant, working through him and John, with the God of the old covenant. John writes in his first letter (2:1–5) that we must come to know Christ by keeping his commandments. And in John 15:1–8, we hear the parable of the lost sheep. The introit is thus connected more to the themes of the season than to specific references in the readings.

Conclusions

We can conclude that the introit texts were originally chosen to reflect the sense of the season for which they were written. In addition, there are some instances where the texts reflect specific ideas portrayed in the readings, which is especially prominent in the feasts of the Lord. However, there does not seem to be in the original plan an overall effort on the part of the composers of the introits to make a direct link to the readings of ordinary Sundays. Within the seasons, any reference to a reading in the introit seems to be coincidental. In addition, some obvious opportunities for bringing out a particular theme in connection to certain readings are not taken. For example, on Good Shepherd Sunday (the Second Sunday after Easter or the Fourth Sunday of Easter in the new system) the obvious opportunity to choose a scripture text about the Good Shepherd is not taken. In this way, the introit antiphon and the chosen psalm augment and complement the readings within the season, rather than making direct reference to the readings. The three-year cycle does not seem to have obscured that application.

It should be mentioned, however, that the texts of the communion antiphons, which would have been assembled at about the same time as the introits, are much closer linked to the readings throughout the year. This makes sense, since the readings have been proclaimed at Mass before the time of communion, and continuing a theme heard in the readings would carry that theme to the end of the Mass. Theologically speaking, we partake of the word during the readings, and we partake of the Word in communion. However, applying such a theme at the beginning of Mass, before the readings have actually been heard, makes no sense at all, unless the theme is well known, as it would be in a feast of the Lord. Thus, the texts of the introits tend to be more general, and the texts of the communions more specific.

One of the problems in dealing with the introit texts is the way in which they were applied throughout history. Originally, the antiphon and a considerable portion of the psalm were performed. Since about 1000, the importance of the psalm has diminished, and much of the thematic unity within each introit was lost. It is only in recent decades that we have experienced a resurging interest in psalmody as connected to this part of the Mass.

Part II

Metrical Psalmody

Chapter 7

Metrical Psalms

In the introduction to his *New Metrical Psalter*, Christopher Webber states, "The increasing use of the Psalter in the liturgy makes it desirable that there be musical settings which can be easily used by any congregation. Anglican chant, plainsong, and the Gelineau method all require an attention to phrasing which is quite different from the set relationship between words and music of the usual hymn . . . . The metrical method, on the other hand, fits the psalms to simple, and in most cases, familiar melodies. Most metrical psalms can be easily sung the first time they are presented."[1]

Metrical psalmody grew out of the need to provide appropriate congregational songs with biblical texts for Protestants after the Reformation. In the beginning, all British metrical hymns were psalms, and the Presbyterian Church retained the tradition of exclusive use of psalmic texts for hymns the longest.[2] Metrical psalters also appeared in French, German, and Dutch, as Protestant congregations found this new form of praise to be an effective vehicle for singing the psalms. Over the centuries, many Churches added hymns to their repertoire, diluting and in many ways replacing the psalms, while adding content important to each Church's doctrine. Julian's *Dictionary of Hymnology* (1907) states that between 1414 and 1889, 326 complete or partial versions of the metrical psalter were written.[3] The last century has seen a marked slowdown in this activity, and it is only since the liturgical renewal of the 60s and 70s that the subject has been revived.

The Catholic Church before the Second Vatican Council had no use for metrical psalmody, since the Church language was Latin and the congregation was not involved in the singing of the proper parts of the Mass or the chants of the office. However, with a renewed emphasis on congregational participation and the use of the psalter in the vernacular, we must reexamine metrical psalmody.

Most congregations are already familiar with the great wealth of responsorial psalms, sung between the readings, where the people sing a short refrain in response to a psalmist's verses. This form of psalmody recalls the original form of the gradual psalm at a time when Latin was still the language of the people. The documents also state clearly that the congregation should participate in the other parts of the proper of the Mass, most importantly the introit and communion antiphons.[4] Several poets and musicians have tried to compose practical settings of these parts of the Mass, but they are using either chant or a chant derivative, or presenting these parts in a responsorial form with either solo or choir verses and a congregational response. In the previous treatise on the origin and early development of the introit, we learned that the original form of the introit was antiphonal psalmody, where the antiphon was sung at the beginning and at the very end, framing a complete chanting of a psalm and doxology. Would it not be appropriate to reexamine the use of metrical psalmody in an antiphonal medium?

The Poetry of the Hebrew Psalter

Before we can answer this question, we must ask ourselves what happens to biblical prose when it is translated from Hebrew into another language, and when this translation is then metricized. It will become clear that any translation, metrical or not, is a compromise, trading original poetic form, beauty, and content with understanding and utility. Unfortunately, most biblical translators are not poets, and most poets are not translators, and thus many of the elements of the poetry of the psalms get lost in almost all translations. And even if a translation were done poetically, there is always the danger that the poet would superimpose his own poetic mind onto the psalmist's, creating a personal mixture of ideas that might not be appropriate for scriptural readings in public worship.

We can extend this train of thought to music in general, considering that the original language of a composition is intimately connected with the music. When the text is presented in translated form (for example, when singing a Palestrina motet or a Verdi opera in English), an important element of the music is changed.

Two psalters that stand out as excellent translations and poetic texts are the psalter from *The New Jerusalem Bible* and the *Grail Psalter*. *The New Jerusalem Bible* takes great care not only to present an authentic translation, but also to portray the psalms as English works of literary value. The *Grail Psalter* tries to imitate the musical rhythm of Hebrew poetry, which is characterized not by the number of syllables in each line, but by the number of accentuated syllables. When set to Gelineau tones, this psalter produces a musical result that is difficult to reproduce with any of the other psalters.

The general mood of a psalm is often the easiest element to copy in a translation. Even the overall structure, so much a part of particular psalm types, is represented in most translations. However, it is in the smaller structures of parallelism (saying things or concepts in two distinct ways), word pairs, imagery, and phonetic devices that translators have the most difficulty, and these are the areas of poetry that are lost or diluted even more in metrical settings.

For those who wish to pursue an in-depth study on the subject, I can recommend S. Gillingham's excellent book, from which I have taken some of the following illustrations.

As an example of parallelism, let us take Psalm 8: There are word pairs or examples of parallelism in almost every verse, expounding and amplifying and intensifying certain concepts.

v. 2 Children / babes (word pair)

v. 2b To foil the enemy, / to silence the foe and the rebel. (parallelism)

v. 3 When I look at the heavens, the work of your fingers, / the moon and the stars that you established. (parallelism, also word pair moon / stars)

v. 4 What are human beings that you are mindful of them, / mortals that you care for them? (parallelism)

v. 5 Yet you have made them little lower than God, / and crowned them with glory and honor. (parallelism by amplification, also word pair glory / honor)

v. 6 You have given them dominion over the works of your hands; / you have put all things under their feet. (parallelism, also word pair of hands / feet)

v. 7, 8 word pairs between land animals and air and sea animals

Examples of imagery in Psalm 8 are listed below.

v. 1 "Sovereign" and "majestic" imply royal character.

v. 2 Praise from children and babes foils the enemy, meaning the smallest praise can accomplish much.

v. 3 The heavens are the work of God's fingers (not hands).

v. 5 Human beings are little lower than God and crowned with glory and honor; again a royal character, this time shared by God with humanity (also "dominion," v. 6).

v. 6 All things under their feet: the earth is subdued by being subservient to human beings, borrowing imagery from Egyptian traditions.[5]

The Hebrew language of the psalter is filled with wordplay. It becomes clear that Hebrew is a language to be listened to rather than read.

Psalm 93:4

Mightier than the thunders of many waters
    miqqolot mayim rabbim
Mightier than the waves of the sea
    'addirim misb're yam
The Lord on high is mighty!
    'addir bammarom 'adonay

This example contains assonances in the sounds im, am, and om, and alliteration in the repeated consonants r, m, and y. Onomatopoeia is present in sounds resembling the thundering and roaring of the waves.[6]

Psalm 93:3

The floods have lifted up, O Lord,
    nas'u n'harot 'adonay
the floods have lifted up their voice,
    nas'u n'harot qolam
the floods lift up their roaring.
    yis'u n'harot dokyam

Again, we find assonance in the interplay of a-u, a-o, and o-a; alliteration in the use of the letter n in the first line; and onomatopoeia in the imitation of waves.[7] In addition, there is a further wordplay: adonay + qolam=dokyam (the first half of first word and the second half of second word).

Metrical Psalters

While the English language can use all of these poetic and phonetic devices and English poetry is filled with them, it is very difficult to reproduce them in a translation that tries to be faithful to an original text, especially when this translation is further altered in a metrical setting. However, metrical settings can add a device that is not explored in Hebrew psalmody: rhyme. While Hebrew poetry achieves aural satisfaction through phonetic devices, much of traditional English poetry achieves a different type of aural satisfaction through rhyme.

Metrical versions of the psalter present a great challenge, for they require a deep understanding of the psalms as well as poetic ability to create a work that does not become a personal stamp. However, the universal utility of metrical psalms provides a general appeal to congregations, making it possible to sing these ancient texts in pleasing meters and rhymes. The fact that some of the earliest settings of metrical psalms have stayed in the common repertoire for centuries point to their success in this regard.

For this project, an analysis of the history of English metrical psalmody is needed. As we will see, metrical psalters provided Protestant congregations with basic congregational song, and these settings were often the only vehicle making the psalms accessible to the common people. Before Parliament passed the Act of Supremacy in 1534, formally breaking England from Rome and setting Henry VIII as head of the Church of England, there were already some Protestant pockets in English religious life. William Tyndale could not publish an English translation of the New Testament at home; this was done in Worms, Germany, in 1525. In 1530, he followed by publishing the Pentatuch in English. The Protestant element took a strong foothold after 1534, however, and Miles Coverdale published the first complete English Bible on English soil and dedicated it to Henry VIII.

Sternhold's Psalter: The first attempt at setting a large number of psalms in metrical form occurred in Geneva in 1539, when John Calvin published 30 psalm settings by Clement Marot. Thomas Sternhold was the first Englishman to publish a metrical psalter, around 1548, containing 19 psalms, titled "Certayne Psalmes chose out of the Psalter of David, and drawe into English metre, by Thomas

Sternhold grome of Ye Kynges Maiesties roobes." A posthumous edition of 1549 contained 37 psalms by Sternhold and an additional seven by John Hopkins.

The Anglo-Genevan Editions: When Mary became Queen in 1553, many of the Protestant leaders fled the country. A very successful colony of English Protestants was established in Geneva, and the Calvinistic influence made itself felt in the four Anglo-Genevan editions of the psalter. All of them contained the original 44 Sternhold and Hopkins and added English translations of Genevan psalms by William Whittingham, John Pullain, and William Kethe.

Sternhold and Hopkins: When Queen Mary died in 1558 and Elizabeth I ascended the throne, most Protestant leaders returned from exile. John Daye went to work on an Anglo-Genevan psalter, which was to influence hymnody for the next two centuries. After publications of two incomplete psalters in 1560 and 1561, Daye finished the first complete English psalter in 1562. It contained the core Sternhold and Hopkins psalms, additional psalms by Hopkins, and the rest English translations of Genevan psalms. Known as the "Sternhold and Hopkins Psalter," it received 600 editions and was used extensively until the last publication in 1828.

A few verses of Psalm 27 show the language of the Sternhold and Hopkins Psalter.

Psalm 27

The Lord is both my health and light,
Shall man make me dismayed?
Since God doth give me strength and might,
Why should I be afraid?

While that my foes with all their strength
Began with me to brawl,
Thinking to eat me up, at length
Themselves have caught the fall.

Though they encamped against me lie,
My heart is not afraid;
And if in battle they will try,
I trust in God for aid.

Scottish Psalter of 1564/1635: In 1564, the General Assembly of the Church of Scotland published a psalter that leaned heavily on the Sternhold and Hopkins version. The edition of 1635 by Edward Millar added music, an astonishing 104 different tunes. These psalters have a greater variety in meter than the Sternhold and Hopkins and also included 21 settings of Scottish origin. However, the general opinion about the poetry is rather low. There seems to be a slavish adherence to literal translation at the expense of poetic beauty.

Psalm 47*

Let all folk with joy
Clap hands and rejoice,
And sing unto God
With most cheerful voice.
For high is the Lord,
And fear-ed to be,
The earth over all
A great King is he.

In daunting the folk
He hath so well wrought
That under our feet
Whole nations are brought.
An heritage fair,
He chose us to move,
Which Jacob enjoyed,
Whom he did so love.

Our God is gone up
With trumpet and fame,
With sound of the trump
To witness the same.
Sing praises to God,
Sing praises, I say:
To this our great King,
Sing praises alway.

*By William Kethe. Old 47th, probably from the Anglo-Genevan Psalter of 1561.

Bay Psalm Book: "The Whole Booke of Psalmes Faithfully Translated into English Meter" was published in Cambridge, Massachusetts, in 1640. It was the first book printed in the colonies as well as the first book written entirely there. The editorial committee of 30 clergymen included John Cotton, John Eliot, Richard Mather, and Thomas Weld. This book was printed without music but referred to tunes found in the Ravenscroft Psalter of 1621. It was in use for over 100 years and enjoyed several editions. However, the poetry again is rather poor and shows a slavish adherence to literal translation, a mark of the time.

Psalm 19

The heavens doe declare
the majesty of God:
also the firmament shews forth
his handy-work abroad.

Day speaks to day, knowledge
night hath to night declar'd.
There neither speach nor language is,
where their voyce is not heard.

Through all the earth their line
is gone forth, & unto
the utmost end of all the world,
their speaches reach also.

A tabernacle hee
in them pitcht for the Sun.
Who Bridegroom like from's chamber goes
Glad Giants-race to run.

The Scottish Psalter of 1650: The General Assembly of the Church of Scotland approved these texts in 1650, and this psalter has been in continuous use since then, largely unaltered. Originally, this was a work of Francis Rous, but, after much scrutiny and revision, little of the original work was left. The Scottish Psalter contains sections of the 1564 version, the Bay Psalm Book, the Westminster version of 1647, Francis Rous, and others. Although the poetry is sometimes awkward, some settings are much beloved and found in many hymnals.

Psalm 27

The Lord's my light and saving health,
Who shall make me dismayed?
My life's strength is the Lord, of whom
Then shall I be afraid?

When as mine enemies and foes,
Most wicked persons all,
To eat my flesh against me rose,
They stumbled and did fall.

Against me though an host encamp,
My heart yet fearless is:
Though war against me rise, I will
Be confident in this.

Tate and Brady: First published in England in 1696, this psalter was the work of Nahum Tate and Nicholas Brady. It contains more variety in meter than Sternhold and Hopkins or the Scottish Psalter of 1650, and, with the addition of many long meters, is less monotonous. Both Brady and Tate were poets, Brady also a clergyman and Tate a playwright, ensuring a more polished text.

Psalm 27

Whom should I fear, since God to me
Is saving health and light?
Since strongly he my life supports,
What can my soul affright?

With fierce intent my flesh to tear,
When foes beset me round,
They stumbled, and their lofty crests
Were made to strike the ground.

Through him my heart, undaunted, dares
With num'rous hosts to cope;
Through him in doubtful straits of war,
For good success I hope.

The Psalms of David Imitated in the Language of the New Testament: Sir Isaac Watts' mastery of poetic language is amply demonstrated in this publication of 1719.

Psalm 27

The Lord of glory is my light,
And my salvation, too;
God is my strength, nor will I fear
What all my foes can do.

One privilege my heart desires;
O grant me an abode
Among the churches of thy saints,
The temples of my God!

There shall I offer my requests
And see thy beauty still;
Shall hear thy messages of love
And there inquire thy will.

The Presbyterian Psalter: This comprehensive publication of 1887 is due to the work of Revs. D. A. Duff, J. M. French, J. F. Hutchison, S. G. Irvine, W. A. McKanzle, M. F. McKirahan, W. T. Meloy, Messrs. P. W. Hill, and John M. Donaldson. Great care was taken to include widely accepted tunes, and 221 melodies were added.

Psalm 19

The glory of the Lord
The heavens declare abroad;
The firmament displays
The handiwork of God;
Day unto day declareth speech,
And night to night doth knowledge teach.

Aloud they do not speak,
They utter forth no word,
Nor into language break;
Their voice is never heard.
Their line through all the earth extends,
Their words to earth's remotest ends.

In them he for the sun
Hath set a dwelling-place;
Rejoicing as a man
Of strength, to run the race;
He, bridegroom like in his array,
Comes from his chamber, bringing day.

To the layman's eye it may seem that each version got successively better. We have to remember, however, that it is folly to take our modern language as the norm against which we measure poetry of past centuries. Much of what we perceive as clumsy and awkward was actually quite polished in ages past.

Contemporary Application

Nichol Grieve, in his revision of the Scottish Psalter of 1650, outlines some of the poetic defects he found, showing that the utility of this psalter for about 300 years far outweighed its poetic faults.[8] This list also presents ideas for current and future versions of metrical psalmody. I am using his list here, adding some of my own categories.

The reader should keep in mind that for every rule there are exceptions, and sometimes poetic creativity will permit the breaking of one guideline or another in order to create a product of greater interest.

Defective Rhymes: Many rhythms are imperfect, faulty, crude, or uncouth. There are too many rhymes of sight, as distinct from sound, which gratify the eye but do not satisfy the ear (for example, rhyming "by" with "majesty"). The rhymes of "me," "be," and "thee" are overworked, as is the adverbial "-ly," which is sometimes used incorrectly only to give a rhyme. "Ever" and "never" are used too much.

Broken Lines: An attempt should be made for the poetic phrase to coincide with the musical line. Sir Isaac Watts said, "I have seldom permitted a stop in the middle of a line, and seldom left the end of a line without one."[9] Broken lines are evident extensively in the 1650 Scottish Psalter, marring cadences of the tunes and obscuring the meaning of the text. It should be added, however, that the occasional use of broken lines is sometimes "metrically valuable by reducing rhythmical monotony."[10]

Inversions: Awkward inversions in the natural and grammatical order of words should be avoided. An example is the awkward placement of the adjective after the noun, as in "reverence meet" or "pastures fair," or of the object before the subject, as in "if we our hearts should harden" or "Ye, so long My Spirit grieving, Never in My rest can share."[11]

Elisions and Elongations: Elisions such as "th'avenging" or "th'uplifter" should be avoided. While the Revised Church Hymnary has a total of seven in the whole book, the 1650 Scottish Psalter has easily the same number in a verse or two. Also, extensive use of the conversational 's and 'll make the text too homely and pedestrian. Elongations, such as "nation" (three syllables) or "congregation" (five syllables) are awkward and should not be used.

Unsuitable, Obsolete, Unfamiliar, Unmusical Terms: "Archaic words often prove an adornment in a song of praise, but not so words which are so archaic as to have become obsolete."[12] The old second-person form singular (thou, thee, thy) has been out of use for about two centuries in English usage outside the Church, and it is questionable whether it should be used in any new versions. When the second form singular was first used in sacred texts, it was the familiar form of address. The remoteness of the archaic form, still applied to address God in some congregations in our days, changes the theology considerably.

Judaism and Christianity: Obviously, the psalms were written in a decidedly Jewish context, and that character must not be changed. It is part of our Christian heritage.[13] On the other hand, phrases like "Thy cross before to guide me," in a familiar paraphrase of Psalm 23, is hardly warranted by the original.[14]

Crude and Alien Metaphors: Words that had a great deal of meaning in the original Hebrew setting are sometimes awkward in English translations. It is therefore important to consult the original Hebrew text, or, in its absence, several good English study Bibles.

Unchristian Sentiments: Here we can include the curse verses (for example, Psalm 137). These are definitely part of the Bible and the prayer of the Church, and they should be understood in light of the totality of the Old Testament. However, it could be argued whether these verses should enter the prayer of congregations without adequate education.

Prose Poetry: Metrical versions often become pedestrian. For instance, "Why dost Thou cast me off?" becomes "Why thrust'th Thou me Thee fro'?" in the 1650 Scottish Psalter. Also, the perfect dactyllic line "Worship the Lord in the beauty of holiness" must be marred when turned into iambics. The extensive use of monosyllabic words sounds simplistic.

Variety of Meter: It is important to include a variety of meters, but not such a great variety as to be become impractical. The 1564 Scottish Psalter was based on 30 different meters, and its successor of

1650 reduced this number drastically to seven. For congregations that made the switch, a great wealth of musical repertoire was lost.

Inclusive Language: Our sensitivity to gender specific language has changed drastically over the last few decades, and this change is still going on. The phrase "Father-love is reigning o'er us, brother-love binds man to man"[15] was perfectly normal to the ears of 1970, but it sounds very awkward to us now. Great care must therefore be taken when dealing with new translations or new settings of old ones that they be sensitive to those who use them while at the same time avoiding any compromise of the message of the Spirit[16] and grammatical integrity. Changing the Trinity to "Source, Word, and Sustainer" may show sensitivity to a certain small but growing element in today's society,[17] but it also reduces the personal dimension of God. Most people would find it more difficult to have a personal relationship with a concept than with an entity that has the human attributes of Father, Son, and Holy Spirit. Many modern hymnals indiscriminately replace every male pronoun, when referring to the Divinity, with the word "God" to the extent that the term itself is reduced to the level of a pronoun. There is also an element of confusion that occurs in sentences like these: "The Lord has done great things for me, and holy is God's name." Here it sounds as though the Lord and God were not the same person. Another way of addressing divine inclusivity might be by directing all psalms as a prayer to God in the second person, even the psalms that talk about God in the third person. In isolated instances this might work, but in the course of the whole psalter this changes the theology considerably. The whole idea of vertical inclusivity (using the male pronoun when referring to the Divinity), then, is an area of greatest challenge and must be dealt with sensitively, creatively, pastorally, theologically, and grammatically. However, horizontal inclusivity, when the male pronoun refers to a human being, is easier to deal with on a theological level. We need to make sure, however, that the meaning of the text is not altered and that grammatical rules are observed. Indiscriminately changing the male pronoun to the plural makes incorrect use of the language and sounds pedestrian (for example, "Will everybody please take their seat?") by mixing singular and plural attributes.

CONCLUSIONS

There are numerous metrical psalters that have been created since 1900, some very good ones just within the last 20 years. I will mention just two.

The Psalter for Christian Worship: Michael Morgan wrote this psalter in 1999, and it is published jointly by Columbia Theological Seminary Witherspoon Press and the Office of Theology and Worship of the Presbyterian Church of the United States. In the preface, the author says that "metrical paraphrases—unlike literal translations—must be faithful to the Scriptures, but they also must balance fidelity with rhyme, meter, and imagery necessary for good poetry. They must also be appealing and considered 'singable' by a congregation." These settings are not literal paraphrases but poems that express the feeling of the psalms in a contemporary setting.

Psalm 27

God, my light and my salvation,
In whose strength my hope is laid;
Confident in my salvation,
I shall never be afraid.

Evil hosts may rise against me,
Wars distress, and flesh decay;
Yet the cruelest death imagined
But begins my song of praise.

Shelter me within the haven
Of thy house all time to come;
On the rock of thy protection,
Let me safely find a home.

Lift me high above the legions
Who would rail against thy word;
O'er the tumult of division
Make my cry for peace be heard.

A New Metrical Psalter: This work by Christopher Webber and published by Church Publishing is actually a selection of psalms from a complete set by the author. These settings are arranged with lists of Sundays and feasts for which they might be appropriate. The text is quite literally arranged, while still observing good style and poetry. The only drawback is the limited number of meters, only three.

Psalm 27

My light, my Savior is the Lord,
Of whom should I have any fear?
He is the stronghold of my life,
Whom should I dread if he is near?

When evildoers sought my life
And in their malice drew around,
My adversaries and my foes,
They stumbled and fell to the ground.

Though hostile tents encircle me,
My heart will never be dismayed;
Though war break out against my life,
My trust in God will never shake.

One thing alone I ask of God:
To dwell in his most holy place,
To seek him in his temple and
Enjoy the beauty of his face.

Chapter 8

Metrical Introits

The introit antiphons are texts assigned to the entrance rite of the Roman Catholic liturgy. They appear in all missals and Sacramentaries in the form of short sentences, usually unique to the particular day, which are spoken when there is no music. In musical practice, however, they are frequently replaced by an opening hymn, which may or may not reflect the text of the assigned introit antiphon.

The antiphons are coupled with psalms. In about two-thirds of all introits, the antiphon is taken from that psalm. Originally, the whole psalm was sung, but over the centuries, this practice fell into disuse.

The *General Instruction of the Roman Missal* (2000) echoes all earlier pertinent documents in lifting up the value of the introit, since each text prepares the congregation internally for what is to follow.[1] The introit antiphons reflect either a specific idea found in the readings of the day or, most often, a common theme of the season. The documents are very clear that the singing of the introit antiphon be the norm for the entrance rite in Catholic worship.

The musical settings currently available consist of the Gregorian chant introits as found in the *Graduale Romanum,* designed for choir or schola performance in Latin; a simpler setting for congregations, also in Latin, in the *Graduale Simplex;* and several vernacular versions. In English, there are some notable examples: Paul Ford's *By Flowing Waters,* published by The Liturgical Press, gives a choice of several seasonal introit antiphons (and other chants), in chant form, meant for congregation or a religious community. Ainslie's *Simple Gradual* explores the responsorial idea of alternating a simple congregational refrain with cantorial psalm verses. And a current (as yet incomplete), laudable project by Lynn Trapp and Delores Dufner, OSB, presents the antiphons

in metrical form, sung to well-known hymn tunes, with free psalm
verses for cantor or choir. To my knowledge, there are no comprehensive attempts to set the whole text of the introit, both antiphon
and verses, in a manner that includes the congregation throughout.
This present project, then, attempts to provide metrical settings of
these texts, so that they may be sung by a congregation to familiar tunes.

Before actually embarking on this project, the following
questions had to be be answered:

1. What is the history of the introit; how does this present work reflect
   its original intent?
2. In what ways is a metrical version of the psalms superior or inferior
   to other forms?
3. What happens to the text when it is metricized? What do we have
   to observe in order to respect the integrity of the original text in
   a contemporary application?

1.   This summary of the early history of the introit will
touch on the basic points examined in detail in the first part, "The
Origin and Early Development of the Introit." It is given here as
essential information for those who thought they could escape Part I
of this book.

The introit chant was the last of the Roman chants to be
admitted into the Roman liturgy. The first mention of the chant is
found in Ordo Romanus Primus (692–730), which was a service
directory for the pope's stational Masses in Rome. By stational Masses
we understand the practice of visiting various basilicas on pre-assigned
days of the Church year. In the early days of the Middle Ages, each
church had its own customs, and this directory was necessary in order
to keep papal liturgies uniform. The introit was sung by a schola
cantorum, standing on two sides of the altar steps in two rows, men
in the back, boys in front. At a signal from the pope, the prior scholae
(director) would intone the antiphon, followed by a series of psalm
verses, probably in an antiphonal fashion (alternating from side to side).
When the pope reached the altar steps, he would again signal the
prior scholae; the schola would then finish whatever verse was being
sung, continue with the "Gloria Patri" (doxology), and repeat the
antiphon at the end. The performance of the introit, then, mirrored

antiphonal psalmody of the Liturgy of the Hours as it was sung then and as it is sung to this day. There is not a shred of evidence that suggests that the introit was ever sung in a responsorial form before the last century, as many sources claim.

The introit chant melodies, which were transmitted orally and not committed to paper until about 200 years after the first appearance of chant books, are, along with the communion antiphons, unique among the proper chants, in that they exhibit musical unity and liturgical appropriateness throughout the liturgical year. It makes sense, then, to place the origin of the introit and communion after that of the gradual and offertory. The musical and textual form and style reflects monastic choral writing as we know it today. However, we cannot automatically assume that these chants originated in the monastic tradition. I believe it is much more likely that the music of the Mass and the office developed side by side, possibly using the same musical resources, and that it was in the transformation of Roman urban monasticism into an ecclesial system that the schola cantorum was born. The schola cantorum itself was an ecclesiastical organization established for the development and maintenance of music at the papal court. Later documents refer to the adult singers as "clerici." Boys were added, auditioned from other schools, to live and learn at the schola, thus passing the repertoire on to the next generation. There is no evidence that the schola in the earliest documented days included lay singers other than the boys.

Originally, the introit consisted of an antiphon, all verses of a psalm or a greater portion thereof, a doxology, and a repetition of the antiphon. In later centuries, as processions became shorter and the musical tempo slowed down, the psalm was gradually truncated to one verse. This lost much of the thematic connection to the readings of the day or the season, and the psalm itself diminished in importance. The current missal, for instance, gives only the antiphon text, completely disregarding the psalm. Moreover, one third of all introit antiphon texts come from non-psalmic biblical passages.

For this project, the original antiphonal form of the introit is restored, giving the psalm more prominence. In case of a long psalm, several pertinent verses were chosen. Antiphons and verses were set to the same meter (tune). In performance, the music director is encouraged to alternate the verses (for example, men and women, left and right sides) to bring out the antiphonal character and to elaborate the repeat of the antiphon at the end by re-harmonizing it or adding descants, which are not provided within the context of this project. The tunes are only suggestions and can, of course, be changed to other tunes of the same meters.

2.   Textually speaking, it must be understood that any metrical setting of a psalm is but a compromise and not a substitute. Metrical psalters were not and are not composed to supplant the vernacular versions of the psalter, but to make them accessible for congregational singing. It is sometimes necessary to trade the psalm's original poetic language and imagery for utility. However, the test of history has shown us the usefulness of metrical psalmody. For many Protestant congregations, the main vehicle for knowing and singing the psalms was one or another metrical version of the psalter. Many of these congregations used these psalters exclusively, lifting the popularity of the psalms to new heights.

Musically speaking, it must be understood that metrical settings of the introits, of which psalmody is an important and essential part, are no substitute for the beautiful chant melodies written for those texts in Latin. These melodies in one form or another have been part of the prayer of the Church for almost 1,500 years, uniting our present prayers with those of countless earlier generations in a timeless medium. It is not without reason that one Church document after another upholds Gregorian chant as the ideal song of the Church, providing a "patrimony of inestimable value" that is given "pride of place" above all other forms of music.[2] But it must also be understood that, in order to make the texts available for congregational song, metrical forms of singing are still the most effective and time tested. Metrical introits, again sometimes trading the original beauty and content for utility, constitute a useful alternate to the Gregorian introits, when the physical participation of the congregation is desired.

3.   About two-thirds of all introit antiphon texts are taken from the same psalm as the verses, but, besides a handful of exceptions, these texts are generally not from the beginning of the psalm. The other third of the antiphons is from other Old Testament and New Testament sources. There are several hundred metrical psalters in English. Many of these were researched for this project according to the parameters mentioned above, and some of the settings were

used, if found appropriate. The *New Metrical Psalter* by Christopher Webber was especially useful because of its contemporary language and fidelity to the original text. Others used archaic language or were not sufficiently inclusive but could still serve as a basis for an adaptation. Still others were used for inspiration in making my own humble setting. A great many metrical psalters were mere paraphrases that lost a lot of the original detail and poetic vitality and sometimes even the overall structure.

In order to be faithful to the original text, the point of Hebrew poetry must be reiterated: most psalms follow an overall structure, which must be respected. For instance the praise psalms follow this outline: call to praise / reason for praise / call to praise. Within each verse, also, there are more minute structures in the form of parallelism and word pairs, which a metrical version should try to include. The psalms do not just meditate on a story or express a prayer; the form of the language makes the psalmist's thoughts come alive and be present to us. Finally, however, it must be said that the many phonetic devices used in the original Hebrew psalms are lost in just about every translation, whether metrical or not, and that the true impact of the Old Testament psalms can only be gained through a thorough knowledge of biblical Hebrew.

After agonizing over the question of inclusive language, I decided that there were just too many references to God in the pronoun of the third person to arrive at a suitable and theologically sound alternate. It was, I believe, the best way to respect the spirit of the Hebrew and the grammar of the English language. Horizontal inclusivity, however, was applied throughout.

Part III

Hymn Introits for
the Liturgical Year

Chapter 9

Performance Notes

The form of all of the following introit settings follows that of the earliest documented historical practice:

Antiphon
Psalm Verses
Doxology
Antiphon

The responsorial form of performance suggested by so many contemporary authorities is actually a rather modern invention that is antithetical to the antiphonal practice of this part of the Mass.

These hymn introits, then, respect the original form of the introit. The texts were translated with special sensitivity to the original. The use of several psalm verses restores the original intent and makes thematic unity to the daily or seasonal theme possible. A suggested tune is given for each introit. This can, of course, be substituted with any other appropriate tune of the same meter. For this, you may consult the metrical index of any good hymnal. Some of the suggested tunes may be unfamiliar, but they were chosen here because of the high quality of the music, and their addition would be a boon to any congregation's repertoire. Alternate settings are supplied for any unfamiliar tunes.

It is up to the creativity of the music director or organist to bring out the antiphonal character of these compositions. I would like to suggest bringing out the initial antiphon by a fairly full registration, and then cutting the organ back a bit for the psalm. The psalm verses can be performed antiphonally, alternating between men and women, left side and right side, choir and congregation, and so on. The doxology should be sung by everybody, and the organist may bring out the Trinitarian element by elaborating on the harmonic structure.

The repeat of the antiphon, being the central idea of the setting, should be adequately indicated by a descant, a modulation, or a re-harmonization, and, of course, a fuller organ registration.

The psalm verses were carefully chosen to present these introits as a whole. Therefore, whenever possible, they should be sung in their entirety. However, if it is absolutely necessary, some psalm verses may be omitted. In that case, care must be taken that the general theme is still present and that the thematic movement through the psalm and the doxology and the repeat of the antiphon is still intact.

IMPLEMENTATION AT THE PARISH LEVEL

The beauty of singing the introits is not so much that they expound particular themes found in the readings of the day, but in their continuity throughout the Church year. Other hymns and songs can express individual thoughts and ideas and daily themes much more precisely, but they cannot celebrate the liturgical year as a whole, because they come from different sources and traditions. The introits, on the other hand, use the psalter throughout, and the themes are arranged in such a way that they celebrate each season as a continuous entity, a "seamless garment." Therefore a continual approach to the performance of these texts would be the ideal. As is the case with many ideals, they may work very well in the academic setting of the seminary, college, or university, but on the parish level, a more cautious approach is called for, which, if done well, can also lead to fruitful results.

Because these hymn introits use mostly familiar hymn tunes, it should be fairly easy for congregations to adjust to their use. However, the following points should be followed in order to make implementation at the parish level a success.

Communication and Education: The key to a successful implementation of these settings on the parish level lies in communication and education. The music director must convince the pastor, the worship committee, and the congregation of the benefits of singing the proper texts. The starting point would be the Church documents themselves. *Musicam sacram,* the *New General Instruction of the Roman Missal,* and *Music in Catholic Worship* all list the introit texts as normative for the entrance rite. But it is not important enough *what* the documents say; it is *why* they say it that is essential when trying to convince others of the value of this project.

Why should we sing the introits? Firstly, because they are based on the Judeo-Christian hymn book par excellence, the psalter. No other source of poetry can express the depth of our faith more comprehensively. Secondly, because they help us celebrate the continuity of the liturgical year. Thirdly, the Church, recognizing those facts, wants these texts to be sung. Only when the music director is convinced of these three points will implementation be possible.

This project will work best when it can become a parish project, in other words, when the parish as a whole can take ownership of these texts. This requires the support of the pastor, the interest of the worship committee, and the education of the congregation. I would recommend for the music director to talk with the pastor about this project and to what degree these settings might be useful for their particular parish setting. Together with the pastor, the music director should present this idea to the worship committee. Lastly, a series of bulletin articles could be written about the introits, possibly by members of the worship committee, the pastor, or the music director, or a series of talks could be offered. The antiphonal form of singing, an antiphon framing the psalm and the doxology, is sufficiently foreign to Catholic congregations to warrant this educational process.

Musical Performance: It goes without saying that these settings will only be successful when they are performed musically. A thorough knowledge of and experience in hymn playing is required of the organist. The textual form of these hymn introits is also the musical form. Therefore, the importance of the antiphon should be highlighted, possibly with descants, re-harmonizations, or the choice of stops. In order for the congregation to take ownership of these settings, as in all congregational music, the cantor must know when to back off in order to let the congregation hear itself. I have encountered so many situations where the cantor "eats the microphone," leading to most unmusical and unpleasant results. The microphone should be used as a tool and not as an end in itself. These settings are for congregational singing and not for cantor with congregational accompaniment.

The World Library Publications (WLP) version of these hymn introits, *Introit Hymns for the Church Year,* contains music. The scope of this presentation did not allow me to add musical notation. Therefore, this book is not intended to be a hymnal. If a practical performance is intended, the World Library Publications version should be consulted.

Liturgical Performance: The entrance rite calls for music to cover the procession. In an ideal world, this music would stop as soon as the celebrant reaches the chair, but we know that the liturgical world is far from ideal. However, there is nothing that prevents the music from continuing after the priest arrives at his destination; the documents' main concern is that the processional activity be covered by music. When a hymn or a song is composed as a continuous prayer, it would be wrong to cut it at some point simply because the action, which it is designed to cover, has come to an end. The introit is just as much a liturgical action as the procession itself. Besides, when multiple verses are printed in a program and only a few are actually performed, it might actually undermine the congregation's sense of the need for participation.

On the other hand, if the action continues beyond the length of the music, the music must be extended in a musically satisfying way. For many organists this is an opportunity to play interludes and modulations, which for these settings work very well, especially when placed between the psalm verses and the doxology or before the final antiphon, thus highlighting the architecture of the composition. Repeating verses after the end in order to extend the music will not work, since this destroys the form of the introit.

When sung Sunday after Sunday, these texts will support a sense of continuity throughout the liturgical year. Where it is not possible to sing the introits with that frequency, strategic settings may be chosen, which, when taken together, can still bring out this continuity.

Pastoral Performance: As the reader might have noticed, I have taken the musical, liturgical, and pastoral judgment as found in *Music in Catholic Worship* and applied them here to the implementation of the hymn introits on the parish level. The pastoral judgment has always perplexed me, not so much because of what it is, but because of how it is applied. How many times have we seen the pastoral judgment used (or misused) as a means of making an exception in the other two categories? How many times have we seen poor music chosen for a liturgy because it was "pastoral," or poorly placed music (for example, an "Ave Maria" at communion) for the same reason? The three categories of musical, liturgical, and pastoral are meant not as ends in themselves, but they are designed to be applied together as one entity, to go hand in hand. All liturgical music must be all three: musical, liturgical, and pastoral. Music that is pastoral will speak to the particular needs of a particular congregation at a particular time, but it will only be effective if it is also musical and liturgical.

My main concern in pastoral performance of these settings would be the frequency with which they might be applied on the parish level. While individual settings can be just as effective as hymns and songs, it is in their frequent application that most of the benefit resides. However, singing these introits too frequently may at first result in consternation and resistance on the part of the congregation. I would, therefore, suggest a gentler approach. For some congregations, that could mean once a month, then increasing the frequency gradually. Other congregations may initially be able to implement this program on a biweekly level. Some of the hymn tunes suggested are somewhat unfamiliar, and the alternate settings may be used instead.

I do not dare suppose that there will be many parishes that will substitute my Christmas introit settings for the traditional "Adeste fideles" or my Easter setting for "Jesus Christ is risen today." These are so ingrained in today's popular liturgical mind that an abrupt substitution would cause consternation. Also, it is questionable whether these feasts would be a good forum to teach congregations about the continuity of liturgical texts, since many people who attend on those days are continually absent from regular Sunday worship. Nevertheless, I included them for completeness and with the hope that one parish or another might benefit from these settings.

One text that always struck me as an odd choice was the psalm for the Midnight Mass at Christmas (Psalm 2:1–6). While there is continuity in that psalm leading up to the triumph of the Nativity, the beginning of the psalm is antithetical to the baby-in-the-manger expectations of just about any congregation:

O, why do the nations rage
And the people vainly plot,
That in triumph they would wage
War against their King and God?

His Anointed they deride,
And the rulers, plotting, say:
"Their dominion be defiled;
Let us cast their bonds away."

But the Lord will scorn them all,
Laughing from his throne on high.
Soon his wrath strikes them with fear,
When in anger he replies:

"I have set my King to reign
All according to my will;
My Anointed I maintain
High on Zion's holy hill."

When this setting is seen in the context of the surrounding Masses, however, the text looks very appropriate. In a parish where the liturgical celebration of each of the four Christmas Masses is very much alive, this setting will actually enhance the Christmas celebration. However, for most parishes I would recommend some additional education before embarking on this introit. The introit for Christmas Day might work just as well.

The introit for the Midnight Mass makes more sense when taken in the historical context of the feast. It was instituted under Sixtus (432–440) in the midst of various barbarian invasions (410 Rome is sacked by the Goths; 452 Attila the Hun ravages Northern Italy; 455 Vandals pillage Rome for 14 days).

Advent

While the tune for the First Sunday of Advent is fairly general, all the others have an association with the season. *Winchester New* is used on the Second Sunday and as an alternate tune for the Third Sunday; *Gaudeamus pariter*, one of my favorite tunes often found attached to Advent hymns, is suggested for the first tune on the Third Sunday; and *Winchester Old*, a traditional English Christmas carol, is applied to the text of the Fourth Sunday. The text for the Third Sunday was a bit long for *Winchester New*, which was actually my first setting for that introit. *Gaudeamus pariter* supplied enough lines to fit the text of the antiphon more succinctly, but I kept *Winchester New* as an alternate tune.

Christmas and Christmas Season

All of the tunes in this season have a decidedly Christmas character except for *Festal Song* and *St. George* (Christmas Dawn, Second Sunday after Christmas) and *Coronation* (Baptism of the Lord). *Puer nobis nascitur* was chosen for the Vigil of Christmas. I have already mentioned the problematic text of the Midnight introit; *Nun komm, der Heiden Heiland,* my first tune, fits this text very nicely. The alternate tune, *Forest Green,* may sound a bit too pastoral for the militancy of that text but has a stronger Christmas association. The use of *Carol* as a tune for Christmas Day makes this a very useful setting. I am particularly fond of the first tune for Mary, Mother of God, *Gabriel's Message,* which sets this text quite nicely.

Lent and Holy Week

The tune *Erhalt uns, Herr,* which has a close association with the Lenten season, is used on Ash Wednesday. Originally, I had a different tune for the Fifth Sunday, but then I realized that one of the most beloved of all passion tunes would be left out, so I reset the text to *Passion Chorale.* The setting for the Mass of the Lord's Supper, *Duguet,* was chosen to bring out the eucharistic theme. This introit actually grew out of my first experiment (called feasibility study). Settings for Palm Sunday and Good Friday are obviously missing, since there are no introits on those days, and the same is the case for the Easter Vigil.

Easter, Easter Season, and Solemnities after the Easter Season

When I chose *Lauda anima* for the introit of Easter Sunday, the tune and the text made a fitting marriage. However, because of the strong Easter connection with *Easter Hymn,* I created an alternate setting to that tune. *Lasst uns erfreuen,* which appears three times in this season, is very appropriate because of its many "alleluias." I find *Graefenberg* a very useful and tuneful alternative to many other Common Meter tunes, which can often sound square and boring, especially after many verses.

Ordinary Time

As the great variety in meters might suggest, this was the last season of the temporal cycle I worked on. These settings include many familiar tunes like *Duke Street, McKee, Old 100th, St. Denio, Erhalt uns, Herr, Kingsfold, St. Catherine,* and *Diademata,* but also some less familiar but strong tunes like *Repton* and *Laudate Dominum,* for which alternate tunes are given as well. The tunes for the solemnity of Christ the King are *Duke Street* and *Mit Freuden zart,* which bring out the character or the feast perfectly.

Sanctoral Cycle

For my doctoral dissertation I left out the sanctoral cycle, which I was glad to finish for this book. Many of the psalms used elsewhere were applied to the sanctoral feasts, hence the application of most of the tunes to the settings in this group. I was happy to get another chance to suggest *Gabriel's Message* and *Mit Freuden zart.* In general, though, I must say that this cycle contains a high density of lesser known tunes. However, besides the feasts that are obligatory, most of these days are commemorated by Sunday congregations only once every seven years, and when they do fall on a Sunday, these settings would be surrounded by tunes from the temporal cycle that are better known. So what looks like a less familiar group will in context actually not have such a strong impact.

Chapter 10

Advent/Christmas Cycle

FIRST SUNDAY OF ADVENT

Ad te levavi animam meam: Deus meus, in te confido, non erubescam:
neque irrideant me inimici mei: etenim universi qui te exspectant,
non confundentur. Ps. Vias tuas, Domine, demonstra mihi: et semitas
tuas edoce me.

*Unto you have I lifted up my soul. O my God, I trust in you, let me not be
put to shame; do not allow my enemies to laugh at me; for none of those who
are awaiting you will be disappointed. V. Make your ways known unto me,
O Lord, and teach me your paths.*

Meter: SM
Suggested Tune: St. Bride

Antiphon:
> To you, O Lord, I pray;
> I trust in your great name.
> Let not my enemies exult
> Nor put my soul to shame.

Verses:
> Reveal your ways to me
> And guide me in right paths.
> That you may teach me in your truth,
> O Lord, is all I ask.
>
> In pity, Lord, recall
> Your mercies manifold.
> Remember me in your great love
> As in the days of old.

I pray that you forgive
The failings of my youth,
And do not cease to think of me
In grace and love and truth.

Doxology: Give glory to our God,
               The Father, and the Son,
               And also to the Paraclete,
               Eternal Three-in-One.

Antiphon: Psalm 25:1–3a, CT
Verses: Psalm 25:4–7, Doxology: CT
© 2005 World Library Publications

SECOND SUNDAY OF ADVENT

Populus Sion, ecce Dominus veniet ad salvandas gentes: et auditam
faciet Dominus gloriam vocis suae, in laetitia cordis vestri. Ps. Qui
regis Israel, intende: qui deducis velut ovem Jacob.

*People of Zion, behold, the Lord is coming to save all nations; and the Lord
shall cause you to hear his majestic voice for the joy of your heart. V. Shepherd
of Israel, hear us, you who lead Joseph like a flock.*

Meter: LM
Suggested Tune: Winchester New

Antiphon: Behold, O Zion, God will come
               To save the nations of the earth.
               Your hearts will quicken at the sound
               Of his majestic, glorious voice.

Verses: O Israel's Shepherd, hear our prayer.
               You guided Joseph like a flock.
               In all your splendor show yourself,
               Who rides above the heavenly host.

You brought a vine from Egypt's land,
Removed the nations by your hand.
You blessed your vine with ample room,
It took deep root and filled the land.

The hills were sheltered in its shade,
Its boughs like mighty cedars stood;
It stretched its branches to the sea,
And to the river went its shoots.

Why have you broken down its walls
That passers-by its treasures loot,
The wild boar ravages its roots,
And forest beasts devour its fruit?

O bring us back, O Lord of hosts.
From heaven behold and tend your vine.
Regard the stock your hand has set
And planted after your design.

Doxology: To God the Father, God the Son,
And God the Spirit praises be,
Who was before the world began,
Is now and in eternity.

Antiphon: Isaiah 30:19, 30, CT
Verses: Psalm 80:1, 8–15, Doxology: CT
© 2005 World Library Publications

Third Sunday of Advent

Gaudete in Domino semper: iterum dico, gaudete: modestia vestra
nota sit omnibus hominibus: Dominus prope est. Nihil soliciti sitis:
sed in omni oratione petitiones vestrae innotescant apud Deum.
Ps. Benedixisti, Domine, terram tuam: avertisti captivitatem Iacob.

*Rejoice in the Lord always; again I say, rejoice. Let your forbearance be
known to all men. The Lord is at hand. Do not be anxious over anything;*

but in all manner of prayer, let your requests be made known unto God.
V. Lord, you have blessed your land. You have put an end to Jacob's captivity.

First Setting
Meter: 76 76 D
Suggested Tune: Gaudeamus pariter

Antiphon: Come, rejoice in God our King;
       Sing, your voices raising.
       I repeat again: Rejoice!
       Sing with jubilation!
       Let your gentleness be known;
       Lo, the Lord is coming.
       Do not worry, but with thanks
       Let your prayers be summoned.

Verses: Lord, you favored once your land,
       Brought back Jacob's fortunes
       And forgave your people's sins,
       Pardoned their transgressions.
       You withdrew from them your wrath,
       Turned from your hot anger.
       Now restore us, saving God;
       Let your rage not linger.

       Mercy, love, and faithfulness
       Have met in God's presence;
       Peace and justice have embraced,
       Have become one essence.
       Faithfulness springs from the earth;
       Justice rains profusely
       And shall walk before our God;
       Peace shall follow closely.

Doxology: Glory to the Triune God:
       Praises to the Father;
       Praises also to the Son,
       Who became our brother;

Sing the Holy Spirit's praise,
Peaceful dove, descending;
As at first it was, is now,
And will be unending.

Antiphon: Philippians 4:4–6, CT
Verses: Psalm 85:2–5, 11–12, 14, Doxology: CT
© 2005 World Library Publications

Second Setting
Meter: LM
Suggested Tune: Winchester New

Antiphon: Rejoice in Yahweh every day.
"Rejoice, rejoice!" again I say.
Proclaim to all the Lord is near,
Be steadfast, pray, and never fear.

Verses: O Lord, you favored once our land,
Changed Jacob's fortunes by your hand,
Forgave your people's guilt within,
In mercy covered all their sin.

You took away your fiery wrath,
Withdrew from anger's fiercest path.
O Savior God, restore us now,
No longer your displeasure show.

Will you be angry evermore,
Your wrath upon us ever pour?
Will you not quicken us that we
May praise our God eternally?

Show us, O Lord, your faithful love,
Pour your salvation over us.
To faithful souls the Lord speaks peace
If they renounce their wickedness.

Doxology: To God, the Triune One, we raise
                Eternal hymns of endless praise.
                O Father, Son, and Paraclete,
                We praise your name in word and deed.

Antiphon: Philippians 4:4–6, CT
Verses: Psalm 85:1–8, Doxology: CT
© 2005 World Library Publications

FOURTH SUNDAY OF ADVENT

Rorate caeli desuper, et nubes pluant iustum: aperiatur terra, et germinet Salvatorem. Ps. Caeli enarrant gloriam Dei: et opera manuum eius annuntiat firmamentum.

Skies, let the Just One come forth like the dew, let him descend from the clouds like the rain. The earth will open up and give birth to our Savior. V. The heavens declare the glory of God, and the firmament proclaims the work of his hands.

Meter: CM
Suggested Tune: Winchester Old

Antiphon: O heavens, let the Just One come
               Like rain from clouds above.
               The earth will be unsealed and yield
               Our Lord who saves and loves.

Verses: The heavens declare your glory, Lord,
               The work your hands have made;
               Day after day your power is shown
               And night by night displayed.

               There is no utterance or speech,
               No voice is ever heard,
               Yet to all nations comes the sound,
               To every place their word.

Forth like a bridegroom comes the sun
From its appointed place,
And like a hero on his course
Rejoices in the race.

It runs from East to farthest West
To make its course complete,
And nothing in the world beneath
Escapes its scorching heat.

Doxology: Give glory to the Father, Son,
And Spirit equally,
As from the first it was, is now,
And evermore shall be.

Antiphon: Isaiah 45:8, CT, © 2005 World Library Publications
Verses: Psalm 19:1–6, Doxology: NMP alt.
© 1986 Christopher Webber

Christmas: Vigil Mass

Hodie scietis, quia veniet Dominus, et salvabit nos: et mane videbitis
gloriam eius. Ps. Domini est terra, et plenitudo eius: orbis terrarum,
et universi qui habitant in eo.

*Today you will know that the Lord is coming to save us; and tomorrow
you will see his glory. V. The earth is the Lord's and the fulness thereof;
the world, and all those who dwell therein.*

Meter: LM
Suggested Tune: Puer nobis

Antiphon: Today it will be known to you:
Our Savior comes to rule the earth.
Tomorrow you will sing his praise,
When you behold his glorious birth.

Verses: All the whole earth belongs to God,
Its people all are his to keep;
For he has placed it on the seas
And made it firm upon the deep.

"Who can ascend the hill of God?
And who can stand within his walls?"
"All those who have clean hands, pure hearts,
And have not sworn by what is false."

"All these the Lord himself will bless,
And he will give them just reward."
Such, God of Jacob, are the ones
Who seek the presence of the Lord.

Lift up your heads, eternal gates;
Lift up your everlasting door;
The King shall come. "Who is the King?"
"The mighty Lord, the Conqueror."

Doxology: All glory to the Father, Son,
And to the Holy Spirit be;
As from the first it was, is now,
And will be for eternity.

Antiphon: Exodus 16:6, 7; Isaiah 35:4, CT
© 2005 World Library Publications
Verses: Psalm 24:1–8, Doxology: NMP
© 1986 Christopher Webber

CHRISTMAS: MASS AT MIDNIGHT

Dominus dixit ad me: Filius meus es tu, ego hodie genui te. Ps. Quare fremuerunt gentes: et populi meditati sunt inania.

The Lord said unto me: You are my Son, today I have begotten you.
V. Why do the nations conspire and the peoples plot in vain?

Meter: 77 77
Suggested Tune: Nun komm der Heiden Heiland

Antiphon: I proclaim the Lord's decree;
                         God said this in words of truth:
                         "You are my beloved Son,
                         Yes, I have begotten you."

Verses: O, why do the nations rage
                         And the people vainly plot,
                         That in triumph they would wage
                         War against their King and God?

His Anointed they deride,
And the rulers, plotting, say:
"Their dominion be defied;
Let us cast their bonds away."

But the Lord will scorn them all,
Laughing from his throne on high.
Soon his wrath strikes them with fear,
When in anger he replies:

"I have set my King to reign
All according to my will;
My Anointed I maintain
High on Zion's holy hill."

Doxology: Glory be to the Father, Son,
And the Spirit, with them One;
As we worship and adore,
We will sing for evermore.

Antiphon: Psalm 2:7, *The Psalter,* Philadelphia, 1912
Verses: Psalm 2:1–6, *The Psalter,* Philadelphia, 1912
Doxology: CT, © 2005 World Library Publications

Alternate Tune
Meter: CMD
Suggested Tune: Forest Green

Antiphon: The Lord announced his just decree
             In words of grace and truth:
             "You are my own beloved Son,
             I have begotten you."
Verses: Why do the nations fly in rage
             And people vainly plot,
             That in false triumph they wage war
             Against their King and God?

             The Lord's Anointed they deride,
             And rulers, plotting, say:
             "Let their dominion be defied;
             We cast their bonds away."
             Behold, the Lord will scorn them all
             And mock them from on high.
             And soon his wrath strikes them with fear,
             When angrily he cries:

             "I have installed my King to reign
             According to my will;
             My own Anointed I maintain
             On Zion's holy hill."
             "You are my own beloved Son,
             I have begotten you.
             You will possess all nations and
             The whole creation, too."

Doxology: Give glory to our loving God,
             The Father, and the Son,
             And also to the Paraclete,
             Eternal Three-in-One.

Antiphon: The Lord announced his just decree
             In words of grace and truth:
             "You are my own beloved Son,
             I have begotten you."

Antiphon: Psalm 2:7, CT
Verses: Psalm 2:1–6, Doxology: CT
© 2005 World Library Publications

Christmas: Mass at Dawn

Lux fulgebit hodie super nos: quia natus est nobis Dominus: et
vocabitur Admirabilis, Deus, Princeps pacis, Pater futuri saeculi: cuius
regni non erit finis. Ps. Dominus regnavit, decorem indutus est:
indutus est Dominus fortitudinem, et praecinxit se.

Radiant light will shine upon us today, for the Lord is born unto us.
He shall be called Wonderful God, Prince of Peace, Father of the worlds
to come. His reign shall have no end. V. The Lord reigns, he is enrobed
with majesty; the Lord is clothed with strength, he has girded himself.

Meter: SM
Suggested Tune: St. Michael

Antiphon: A radiant light has come:
             The Lord is born today!
             He will be called Most Wonderful
             And Prince of Peace always.

Verses: The Lord himself is King,
             In glorious robes arrayed;
             Arrayed in glory, clad in strength,
             In majesty displayed.

             He set the world in place
             By his most sure command;
             Your throne has stood, eternal Lord,
             Since first the world began.

The floods lift up their voice,
Lift up their pounding waves,
But mightier than the flood is God
Who dwells on high and saves.

Your testimonies, Lord,
Are fixed most certainly,
And holiness adorns your house
To all eternity.

Doxology: Give God the Father praise,
And praise to God the Son,
To God the Spirit equal praise:
Eternal Three-in-One.

Antiphon: Isaiah 9:2, 6; Luke 1:33, CT
© 2005 World Library Publications
Verses: Psalm 93:1–5, Doxology: NMP, © 1986 Christopher Webber

CHRISTMAS: MASS DURING THE DAY

Puer natus est nobis, et filius datus est nobis: cuius imperium super humerum eius: et vocabitur nomen eius, magni consilii Angelus. Ps. Cantate Domino canticum novum: quia mirabilia fecit.

Unto us a child is born, unto us a son is given. Dominion is on his shoulders, and his name shall be called the Angel of Great Counsel. V. Sing unto the Lord a new song, for he has accomplished wondrous deeds.

Meter: CMD
Suggested Tune: Carol

Antiphon: For us a Child of hope is born,
To us a Son is given;
All peoples shall obey his word,
And all the hosts of heaven.

His name shall be the Prince of Peace,
For evermore adored,
The Wonderful, the Counselor,
The great and mighty Lord.

Verses:

O sing a new song to our Lord,
He has done wondrous deeds.
His right hand and his holy arm
Have gained the victory.
The Lord displayed his saving power
And truth and constancy;
He has revealed his justice and
His strength for all to see.

To Israel's house God has recalled
His faithfulness and love.
The farthest ends of earth have seen
The victory from above.
Make joyful noises to the Lord,
Break forth in harmony.
Sing praises to the Lord our God
With lyre and melody.

Doxology:

All glory be to God on high
And on the earth below.
The Triune Godhead be proclaimed
And evermore adored.
Give glory to our loving God,
The Father, and the Son,
And also to the Paraclete,
Eternal Three-in-One.

Antiphon: Isaiah 9:6, CT
Verses: Psalm 98:1–5, Doxology: CT
© 2005 World Library Publications

The Holy Family of Jesus, Mary, and Joseph

Deus in loco sancto suo: Deus, qui inhabitare facit unanimes in domo: ipse dabit virtutem et fortitudinem plebi suae. Ps. Exsurgat Deus, et dissipentur inimici eius: et fugiant qui oderunt eum, a facie eius.

God is in his holy dwelling place; the God who causes us to dwell together, one at heart, in his house; he himself will give power and strength to his people. V. Let God arise, and let all enemies be scattered; and let those who hate him flee before his face.

Meter CMD
Suggested Tune: Forest Green

Antiphon: Our God dwells in his holy place,
             The God, who wills that we
             Should live together, one in heart,
             In love and harmony.
             He gives his people power and strength
             And confidence and might;
             They glorify his holy name
             And worship day and night.

Verses: Let God arise and strike his foes;
             Let those who hate him flee;
             Let them, like smoke the wind blows off,
             All vanish speedily.
             Before God let the wicked melt
             As wax does in the flame,
             But let the righteous dance for joy
             And offer God acclaim.

             Sing praise to God, exalt his name
             Who rides the clouds on high,
             The Lord who dwells in holiness
             Yet hears the widow's cry.

God brings the solitary home
And breaks the prisoner's bands;
But rebels who reject the Lord
Shall live in arid lands.

Doxology: All glory be to God on high
And on the earth, the Lord
In Triune Godhead be proclaimed
And evermore adored.
Give glory to the Father, Son,
And Spirit equally;
As from the first it was, is now,
And evermore shall be.

Antiphon: Psalm 68:6, 7, 36, CT, © 2005 World Library Publications
Verses: Psalm 68:2–7, Doxology: NMP
© 1986 Christopher Webber

THE BLESSED VIRGIN MARY, THE MOTHER OF GOD

Salve, sancta Parens, enixa puerpera Regem, qui caelum terramque
regit in saecula saeculorum. Ps. Eructavit cor meum verbum bonum:
dico ego opera mea regi.

*Hail holy Mother, the Child-Bearer who has brought forth the King, the
ruler of heaven and earth for ever. V. My heart overflows with a goodly
theme; I address my works to the King.*

First Setting
Meter: 10 10 12 10
Suggested Tune: Gabriel's Message

Antiphon: Hail, Holy Mother of the universe,
You bore the King of heaven and of earth,
Who rules for evermore. May all your praises sing:
Most highly favored Lady. Gloria!

Verses: My heart is overcome by noble themes,
My song of songs is only for the king!
And as a writer's nimble pen, my soul may sing:
Most highly favored Lady. Gloria!

O hearken, daughter, fair and lovely one,
Forget the people of your land and home,
Leave father, mother, brothers, sisters all behind.
Most highly favored Lady. Gloria!

With golden robes you are bedecked today,
And by the king adored, in rich array.
Your followers will come with joy before the Lord.
Most highly favored Lady. Gloria!

Doxology: Give glory to the Father, and the Son,
The Spirit equally, the Three-in-One,
For as it was in the beginning and is now,
It will be for all ages. Gloria!

Antiphon: Sedulius, CT
Verses: Psalm 45:2, 11–12, 14–16, Doxology: CT
© 2005 World Library Publications

Second Setting

Meter: CM
Suggested Tune: Winchester Old

Antiphon: Hail, Holy Mother of the world,
You bore our Savior King,
Who rules in heaven and on earth.
May all your praises sing.

Verses: My heart is stirred by noble themes,
My song is for the king!
And as a writer's nimble pen
May my soul freely sing.

O hearken, daughter, listen well,
O fair and lovely one,
Forget the people of your land
And leave your father's home.

With golden robes you are bedecked
And by the king adored,
And those who follow you will come
With joy before the Lord.

Doxology: Give glory to our loving God,
The Father, and Son,
And also to the Paraclete,
Eternal Three-in-One.

Antiphon: Sedulius, CT
Verses: Psalm 45:2, 11–12, 14–16, Doxology: CT
© 2005 World Library Publications

Second Sunday after Christmas

Dum medium silentium tenerent omnia, et nox in suo cursu medium
iter haberet, omnipotens sermo tuus, Domine, de caelis a regalibus
sedibus venit. Ps. Dominus regnavit, decorem indutus est: indutus est
Dominus fortitudinem, et praecinxit se.

*While a profound silence enveloped all things and night was in the midst
of her course, your all-powerful Word, O Lord, leaped down from your royal
throne. V. The Lord reigns, he is enrobed with majesty; the Lord is clothed
with strength, he has girded himself.*

Meter: SM
Suggested Tune: St. George

Antiphon: While silence covered all,
And half-spent was the night,
Your mighty Word, O Lord of hosts,
Leaped from your throne of might.

Verses:
> You are the Ruler, Lord,
> In glorious robes arrayed;
> Arrayed in glory, clad in strength,
> In majesty displayed.
>
> You set the world in place
> By your most sure command;
> Your throne has stood, eternal Lord,
> Since first the world began.
>
> The floods lift up their voice,
> Lift up their pounding waves,
> But mightier than the flood is God
> Who dwells on high and saves.
>
> Your testimonies, Lord,
> Are fixed most certainly,
> And holiness adorns your house
> To all eternity.

Doxology:
> Give God the Father praise,
> And praise to God the Son,
> To God the Spirit equal praise:
> Eternal Three-in-One.

Antiphon: Wisdom 18:14–15, CT, © 2005 World Library Publications
Verses: Psalm 93:1–5, Doxology: NMP
© 1986 Christopher Webber

THE EPIPHANY OF THE LORD

Ecce advenit dominator Dominus: et regnum in manu eius, et
potestas, et imperium. Ps. Deus, iudicium tuum regi da: et iustitiam
tuam filio regis.

*Behold, the Sovereign Lord is coming; kingship, government, and power
are in his hands. V. Endow the King with your judgment, O God, and the
King's son with your righteousness.*

Meter: CM
Suggested Tune: Winchester Old

Antiphon: Behold, the Sovereign Lord is nigh,
        Comes swiftly to our land;
        All kingship, government, and power
        Are in his holy hand.

Verses: Send us, O God, the king whose reign
        Will make your justice known,
        Who will deal fairly with your land,
        The poor, and all your own.

        From Tarshish, Saba, from the isles,
        Arabia, all kings
        Shall come, bow down to him, and serve,
        And make their offerings.

        And let the Chosen One, O Lord,
        Save those oppressed by strife,
        Have pity on the weak and poor
        And offer them new life.

        Long live your Chosen One! Let prayers
        Be offered up always;
        May all people bless his Name
        Throughout the length of days.

Doxology: Give glory to the Father, Son,
        And Spirit equally;
        As from the first it was, is now,
        And evermore shall be.

Antiphon: Malachi 3:1; 1 Chronicles 29:12, CT
© 2005 World Library Publications
Verses: 1. Psalm 72:1–2, 10–13, 17
Doxology: NMP
© 1986 Christopher Webber

THE BAPTISM OF THE LORD

Dilexisti iustitiam, et odisti iniquitatem: propterea unxit te Deus, Deus tuus, oleo laetitiae prae consortibus tuis. Ps. Eructavit cor meum verbum bonum: dico ego opera mea regi.

You have loved justice and hated iniquity: therefore God, your God, has anointed you with the oil of gladness above your companions. V. My heart overflows with a goodly theme; I address my works to the King.

Meter: CM
Suggested Tune: Coronation

Antiphon: All justice you have loved and taught,
               But scorned iniquity,
               So God anoints and raises you
               Above your company.

Verses: My heart is stirred by noble themes,
               My song is for the king!
               And as a writer's numble pen
               May my soul freely sing.

               Fairer than all of humankind
               Are you, O Majesty!
               And full of grace your lips, for God
               Blessed you eternally!

               And I will sing for evermore
               And let your praises ring,
               Proclaim your praises far and wide
               For all to join and sing.

Doxology: Give glory to our loving God,
               The Father, and the Son,
               And also to the Paraclete,
               Eternal Three-in-One.

Antiphon: Psalm 45:8, CT
Verses: Psalm 45:2–3, 18, Doxology: CT
© 2005 World Library Publications

Chapter 11

Lent/Easter Cycle

Ash Wednesday

Misereris omnium, Domine, et nihil odisti eorum quae fecisti,
dissimulans peccata hominum propter paenitentiam, et parcens illis:
quia tu es Dominus Deus noster. Ps. Miserere mei Deus, miserere
mei: quoniam in te confidit anima mea.

*Your mercy extends to all things, O Lord, and you despise none of the things
you have made. You overlook human sins for the sake of repentance. You
grant them your pardon, because you are the Lord our God. V. Be merciful
to me, O God, be merciful to me, for my soul confides in you.*

Meter: LM
Suggested Tune: Erhalt uns, Herr

Antiphon:	O Lord, your mercy does extend
	To everything formed by your hand.
	You set repentant sinners free;
	O Lord and God, now pardon me.
Verses:	Be merciful, O Lord, to me,
	My soul to you for refuge flees;
	In shadows of your wings I'll lie,
	Until destroying storms pass by.
	I cry to you, O Majesty!
	Fulfill your promises to me.
	Descend from heaven with constancy,
	That none may hurt or harry me.

Though I am caught in lions' jaws,
Their teeth like arrows, tongues like swords,
I praise you, Lord above the sky,
Let not your glory pass me by.

My heart is steadfast, God and King,
I will make melody and sing.
With harp and lyre in gratitude,
I'll wake the dawn, for it is good.

Doxology: To God, the Triune One, we raise
Eternal hymns of endless praise.
O Father, Son, and Paraclete,
We praise your name in word and deed.

Antiphon: Wisdom 11:24–25, 27, CT
Verses: Psalm 57:2–6, 8–9, Doxology: CT
© 2005 World Library Publications

First Sunday of Lent

Invocabit me, et ego exaudiam eum: eripiam eum, et glorificabo eum: longitudine dierum adimplebo eum. Ps. Qui habitat in adiutorio Altissimi, in protectione Dei caeli commorabitur.

When he calls on me, I will answer him; I will rescue him and honor him; with long life will I satisfy him. V. He who abides in the shelter of the Most High shall remain under the protection of the God of Heaven.

Meter: 87 87 D
Suggested Tune: In Babilone

Antiphon: When they call in tribulation,
I will surely hear their prayer,
Answer them and be with them in
Every trouble and despair.

I will rescue them and free them,
Give them honor from above,
And fulfill them with a long life,
Showing them my saving love.

Verses: All within the Lord's protection,
                   In the shadow of his throne,
                   Say, "You are my Lord and refuge.
                   My trust is in you alone."
                   From the snares of hell he frees you
                   And from deadly pestilence;
                   Faithfulness your shield and buckler,
                   Sheltered under Yahweh's wings.

                   Nightly terrors bring no fear, nor
                   Yet by day the arrow's flight,
                   Nor the scourges of the noontime,
                   Nor the plague that stalks at night.
                   God has given to his angels
                   A most sure and strict command:
                   To protect you, lest you stumble,
                   And to bear you in their hand.

Doxology: To the Father sing your praises,
                   Who made land and sky and sea;
                   Also praises to the Son who
                   Saved us from the enemy;
                   Praises to the Holy Spirit,
                   Who helps us in time of need;
                   As it was in the beginning,
                   It will be eternally.

Antiphon: Psalm 91:15–16, CT
Verses: Psalm 91:1–6, 11–12, Doxology: CT
© 2005 World Library Publications

Second Sunday of Lent

Tibi dixit cor meum, quaesivi vultum tuum, vultum tuum, Domine, requiram: ne avertas faciem tuam a me. Ps. Dominus illuminatio mea, et salus mea: quem timebo?

My heart declared to you: "Your countenance have I shought; I shall ever seek your countenance, O Lord; do not turn your face from me." V. The Lord is my light and my salvation; whom shall I fear?

Meter: LM
Suggested Tune: Breslau

Antiphon:
My heart declared to you, O Lord:
"Your countenance my soul has sought;
My heart shall ever seek your face;
Do not reject me, O my God."

Verses:
My light, my Savior is the Lord,
Of whom should I have any fear?
He is the stronghold of my life;
Whom should I dread if he is near?

When evildoers seek my life
And in their malice draw around,
My adversaries and my foes
Will stumble and fall to the ground.

Though hostile tents encircle me,
My heart will never be dismayed;
Though war rise up against my life,
I will trust God, not be afraid.

One thing alone I ask of God:
To dwell in his most holy place,
To seek him in his holy court
And see his beauty face to face.

Doxology: All glory to the Father, Son,
                 And to the Holy Spirit be;
                 As from the first it was, is now,
                 And will be for eternity.

Antiphon: Psalm 27:8, 9, CT, © 2005 World Library Publications
Verses: Psalm 27:1–4, Doxology: NMP
© 1986 Christopher Webber

THIRD SUNDAY OF LENT

Oculi mei semper ad Dominum, quia ipse evellet de laqueo pedes
meos: respice in me, et miserere mei, quoniam unicus et pauper
sum ego. Ps. Ad te, Domine, levavi animam meam: Deus meus,
in te confido, non erubescam.

*My eyes are forever turned towards the Lord; for he shall release my feet
from the snare; look upon me and have mercy on me, for I am abandoned
and destitute. V. Unto you, O Lord, have I lifted up my soul; O my God,
I trust in you, let me not be put to shame.*

Meter: SM
Suggested Tune: St. Bride

Antiphon: My eyes are fixed on God;
                 From snares he rescues me.
                 Behold my poor and lonely soul;
                 Have mercy, Lord, on me.

Verses: To you, O Lord, I pray,
                 I trust in your great name.
                 Let not my enemies exult,
                 Nor put my soul to shame.

                 Reveal your ways to me
                 And guide me in right paths.
                 That you may teach me in your truth,
                 O Lord, is all I ask.

In pity, Lord, recall
Your mercies manifold.
Remember me in your great love
As in the days of old.

I pray that you forgive
The failings of my youth,
And do not cease to think of me
In grace and love and truth.

Doxology: Give glory to our God,
The Father and the Son,
And also to the Paraclete,
Eternal Three-in-One.

Antiphon: Psalm 25:15, 16, CT
Verses: Psalm 25:1, 2, 4–7, Doxology: CT
© 2005 World Library Publications

FOURTH SUNDAY OF LENT

Laetare Jerusalem: et conventum facite omnes qui diligitis eam:
gaudete com laetitia, qui in tristitia fuistis: ut exsultetis, et satiemini
ab uberibus consolationis vestrae. Ps. Laetatus sum in his quae diacta
sunt mihi: in domum Domini ibimus.

Rejoice, O Jerusalem; and gather round, all you who love her; rejoice in
gladness, after having been in sorrow; exult and be replenished with the
consolation flowing from her motherly bosom. V. I rejoiced when it was said
unto me: "Let us go to the house of the Lord."

Meter: LM
Suggested Tune: Truro

Antiphon: Rejoice, Jerusalem! and come,
All those who love her glorious face.
Rejoice, distressed and mournful souls,
And be consoled by her embrace.

Verses:

Jerusalem: with what great joy
I heard them say, "Let us go there!"
And now at last we take our stand
Within her gates to make our prayer.

Jerusalem: a city built
To be a place of unity;
The tribes go up, the tribes of God,
To praise God's name eternally.

Jerusalem: within your walls
The thrones of justice serve God's will;
The ancient thrones of David's house
Stand and unite God's people still.

Jerusalem: pray for her peace:
"May all who love you find success;
Peace be to all within your walls,
And in your towers quietness."

Jerusalem: for comrades' sake
My prayers for you will never cease;
Because God's house is standing here,
I pray forever for your peace.

Doxology:

All glory to the Father, Son,
And to the Holy Spirit be;
As from the first it was, is now,
And will be for eternity.

Antiphon: Isaiah 66:10, 11, CT, © 2005 World Library Publications
Verses: Psalm 122, Doxology: NMP
© 1986 Christopher Webber

Fifth Sunday of Lent

Iudica me Deus, et discerne causam meam de gente non sancta: ab homine iniquo et doloso eripe me: quia tu es Deus meus, et fortitudo mea. Ps. Emitte lucem tuam, et veritatem tuam: ipsa me deduxerunt, et adduxerunt in montem sanctum tuum, et in tabernacula tua.

Vindicate me, O God, and defend my cause against an ungodly nation; from wicked and deceitful men deliver me, for you are my God and my strength. V. Send forth your light and your truth; these have led me and brought me to your holy mountain and to your dwelling place.

Meter: 76 76 D
Suggested Tune: Passion Chorale

Antiphon: Give judgment, Lord my Savior,
O God, defend my cause
Against a faithless people,
Which honors not your laws.
From those who are deceiving,
O Lord, deliver me;
You are my God, my refuge,
My strength eternally.

Verses: Your light and truth deliver,
O let them lead me still
To your most holy dwelling
Upon your holy hill.
I will go to your altar,
O God, with great delight,
Praise you with harp and psalter,
For it is good and right.

My soul, why are you heavy,
So full of turbulence?
Trust God. My tongue shall praise him,
My help and confidence.

Doxology: All praise to God the Father,
                   The Son and Spirit be,
                   Who was from the beginning,
                   And is eternally.

Antiphon: Psalm 43:1–2a, CT
Verses: Psalm 43:3–5, Doxology: CT
© 2005 World Library Publications

Holy Thursday: Chrism Mass

Dilexisti iustitiam, et odisti iniquitatem: propterea unxit te Deus,
Deus tuus, oleo laetitiae prae consortibus tuis. Ps. Eructavit cor meum
verbum bonum: dico ego opera mea regi.

You have loved justice and hated iniquity. Therefore God, your God,
has anointed you with the oil of gladness above your companions.

Meter: LM
Suggested Tune: Deus tuorum militum

Antiphon: All justice you have loved and taught
                   But hated all iniquity,
                   So God anoints and raises you
                   Above your human company.

Verses: My heart is stirred by noble themes,
                   My song is for my Lord, the King!
                   And as a writer's nimble pen,
                   May my soul freely shout and sing.

                   Among your friends and family,
                   The fairest and most radiant,
                   The Lord blessed you abundantly
                   With grace upon your lips and hands.

Girded with strength and majesty
And splendor from the highest place,
Your cause is truth and gentleness
And uprightness and love and grace.

Therefore the Lord anointed you
With oil of joy and grace untold.
The sweetest fragrance will exude
From head and hands, from heart and soul.

And we will sing for evermore
And let your glorious praises ring,
Proclaim your name in all the earth
For everyone to join and sing.

Doxology: All glory to the Father, Son,
And to the Holy Spirit be,
Who was before the world began,
Is now, and reigns eternally.

Antiphon: Psalm 45:8, CT
Verses: Psalm 45:2–5, 8b–9a, 18, Doxology: CT
© 2005 World Library Publications

Holy Thursday: Evening Mass
of the Lord's Supper

Nos autem gloriari oportet, in cruce Domini nostri Iesu Christi: in
quo est salus, vita, et resurrectio nostra: per quem salvati, et liberati
sumus. Ps. Deus misereatur nostri, et benedicat nobis: illuminet
vultum suum super nos, et misereatur nostri.

*Let our glory be in the cross of our Lord Jesus Christ; in him we have
salvation, life, and resurrection; through him we are rescued and set free.
V. May God have mercy on us and bless us; may he cause his face to shine
upon us, and may he have mercy on us.*

Meter: LM
Suggested Tune: Duguet

Antiphon: Then let us glory in the cross
              Of Jesus Christ, who sets us free;
              He rescues us and gives us life
              That we may sing eternally.

Verses: My God be merciful to us,
              Bless us, shine on us from above;
              Let all earth's people know your ways,
              All nations know your saving love.

              Let all the nations praise you, Lord,
              Let them praise you, be glad, and sing;
              You judge with equity all lands
              And rule the nations as their king.

              Let all the nations praise you, Lord,
              And may the earth yield its increase;
              Then God, our God, will bless our land
              And nations worship him in peace.

Doxology: Then praise the Father, praise the Son,
              And praise the Spirit equally,
              Who was before the light of day,
              Is now, and reigns eternally.

Antiphon: Galatians 6:14, CT, © 2005 World Library Publications
Verses: Psalm 67, Doxology: NMP
© 1986 Christopher Webber

Easter Sunday

Resurrexi, et adhuc tecum sum, alleluia: posuisti super me manum
tuam, alleluia: mirabilia facta est scientia tua, alleluia, alleluia.
Ps. Domine probasti me, et cognovisti me: tu cognovisti sessionem
meam, et resurrectionem meam.

I am risen, and I am always with you, alleluia; you have placed your hand upon me, alleluia; your wisdom has been shown to be most wonderful alleluia, alleluia. V. O Lord, you have searched me and know me; you know when I sit down and when I rise up.

First Setting
Meter: 87 87 87
Suggested Tune: Lauda anima

Antiphon: Alleluia! Christ is risen
And is always with his fold!
Alleluia! He is with us,
Placed his hands on young and old.
Alleluia! May God's wisdom
To eternity be told.

Verses: Alleluia! Lord, you search me,
And you know my every way,
Know my sitting, know my rising,
Know my thoughts from far away,
Know my walking, know my sleeping
Through the night and all the day.

Lord, you know the words I'm speaking
Long before they are proclaimed.
Lord, you are before, behind me,
Blessing me by your own hand.
Such great knowledge is too lofty
For my soul to understand.

Lord, where could I flee your Spirit?
Where could I escape from you?
If I scale the highest heavens,
Lands of death, deep oceans, too,
Even there your hand will guide me;
Your right hand draws me to you.

Doxology: Glory be to God the Father,
             And to Jesus Christ, his Son,
             Glory to the Holy Spirit,
             Triune God, the Three-in-One.
             As it was in the beginning,
             It endures as ages run.

Antiphon: Psalm 139:18, 5, 6, CT
Verses: Psalm 139:1–10, Doxology: CT
© 2005 World Library Publications

Second Setting
Meter: 77 77 with Alleluias
Suggested Tune: Easter Hymn

Antiphon: Christ is risen from the grave, alleluia,
             And remains with us always, alleluia.
             God has placed his hands on me, alleluia,
             Shown his wisdom wondrously, alleluia.

Verses: Lord, you search and know my ways, alleluia,
             Know my thoughts from far away, alleluia,
             When I walk and when I lie, alleluia,
             When I live and when I die, alleluia.

             Lord, you know the word I speak, alleluia,
             Long before I utter it, alleluia.
             Lord, you are before, behind, alleluia,
             Ever blessing humankind, alleluia.

             Where could I flee from your glance, alleluia?
             Or escape your countenance, alleluia?
             If in heaven or vale or hill, alleluia,
             You are there to guide me still, alleluia.

Doxology: Glory to the Three in One, alleluia,
             God the Father, God the Son, alleluia,
             God the Holy Paraclete, alleluia,
             Who endures eternally, alleluia.

Antiphon: Psalm 139:18, 5, 6, CT
Verses: Psalm 139:1–10, Doxology: CT
© 2005 World Library Publications

Second Sunday of Easter

Quasi modo geniti infantes, alleluia: rationabiles, sine dolo lac concupiscite, alleluia, alleluia, alleluia. Ps. Exsultate Deo adiutori nostro: iubilate Deo Iacob.

As newborn babes, alleluia, long for pure spiritual milk, alleluia, alleluia, alleluia. V. Rejoice in honor of God our helper; shout for joy to the God of Jacob.

Meter: CM
Suggested Tune: Graefenberg

Antiphon: As newborn infants long for milk,
              We seek our heavenly food,
              Which strengthens, gives eternal life;
              O taste, the Lord is good.

Verses: A loud shout raise to Jacob's God,
              Rejoice in God our King;
              Sound timbrels, pluck the merry harp,
              And play the lyre and sing.

              Blow on the ram's horn on our feast,
              The full moon and the new;
              This is a law of Jacob's God
              And Israel's statute, too.

              When Joseph came from Egypt, he
              Received the solemn charge.
              A great voice said, "I eased your load,
              And set your feet at large."

"I am the Lord who brought you out
Of Egypt and I said,
If you would open wide your mouth,
You will be truly fed."

Doxology: Give glory to the Father, Son,
                 And Spirit equally;
                 As from the first it was, is now,
                 And evermore shall be.

Antiphon: 1 Peter 2:2–3, CT, © 2005 World Library Publications
Verses: Psalm 81:2–7, 11, Doxology: NMP alt.
© 1986 Christopher Webber

THIRD SUNDAY OF EASTER

Iubilate Deo omnis terra, alleluia: psalmum dicite nomini eius, alleluia:
date gloriam laudi eius, alleluia, alleluia, alleluia. Ps. Dicite Deo,
quam terribilia sunt opera tua, Domine! in multitudine virtutis tuae
mentientur tibi inimici tui.

*Shout joyfully to God, all the earth, alleluia; sing a psalm to his name,
alleluia; praise him with magnificence, alleluia, alleluia, alleluia. V. Say to
God: "How awesome are your deeds, O Lord! In the greatness of your power
your enemies will be convicted of lying to you."*

Meter: LM w/Alleluias
Suggested Tune: Lasst uns erfreuen

Antiphon: All people of the earth, rejoice,
                 Praise God, and raise a joyful voice,
                 Alleluia, alleluia.
                 Sing psalms, and glorify his name,
                 Give joyful praises all the same.
                 Alleluia, alleluia, alleluia, alleluia, alleluia.

Verses: Proclaim to God, "Your deeds are great,
               Your enemies are soon dismayed."
               Alleluia, alleluia.
               All earth reveres and worships you,
               Adores, and sings your praises, too.
               Alleluia, alleluia, alleluia, alleluia, alleluia.

               Come, witness all our Lord has done,
               He is the awesome Holy One.
               Alleluia, alleluia.
               He turned the sea into dry land,
               They passed through it at his command.
               Alleluia, alleluia, alleluia, alleluia, alleluia.

Doxology: To God, the Triune One, we raise
               Eternal songs of joyful praise.
               Alleluia, alleluia,
               O Father, Son, and Paraclete,
               We praise your name in word and deed.
               Alleluia, alleluia, alleluia, alleluia, alleluia.

Antiphon: Psalm 66:1–2, CT
Verses: Psalm 66:3–6, Doxology: CT
© 2005 World Library Publications

FOURTH SUNDAY OF EASTER

Misericordia Domini plena est terra, alleluia: verbo Dei caeli firmati
sunt, alleluia, alleluia. Ps. Exsultate iusti in Domino: rectos decet
collaudatio.

*The earth is full of the mercy of the Lord, alleluia; by the word of the Lord,
the heavens were established, alleluia, alleluia. V. Rejoice in the Lord,
O you righteous! Praising befits those who are upright.*

Meter: SM
Suggested Tune: Festal Song

Antiphon: The mercy of the Lord
             Replenishes the world.
             The heavens above were fashioned by
             The Lord's almighty word.

Verses: You upright in the Lord,
             Rejoice, let praises ring,
             Give thanks to Yahweh with the lyre,
             Make melody and sing.

             Compose a song to God,
             Play strings with great finesse.
             His word is honest, and he works
             His deeds in uprightness.

             Let all the earth fear God,
             Let everyone admire;
             For when he spoke, the earth was made
             And stood at his desire.

Doxology: Give glory to our God,
             The Father, and the Son,
             And also to the Paraclete,
             Eternal Three-in-One.

Antiphon: Psalm 33:5b–6, CT
Verses: Psalm 33:1–4, 8–9, Doxology: CT
© 2005 World Library Publications

Fifth Sunday of Easter

Cantate Domino canticum novum, alleluia: quia mirabilia fecit
Dominus, alleluia: ante conspectum gentium revelavit iustitiam suam,
alleluia, alleluia. Ps. Salvavit sibi dextera eius: et brachium sanctum eius.

*Sing to the Lord a new song, alleluia; for the Lord has accomplished
wondrous deeds, alleluia; he has revealed his justice in the sight of the*

gentiles, alleluia, alleluia. V. His right hand and his holy arm have given him victory.

Meter: CM
Suggested Tune: St. Magnus

Antiphon: O sing a new song to the Lord,
               He has done wondrous deeds.
               His right hand and his holy arm
               Have gained the victory.

Verses: The Lord displayed his saving power
               And truth and constancy;
               He has revealed his justice and
               His strength for all to see.

               To Israel's house God has recalled
               His faithfulness and love.
               The farthest ends of earth have seen
               The victory from above.

               Make joyful noises to the Lord,
               Break forth in harmony.
               Sing praises to the Lord our God
               With lyre and melody.

Doxology: Give glory to our loving God,
               The Father, and the Son,
               And also to the Paraclete,
               Eternal Three-in-One.

Antiphon: Psalm 98:1, CT
Verses: Psalm 98:2–5, Doxology: CT
© 2005 World Library Publications

SIXTH SUNDAY OF EASTER

Vocem iucunditatis annuntiate, et audiatur, alleluia: nuntiate usque ad extremum terrae: liberavit Dominus populum suum, alleluia, alleluia. Ps. Iubilate Deo omnis terra: psalmum dicite nomini eius, date gloriam laudi eius.

Spread the news with a voice of joy; let it be heard, alleluia; speak it out to the very ends of the earth; the Lord has liberated his people, alleluia, alleluia. V. Shout joyfully to God, all the earth; sing a psalm to his name; praise him with magnificence.

Meter: LM w/Alleluias
Suggested Tune: Lasst uns erfreuen

Antiphon: Come, spread the news with shouts of joy,
                 Let it be heard with every cry:
                 Alleluia, alleluia!
                 Speak to the ends of earth with glee:
                 The Lord has set his people free.
                 Alleluia, alleluia! Alleluia, alleluia! Alleluia!

Verses: All people of the earth, rejoice,
                 Praise God, and raise a joyful voice.
                 Alleluia, alleluia.
                 Sing psalms and glorify his name,
                 Give joyful praises all the same.
                 Alleluia, alleluia, alleluia, alleluia, alleluia.

                 Proclaim to God, "Your deeds are great,
                 Your enemies are soon dismayed."
                 Alleluia, alleluia.
                 All earth reveres and worships you,
                 Adores, and sings your praises, too.
                 Alleluia, alleluia, alleluia, alleluia, alleluia.

Come, witness all our Lord has done,
He is the awesome Holy One.
Alleluia, alleluia.
He turned the sea into dry land,
They passed through it at his command.
Alleluia, alleluia, alleluia, alleluia, alleluia.

Doxology: To God, the Triune One, we raise
Eternal songs of joyful praise.
Alleluia, alleluia,
O Father, Son, and Paraclete,
We praise your name in word and deed.
Alleluia, alleluia, alleluia, alleluia, alleluia.

Antiphon: Isaiah 48:20, CT
Verses: Psalm 66:1–6, Doxology: CT
© 2005 World Library Publications

THE ASCENSION OF THE LORD

Viri Galilaei, quid admiramini aspicientes in caelum? alleluia:
quemadmodum vidistis eum ascendentem in caelum, ita veniet,
alleluia, alleluia, alleluia. V. Omnes gentes plaudite manibus:
iubilate Deo in voce exsultationis.

Men of Galilee, why are you gazing in astonishment at the sky? alleluia;
just as you have seen him ascend into heaven, so, in like manner, shall he
return, alleluia, alleluia alleluia. V. All nations, clap your hands; shout unto
God with a voice of joy.

Meter: SM
Suggested Tune: Swabia

Antiphon: O men of Galilee,
Why gaze into the sky?
Just as the Lord ascended, so
He will return from high.

Verses: All peoples, clap your hands,
To God with joy now sing.
The Lord, the Awesome, the Most High,
O'er all the earth is King.

God has gone up with shouts
Amid the trumpet's blast.
Sing praise to God our King, sing praise,
And let this music last.

The Lord rules over all;
He sits upon his throne.
All princes of the earth shall kneel
And honor him alone.

Doxology: Give glory to our God,
The Father, and the Son,
And also to the Paraclete,
Eternal Three-in-One.

Antiphon: Acts 1:11, CT
Verses: Psalm 47:2–3, 6–10a, Doxology: CT
© 2005 World Library Publications

Seventh Sunday of Easter

Exaudi, Domine, vocem meam, qua clamavi ad te, alleluia: tibi dixit cor meum, quaesivi vultum tuum, vultum tuum, Domine, requiram: ne avertas faciem tuam a me. Ps. Dominus illuminatio mea, et salus mea: quem timebo?

Hearken, O Lord, unto the voice which has called out to you, alleluia; my heart declared to you: "Your countenance have I shought; I shall ever seek your countenance, O Lord; do not turn your face from me." V. The Lord is my light and my salvation; whom shall I fear?

Meter: LM
Suggested Tune: Duke Street

Antiphon: My heart declared to you, O Lord:
             "Your countenance my soul has sought;
             My heart shall ever seek your face;
             Do not reject me, O my God."

Verses: My light, my Savior is the Lord,
             Of whom should I have any fear?
             He is the stronghold of my life;
             Whom should I dread if he is near?

             When evildoers seek my life
             And in their malice draw around,
             My adversaries and my foes
             Will stumble and fall to the ground.

             Though hostile tents encircle me,
             My heart will never be dismayed;
             Though war rise up against my life,
             I will trust God, not be afraid.

             One thing alone I ask of God:
             To dwell in his most holy place,
             To seek him in his holy court
             And see his beauty face to face.

Doxology: All glory to the Father, Son,
             And to the Holy Spirit be;
             As from the first it was, is now,
             And will be for eternity.

Antiphon: Psalm 27:8, 9, CT, © 2005 World Library Publications
Verses: Psalm 27:1–4, Doxology: NMP
© 1986 Christopher Webber

Pentecost: Vigil Mass

Dum sanctificatus fuero in vobis, congregabo vos de universis terris: et effundam super vos aquam mundam, et mundabimini ab omnibus iniquinamentis vestris: et dabo vobis spiritum novum, alleluia, alleluia. Ps. Benedicam Dominum in omni tempore: semper laus eius in ore meo.

When I vindicate my holiness through you, I will gather you from all the lands, and I will sprinkle clean water upon you, and you shall be cleansed from all your filthiness; and I will give you a new Spirit, alleluia, alleluia. V. I will bless the Lord at all times; his praise shall continually be in my mouth.

Meter: LM
Suggested Tune: Tallis' Canon

Antiphon:

When I will sanctify my name,
From every land I'll gather you,
And with pure water cleanse your souls,
And grant a Spirit that is new.

Verses:

At all times I will bless the Lord;
His praise shall always fill my voice.
My heart extols his glorious name,
The humble listen and rejoice.

Proclaim God's magnitude with me;
Let us exalt his glorious name.
I seek the Lord, and he responds,
Delivers me from fear and shame.

Be radiant as you gaze at him;
Thus may your face reveal no shame.
The paupers cry, the Lord responds,
And rescues them from ill and blame.

Doxology: To God the Father, God the Son,
             And God the Spirit praises be,
             Who was before the world began,
             Is now and in eternity.

Antiphon: Ezekiel 36:23–26, CT
Verses: Psalm 34:2–7, Doxology: CT
© 2005 World Library Publications

Pentecost Sunday

Spiritus Domini replevit orbem terrarum, alleluia: et hoc quod
continet omnia, scientiam habet vocis, alleluia, alleluia, alleluia.
Ps. Exsurgat Deus, et dissipentur inimici eius: et fugiant qui oderunt
eum, a facie eius.

*The Spirit of the Lord has filled the whole world, alleluia; and that which
contains all things, knows every language spoken by humans, alleluia,
alleluia, alleluia. V. Let God arise, and let his enemies be scattered; and let
those who hate him flee before his face.*

Meter: LM w/Alleluias
Suggested Tune: Lasst uns erfreuen

Antiphon: The Spirit of our God and King
             Has filled the world; let voices ring:
             Alleluia, alleluia.
             He fills all things made by our God,
             Knows every language, every thought.
             Alleluia, alleluia, alleluia, alleluia, alleluia.

Verses: Let God arise, and scatter those
             Who scorn his law, his ways oppose.
             Alleluia, alleluia.
             As fire melts wax and smoke recedes,
             They perish when God's face they see.
             Alleluia, alleluia, alleluia, alleluia, alleluia.

But let the righteous shout with glee,
Let them exult in ecstasy.
Alleluia, alleluia.
Let your melodious music ring,
Rejoice in Yahweh, dance and sing!
Alleluia, alleluia, alleluia, alleluia, alleluia.

God helps the orphans, widows, lone;
He gives the desolate a home.
Alleluia, alleluia.
Then prisoners are truly freed,
He leads them to prosperity.
Alleluia, alleluia, alleluia, alleluia, alleluia.

Doxology: To God, the Triune One, we raise
Eternal songs of joyful praise.
Alleluia, alleluia.
O Father, Son, and Paraclete,
We praise your name in word and deed.
Alleluia, alleluia, alleluia, alleluia, alleluia.

Antiphon: Wisdom 1:7, CT
Verses: Psalm 68:1–2, 3–4, 5–6a, 7a, Doxology: CT
© 2005 World Library Publications

Chapter 12

Solemnities after Pentecost

THE MOST HOLY TRINITY, YEAR A & B

Benedicta sit sancta Trinitas, atque individua Unitas: confitebimur ei, quia fecit nobiscum misericordiam suam. Ps. Domine Dominus noster: quam admirabile est nomen tuum in universa terra!

Blessed be the Holy Trinity and its undivided unity; we shall ever give him thanks, for he has dealt with us according to his mercy. V. O Lord, our Governor, how admirable is your name in all the earth!

Meter: 87 87 D
Suggested Tune: Hyfrydol

Antiphon: Blessed be the Triune Godhead,
     Undivided Unity!
     Let us evermore be thankful:
     God has blessed us bounteously.
Verses: Lord, our God and mighty Savior,
     How majestic is your name;
     You arrayed your splendid glory
     Far above the heavenly frame.

     Songs of praise and jubilation
     Fall from infant children's tongues,
     Silencing the lips of evil
     And subduing wicked ones.
     I behold your works in wonder,
     Moon and stars that you prepared.

What are we of human stature,
That our God should mind and care?

Doxology: Sing to God in highest heaven,
Father, Son, and Paraclete.
As it was in the beginning,
And will be eternally.

Antiphon: Blessed be the Triune Godhead,
Undivided Unity!
Let us evermore be thankful:
God has blessed us bounteously.

Antiphon: Tobit 12:6, CT
Verses: Psalm 8:2–5, Doxology: CT
© 2005 World Library Publications

The Most Holy Trinity, Year C

Caritas Dei diffusa est in cordibus nostris, alleluia: per inhabitantem
Spiritum eius in nobis, alleluia, alleluia. Ps. Benedicam anima mea
Domino: et omnia quae intra me sunt, nomini sancto eius.

*The love of God has been poured into our hearts, alleluia; by his Spirit
which dwells in us, alleluia, alleluia. V. Bless the Lord, O my soul; and all
that is within me, bless his holy name.*

Meter: SM
Suggested Tune: St. Thomas (Williams)

Antiphon: The love of God most high
Was poured into our hearts.
The Spirit who dwells in our souls
Accomplished this in us.

Verses: O bless the Lord, my soul;
Your holy name be blessed.
O bless the Lord, my soul; do not
Forget his kindnesses.

Bless God, you mighty ones;
You angels, bless the Lord!
O bless the Lord, you hosts on high,
Obedient to his word.

All peoples, bless the Lord,
And all created things.
In all the places of his reign
O bless the Lord and King.

Doxology: Give God the Father praise,
              And praise to God the Son,
              To God the Spirit equal praise:
              Eternal Three-in-One.

Antiphon: Romans 5:5; 10:11, CT
Verses: Psalm 103:1–2, 20–21, 22, Doxology: CT
© 2005 World Library Publications

The Most Holy Body and Blood of Christ

Cibavit eos ex adipe frumenti, alleluia: et de petra melle saturavit eos, alleluia, alleluia, alleluia. Ps. Exsultate Deo adiutori nostro: iubilate Deo Iacob.

He fed them with the finest of wheat, alleluia; and with honey from the rock he satisfied them, alleluia, alleluia. V. Rejoice in honor of God our helper; shout for joy to the God of Jacob.

Meter: CM
Suggested Tune: Azmon

Antiphon: The Lord provided Israel
              With gifts of finest wheat,
              Gave flowing honey from the rock
              To satisfy their need.

Verses:	A loud shout raise to Jacob's God, Rejoice in God our King; Sound timbrels, pluck the merry harp, And play the lyre and sing.

Blow on the ram's horn on our feast,
The full moon and the new;
This is a law of Jacob's God
And Israel's statute, too.

When Joseph came from Egypt, he
Received the solemn charge.
A great voice said, "I eased your load,
And set your feet at large."

"I am the Lord who brought you out
Of Egypt's land and I said,
If you would open wide your mouth,
You will be truly fed."

Doxology:	Give glory to the Father, Son, And Spirit equally; As from the first it was, is now, And evermore shall be.

Antiphon: Psalm 81:17, CT, © 2005 World Library Publications
Verses: Psalm 81:2–7, 11, Doxology: NMP alt.
© 1986 Christopher Webber

THE MOST SACRED HEART OF JESUS

Cogitationes Cordis eius in generatione et generationem: ut eruat a
morte animas eorum et alat eos in fame. Ps. Exsultate iusti in Domino:
rectos decet collaudatio.

*The thoughts of his heart stand from generation to generation: that he
might deliver their souls from death, and nourish them in times of famine.
V. Rejoice in the Lord, O you righteous! Praising befits those who are upright.*

Meter: SM
Suggested Tune: Festal Song

Antiphon:	Forever in his heart,
	His thoughts are firm indeed:
	That he might save our souls from death
	And nourish us in need.

Verses:	You upright in the Lord,
	Rejoice, let praises ring,
	Give thanks to Yahweh with the lyre,
	Make melody and sing.

Compose a song to God,
Play strings with great finesse.
His word is honest, and he works
His deeds in uprightness.

Let all the earth fear God,
Let everyone admire;
For when he spoke, the earth was made
And stood at his desire.

Doxology:	Give glory to our God,
	The Father and the Son,
	And also to the Paraclete,
	Eternal Three-in-One.

Antiphon: Psalm 33:11, 19, CT
Verses: Psalm 33:1–4, 8–9, Doxology: CT
© 2005 World Library Publications

Chapter 13

Ordinary Time

SECOND SUNDAY IN ORDINARY TIME

Omnis terra adoret te, Deus, et psallat tibi: psalmum dicat nomini tuo, Altissime. Ps. Iubilate Deo omnis terra, psalmum dicite nomini eius: date gloriam laudi eius.

Let all the earth worship you and praise you, O God; may it sing in praise of your name, O Most High. V. Shout joyfully to God, all the earth; sing a psalm in honor of his name; praise him with magnificence.

Meter: LM
Suggested Tune: Duke Street

Antiphon: Let all the earth praise you, O Lord,
                     And worship you with one accord;
                     May we, with song and melody,
                     Praise your great name, O Majesty!

Verses: All people of the earth, rejoice,
                     Praise God, and raise a joyful voice,
                     Sing psalms and glorify his name,
                     Give joyful praises all the same.

                     Proclaim to God, "Your deeds are great,
                     Your enemies are soon dismayed."
                     All earth reveres and worships you,
                     Adores, and sings your praises, too.

Come, witness all the Lord has done,
He is the awesome Holy One;
He turned the sea into dry land,
They passed through it at his command.

Doxology: To God, the Triune One, we raise
Eternal songs of joyful praise.
O Father, Son, and Paraclete,
We praise your name in word and deed.

Antiphon: Psalm 66:4, CT
Verses: Psalm 66:1–6, Doxology: CT
© 2005 World Library Publications

Third Sunday in Ordinary Time, Year A & B

Dominus secus mare Galilaeae vidit duos fratres, Petrum et Andream, et vocabit eos: Venite post me: faciam vos fieri piscatores hominum. Ps. Caeli enarrant gloriam Dei: et opera manuum eius annuntiat firmamentum.

The Lord, walking by the sea of Galilee, saw two brothers, Peter and Andrew, and he called out to them: "Follow me, and I will make you fishers of men." V. The heavens declare the glory of God, and the firmament proclaims the work of his hands.

Meter: CM
Suggested Tune: McKee

Antiphon: The Lord observed two fishermen
While walking by the sea:
"O Peter, Andrew, follow close,
You'll fish for souls," said he.

Verses: The heavens declare your glory, Lord,
The work your hands have made;
Day after day your power is shown
And night by night displayed.

There is no utterance or speech,
No voice is ever heard,
Yet to all nations comes the sound,
To every place their word.

Forth like a bridegroom comes the sun
From its appointed place,
And like a hero on his course
Rejoices in their race.

It runs from East to farthest West
To make its course complete,
And nothing in the world beneath
Escapes its scorching heat.

Doxology: Give glory to the Father, Son,
And Spirit equally,
As from the first it was, is now,
And evermore shall be.

Antiphon: Matthew 4:18–19, CT, © 2005 World Library Publications
Verses: Psalm 19:2–7, Doxology: NMP alt.
© 1986 Christopher Webber

Third Sunday in Ordinary Time, Year C

Adorate Deum, omnes angeli eius: audivat, et laetata est Sion:
et exsultaverunt filiae Iudae. Ps. Dominus regnavit, exsultet terra:
laetentur insulae multae.

*Bow down before God, all you Angels of his. Zion has heard and is glad;
and the daughters of Judah have rejoiced. V. The Lord reigns, let the earth
rejoice; let all the isles be glad.*

Meter: 77 77
Suggested Tune: Luebeck

Antiphon: O bow down before the King,
                 Angel hosts, who worship him.
                 Zion gladly heard the voice;
                 Judah's daughters have rejoiced.

Verses: God is King, let earth rejoice;
                 All you isles, lift up your voice.
                 Clouds of darkness are around,
                 But with God is justice found.

                 Heaven proclaims God's righteousness;
                 Let the world his deeds confess.
                 For, O Lord, you are Most High,
                 Over all the earth and sky.

                 Light is given to the just;
                 Secrets God to them entrusts.
                 All you righteous, praise the Lord,
                 Ever be his name adored.

Doxology: Glory to the Father, Son,
                 And the Spirit, with them One;
                 As we worship and adore,
                 We will sing for evermore.

Antiphon: Psalm 97:6–7, CT
Verses: Psalm 97:1–2, 6, 9, 11–12, Doxology: CT
© 2005 World Library Publications

Fourth Sunday in Ordinary Time

Laetetur cor quaerentium Dominum: quaerite Dominum, et
confirmamini: quaerite faciem eius semper. Ps. Confitemini Domino,
et invocate nomen eius: annuntiate inter gentes opera eius.

*Let the hearts of those who seek the Lord rejoice; seek the Lord and be
strengthened; seek his face for evermore. V. Give thanks to the Lord and call
upon his name; declare his deeds among the gentiles.*

First Setting
Meter: LM
Suggested Tune: Erhalt uns, Herr; Old 100th

Antiphon: Let searching hearts rejoice in God:
Come, glory in his holy name.
Hope in the Lord to find your strength
And in his presence to remain.

Verses: Give thanks to God, invoke his name;
Proclaim his deeds throughout the earth.
Sing praises, lifting up your voice;
Make melody, recount his works.

Recall the deeds the Lord performed,
The miracles that he made known,
O family of Abraham
And Jacob, chosen as his own.

He is our God eternally,
Remembering his covenant;
His judgments are by all proclaimed,
And what he promised us will stand.

Doxology: To God, the Triune One, we raise
Eternal hymns of endless praise.
O Father, Son, and Paraclete,
We praise your name in word and deed.

Antiphon: Psalm 105:3–4, CT
Verses: Psalm 105:1–2, 5–6, 7–8, Doxology: CT
© 2005 World Library Publications

Second Setting
Meter: 10 10 10 10
Suggested Tune: Woodlands, Toulon

Antiphon: Let every heart who seeks the Lord rejoice;
                     Come, glorify his everlasting name.
                     Hope in the Lord, and find your strength in him;
                     Desire with him forever to remain.

Verses: Give thanks to God, invoke his holy name.
                     Proclaim his wondrous deeds to all the earth.
                     Sing praises to the Lord, lift up your voice;
                     Make melody, recount his marvelous works.

                     Recall the wondrous deeds the Lord performed,
                     His miracles, and judgments he made known,
                     O offspring of his servant Abraham,
                     Children of Jacob, chosen as his own.

                     He is the Lord our God eternally,
                     Remembering his faithful covenant;
                     His judgments are in all the earth proclaimed,
                     And what he promised will forever stand.

Doxology: Give praise to God the Father, God the Son,
                     And God the Spirit, ever Three-in-One,
                     Who was from the beginning without end,
                     Is now, and shall be evermore. Amen.

Antiphon: Psalm 105:3–4, CT
Verses: Psalm 105:1–2, 5–6, 7–8, Doxology: CT
© 2005 World Library Publications

Fifth Sunday in Ordinary Time

Venite, adoremus Deum, et procidamus ante Dominum: ploremus
ante eum, qui fecit nos: quia ipse est Dominus Deus noster. Ps. Venite,
exsultemus Domino: iubilemus Deo salutari nostro.

Come, let us worship God and bow down before the Lord; let us shed tears
before the Lord who made us, for he is the Lord our God. V. Come, let us sing
to the Lord; let us make a joyful noise unto God our Savior.

First Setting
Meter: 66 66 88
Suggested Tune: Darwall's 148th

Antiphon: Bow down before the Lord
             And worship him alone.
             Come, kneel before the God
             Who made us as his own.
             Within his hand we are like sheep,
             The flock within the Shepherd's keep.

Verses: Come, sing in harmony
             And make a joyful sound!
             Let us approach the Rock
             And let our praise abound!
             With thankful lips and grateful soul,
             We come before our One and All.

             The Lord our God is great:
             The depths of earth his own,
             The hills, the plains, the sea,
             The sky are his alone.
             He made them all, and by his will
             Was molded every vale and hill.

Doxology: Give God the Father praise,
             And glory to the Son,
             And to the Holy Spirit
             Equal praise be done.
             The God who was and is to be
             For us into eternity.

Antiphon: Psalm 95:6–7, CT
Verses: Psalm 95:1–2, 3–5, Doxology: CT
© 2005 World Library Publications

Second Setting

Meter: 86 886
Suggested Tune: Repton

Antiphon: Bow down before the Lord our God,
               And worship him alone.
               Come, kneel before our gracious God;
               We are the people of his flock,
               The sheep he calls his own.

Verses: Come, sing in glorious harmony
               And make a joyful sound!
               Let us approach the Rock, our God,
               With thankful lips and grateful heart,
               And let our praise abound!

               The Lord our God is great indeed:
               The depths of earth his own,
               The mountaintops, the sea, the land;
               He fashioned all things by his hand,
               Created them alone.

Doxology: Give glory to our loving God,
               The Father, and the Son,
               The Holy Spirit equally,
               The God who rules eternally,
               For ever Three-in-One.

Antiphon: Psalm 95:6–7, CT
Verses: Psalm 95:1–2, 3–5, Doxology: CT
© 2005 World Library Publications

Sixth Sunday in Ordinary Time

Esto mihi in Deum protectorem, et in locum refugii, ut salvum me
facias: quoniam firmamentum meum, et refugium meum es tu: et
propter nomen tuum dux mihi eris, et enutries me. Ps. In te, Domine,
speravi, non confundar in aeternum: in iustitia tua libera me.

Be unto me a protecting God and a house of refuge to save me; for you are my support and my refuge; and for the sake of your name you will lead me and nourish me. V. In you, O Lord, do I trust; let me never be put to shame; deliver me in your righteousness.

Meter: CM
Suggested Tune: St. Anne

Antiphon: Be my protecting, saving God,
      My just security.
      For you are my support, and you
      Will lead and nourish me.

Verses: In you, O Lord, I seek support;
      Let me not be disgraced.
      In righteousness deliver me,
      Attend my needs, make haste.

      The Lord preserves his faithful ones
      But scorns all haughty souls.
      Be strong, and let your heart exult,
      All you who seek the Lord.

Doxology: Give glory to our loving God,
      The Father and the Son,
      And also to the Paraclete,
      Eternal Three-in-One.

Antiphon: Psalm 31:3–4, CT
Verses: Psalm 31:2–3a, 24b–25, Doxology: CT
© 2005 World Library Publications

SEVENTH SUNDAY IN ORDINARY TIME

Domine, in tua misericordia speravi: exsultavit cor meum in salutari tuo: cantabo Domino, qui bona tribuit mihi. Ps. Usquequo, Domine, oblivisceris me in finem? usquequo avertis faciem tuam a me?

O Lord, I have placed my trust in your merciful love; my heart has rejoiced in your salvation. I will sing unto the Lord who has dealt bountifully with me. V. How long will you forget me, O Lord? For ever? How long will you hide your countenance from me?

Meter: SM
Suggested Tune: Swabia

Antiphon: In your most steadfast love,
O Lord, I place my trust.
In your salvation I rejoice;
Your ways are good and just.

Verses: How long, O Lord, how long
Will you abandon me?
Will you forget me evermore
And hide your face from me?

How long must I bear pain
And sorrow night and day?
How long will enemies exult
And triumph in their way?

Respond and answer me,
Give light unto my eyes,
Or I will slumber into death
While enemies rejoice.

Doxology: Give glory to our God,
The Father, and the Son,
And also to the Paraclete,
Eternal Three-in-One.

Antiphon: Psalm 13:6, CT
Verses: Psalm 13:2–5, Doxology: CT
© 2005 World Library Publications

EIGHTH SUNDAY IN ORDINARY TIME

Factus est Dominus protector meus, et eduxit me in latitudinem: salvum me fecit, quoniam voluit me. Ps. Diligam te, Domine, fortitudo mea: Dominus firmamentum meum, et refugium meum, et liberator meus.

The Lord has become my protector; he has brought me forth into free and open spaces; he delivered me, because he was well pleased with me. V. I will love you always, O Lord my strength; the Lord is my support, my refuge, and my deliverer.

Meter: 11 11 11 11
Suggested Tune: St. Denio

Antiphon:	The Lord has become my protector and aid; He brought me from darkness to wide open space. He saved me because he delighted in me, Rewarded me, for I obeyed his decree.
Verses:	I love you, O Lord, my salvation, my friend, My rock, and my refuge who saves and defends, My God, who protects me when I was in need, My shield and the horn of salvation indeed.
	I called on the Lord, "You are worthy indeed!" He saved me from anguish when I was in need; For death's mighty breakers encompassed me round, The torrents of evil and shame did abound.
	Distraught and in anguish, I called on the Lord, I cried for assistance and help to my God. He heard my complaint from his temple above; My cry reached his ears, and my tears reached his love.
Doxology:	So let us adore God the Father and sing Our praise to the Son, who is Savior and King. All praise to the Spirit, who loves and remains, And was from the first and will be for all days.

Antiphon: Psalm 18:19b–21a, CT
Verses: Psalm 18:2–5, 7, CT
© 2005 World Library Publications

Ninth Sunday in Ordinary Time

Respice in me, et miserere mei, Domine: quoniam unicus et pauperum sum ego: vide humilitatem meam, et laborem meum: et dimitte omnia peccata mea, Deus meus. Ps. Ad te, Domine, levavi animam meam: Deus meus, in te confido, non erubescam.

Look upon me and have mercy on me, O Lord; for I am abandoned and destitute; consider my abjection and my labor, and forgive me all my sins, my dear God. V. Unto you, O Lord, have I lifted up my soul; O my God, I trust in you; let me not be put to shame.

Meter: SM
Suggested Tune: St. Michael

Antiphon: Lord, turn your face towards me,
            Abandoned and in need.
            Come, see my tribulations, Lord,
            Forgive my sinful deeds.

Verses: To you, O Lord, I pray,
            I trust in your great name.
            Let not my enemies exult
            Nor put my soul to shame.

            Reveal your ways to me
            And guide me in right paths,
            That you may teach me in your truth,
            O Lord, is all I ask.

            In pity, Lord, recall
            Your mercies manifold.
            Remember me in your great love
            As in the days of old.

I pray that you forgive
The failings of my youth,
And do not cease to think of me
In grace and love and truth.

Doxology: Give glory to our God,
The Father, and the Son,
And also to the Paraclete,
Eternal Three-in-One.

Antiphon: Psalm 25:16, 18, CT
Verses: Psalm 25:1–3a, 4–7, Doxology: CT
© 2005 World Library Publications

TENTH SUNDAY IN ORDINARY TIME, YEAR A & C

Dominus illuminatio mea, et salus mea, quem timebo? Dominus defensor vitae meae, a quo trepidabo? qui tribulant me inimici mei, infirmati sunt, et ceciderunt. Ps. Si consistant adversum me castra: non timebit cor meum.

The Lord is my light and my salvation, whom shall I fear? The Lord is the protector of my life, of whom shall I be afraid? My enemies who trouble me have themselves grown weak and have fallen. V. Though a host camp against me, my heart shall not fear.

Meter: 87 87 D
Suggested Tune: Hyfrydol

Antiphon: Lord, you are my light and Savior;
Who should cause my heart to fear?
You the stronghold of my life, whom
Should I dread if you are near?
Evil forces seek to harm me;
They will stumble, they will fall,
For my God, the Lord of heaven,
Will protect me from them all.

Verses:	Though an army pitch its camp, my
	Heart will steadfastly endure;
	War and battle may o'erpower,
	But my trust in God is sure.
	This alone I ask in pleading,
	This I seek eternally:
	That I may live in his temple,
	There his wondrous face to see.

For he hides me in his shelter
When through troubled days I walk,
Keeps me in the safest chamber,
Sets me high upon a rock.
Now my head is high above all
Evil forces and their ways.
In his temple I will offer
Sacrifice of laud and praise.

Doxology:	To the Father sing your praises,
	Who made land and sky and sea;
	Also praises to the Son who
	Saved us from the enemy;
	Praises to the Holy Spirit,
	Who helps us in time of need;
	As it was in the beginning,
	It will be eternally.

Antiphon: Psalm 27:1–2, CT
Verses: Psalm 27:3–6, Doxology: CT
© 2005 World Library Publications

Tenth Sunday in Ordinary Time, Year B

Si iniquitates observaveris, Domine, quis sustinebit? Quia apud te propitiatio est, Deus Israel. Ps. De profundis clamavi ad te, Domine: Domine, exaudi vocem meam.

O Lord, if you were to take into account our iniquities, who would withstand the test? But forgiveness abides with you, O God of Israel. V. Out of the depths have I cried to you, O Lord; Lord, hear my voice.

Meter: LM
Suggested Tune: Jesu, dulcis memoria

Antiphon: If you should count each sinful deed,
             Lord, who could stand when you appeared?
             But with you is forgiveness found,
             And therefore, Lord, you shall be feared.

Verses: Out of the depths I call to you,
             Lord, hear my voice and heed my prayer.
             Look with compassion on my plea;
             Weigh my petition, Lord, with care.

             More certainly than watchmen wait
             To see the daylight first appear,
             Does my soul wait upon the Lord;
             I wait in trust and holy fear.

             O Israel, wait upon the Lord
             With whom mercy is always found,
             Who pardons us from all our sin,
             And in whom liberty abounds.

Doxology: All glory to the Father, Son,
             And to the Holy Spirit be;
             As from the first it was, is now,
             And will be for eternity.

Antiphon: Psalm 130:3–4, NMP
Verses: Psalm 130:1–2, 5–6, 7–8, Doxology: NMP
© 1986 Christopher Webber

ELEVENTH SUNDAY IN ORDINARY TIME

Exaudi, Domine, vocem meam, qua clamavi ad te: adiutor meus esto,
ne derelinquas me neque despicias me, Deus salutaris meus.
Ps. Dominus illuminatio mea, et salus mea: quem timebo?

*Hearken, O Lord, unto my voice which has called out to you; deign to be my
help, forsake me not, do not despise me, O God my Savior. V. The Lord is my
light and my salvation; whom shall I fear?*

Meter: LM
Suggested Tune: Erhalt uns, Herr

Antiphon: My voice has called to you, O Lord,
Come to my refuge and respond;
Do not forsake or cast me off;
Do not despise me, Savior God.

Verses: My light, my Savior is the Lord,
Of whom should I have any fear?
He is the stronghold of my life;
Whom should I dread if he is near?

When evildoers seek my life
And in their malice draw around,
My adversaries and my foes
Will stumble and fall to the ground.

Though hostile tents encircle me,
My heart will never be dismayed;
Though war rise up against my life,
I will trust God, not be afraid.

One thing alone I ask of God:
To dwell in his most holy place,
To seek him in his holy court
And see his beauty face to face.

Doxology: All glory to the Father, Son,
And to the Holy Spirit be;
As from the first it was, is now,
And will be for eternity.

Antiphon: Psalm 27:7, 9b, CT, © 2005 World Library Publications
Verses: Psalm 27:1–4, Doxology: NMP
© 1986 Christopher Webber

TWELFTH SUNDAY IN ORDINARY TIME

Dominus fortitudo plebis suae, et protector salutarium Christi
sui est: salvum fac populum tuum, Domine, et benedic hereditati tuae,
et rege eos usque in saeculum. Ps. Ad te, Domine, clamabo, Deus
meus ne sileas a me: nequando taceas a me, et assimilabor descenden-
tibus in lacum.

The Lord is the strength of his people, and the guardian of salvation for
his Anointed. Save your people, O Lord, and bless your inheritance; be
their guide for ever. V. Unto you, O Lord, will I cry; O my God, be not silent
with me; if you remain silent, I will become like those who go down into
the grave.

Meter: 11 11 11 11
Suggested Tune: St. Denio

Antiphon: The Lord is the strength of his people, his own;
He is the Protector of his Blessed One.
O rescue your people, your heritage bless,
Forever their Shepherd and guide in distress.

Verses: O Lord, mighty Savior, to you I appeal,
My Rock and my Fortress, O listen to me;
For if you stay silent to my shouts of pain,
I shall be like all those whose life is in vain.

O hearken the sound of my pleading to you,
As I cry for help and assistance anew.
When I lift my hands to the holiest place,
O Lord, be my helper and answer my prayers.

The Lord is my stronghold, my strength, and my shield;
My heart shall confide and to him only yield.
Now that I am freed and revived, I rejoice
And raise grateful songs with melodious voice.

Doxology: All praise to the Father and praise to the Son,
And praise to the Spirit, the great Three-in-One.
As from the beginning, is now without end,
With shouts of great gladness we praise you. Amen.

Antiphon: Psalm 28:8, 9, CT
Verses: Psalm 28:1, 2, 7, Doxology: CT
© 2005 World Library Publications

Thirteenth Sunday in Ordinary Time

Omnes gentes, plaudite manibus: iubilate Deo in voce exsultationis.
Ps. Quoniam Dominus excelsus, terribilis: Rex magnus super
omnem terram.

*All nations, clap your hands; shout unto God with a voice of joy. V. For the
Lord is high and awesome; a great king over all the earth.*

Meter: SM
Suggested Tune: Festal Song

Antiphon: All peoples, clap your hands,
To God with joy now sing.
The Lord, the Awesome, the Most High,
O'er all the earth is King.

Verses: The Lord puts the nations down,
Subdues them under us;
He chose our heritage, the pride
Of Jacob, whom he loves.

God has gone up with shouts
Amid the trumpet's blast.
Sing praise to God our King, sing praise,
And let this music last.

The Lord rules over all,
He sits upon his throne.
All princes of the earth shall kneel
And honor him alone.

Doxology: Give glory to our God,
The Father, and the Son,
And also to the Paraclete,
Eternal Three-in-One.

Antiphon: Psalm 47:1–2, CT
Verses: Psalm 47:3–4, 5–6, 8–10a, Doxology: CT
© 2005 World Library Publications

Fourteenth Sunday in Ordinary Time

Suscepimus, Deus, misericodiam tuam in medio templi tui: secundum nomen tuum Deus, ita et laus tua in fines terrae: iustitia plena est dextera tua. Ps. Magnus Dominus et laudabilis nimis: in civitate Dei nostri, in monte sancto eius.

We have received your mercy, O God, in the midst of your temple; even as your name, so also does your praise extend to the ends of the earth; your right hand is filled with righteousness. V. Great is the Lord and worthy of all praise, in the city of our God, on his holy mountain.

Meter: LM
Suggested Tune: Winchester New

Antiphon: Within your temple, mighty Lord,
                   We ponder and receive your love.
                   Your name and praise surround the earth,
                   And your right hand does what is just.

Verses: Great is the Lord and to be praised
                   In his most awesome holy place;
                   His sacred mountain is the joy
                   Of every land and every race.

                   Mount Zion, center of the earth,
                   On you shall royalty endure;
                   Within its citadels is God.
                   Our stronghold and defense is sure.

Doxology: All glory to the Father, Son,
                   And to the Holy Spirit be;
                   As from the first it was, is now,
                   And will be for eternity.

Antiphon: Psalm 48:10–11, CT
Verses: Psalm 48:2–4, Doxology: CT
© 2005 World Library Publications

Fifteenth Sunday in Ordinary Time

Dum clamarem ad Dominum, exaudivit vocem meam, ab his qui appropinquant mihi: et humiliavit eos, qui est ante saecula, et manet in aeternum: iacta cogitatum tuum in Domino, et ipse te enutriet. Ps. Exaudi Deus orationem meam, et ne despexeris deprecationem meam: intende mihi, et exaudi me.

When I cried out to the Lord, he heeded my call against my assailants; he who is before the beginning of the world and who endures forever has humbled them. Cast your cares upon the Lord, and he will sustain you. V. Hear my prayer, O God, and despise not my supplication; be attentive to me and hear me.

Meter: CMD
Suggested Tune: Kingsfold

Antiphon: I pleaded to the Lord my God,
                    He heard my plaintive call.
                    The Lord who was before the world
                    And governs over all
                    Dispersed the forces that wish harm,
                    Destroyed them utterly.
                    O cast your cares upon the Lord,
                    Our helper in great need.

Verses: Give ear, O Lord, unto my prayer,
                    And hide not from my cry;
                    Attend my sad complaint and hear
                    My restless moan and sigh.
                    For my assailants lift up their voice,
                    I shudder at their cries.
                    False accusations are heaped up,
                    And charges full of lies.

                    With heavy heart I find no ease,
                    Death's terrors overtake,
                    And crushed and bruised by fear and fright,
                    I tremble, shudder, shake.
                    "O had I wings," I sigh and say,
                    "Like some swift dove to roam,
                    Then I would hasten far away
                    To find a peaceful home."

Doxology: All glory be to God on high
                    And on the earth below.
                    The Triune Godhead be proclaimed
                    And evermore adored.
                    Give glory to our loving God,
                    The Father, and the Son,
                    And also to the Paraclete,
                    Eternal Three-in-One.

Antiphon: Psalm 55:17, 20a, 23a, CT
Doxology: CT
© 2005 World Library Publications
Verses: Psalm 55:2–7, *The Psalter*, Philadelphia, 1912, alt.

Sixteenth Sunday in Ordinary Time

Ecce Deus adiuvat me, et Dominus susceptor est animae meae:
averte mala inimicis meis, in veritate tua disperde illos, protector
meus Domine. Ps. Deus in nomine tuo salvum me fac: et in
virtute tua iudica me.

*Behold, God is my helper, and the Lord is the upholder of my soul: turn back
all the evil against my enemies, destroy them in your fidelity, O Lord, the
Protector of my life. V. Save me, O God, by your name, and render justice
unto me in your strength.*

Meter: LM
Suggested Tune: Melcombe

Antiphon: It is the Lord who keeps my life,
              God is the help on whom I call;
              Repel the evil of my foes;
              In faithfulness, destroy them all.

Verses: In your great might and by your name,
              Defend me, save me from despair;
              Give ear to all the words I speak;
              My Savior, listen to my prayer,

              For arrogant and ruthless foes
              Have risen up and press me hard;
              The ruthless ones who sought my life,
              Who hold the Lord in disregard.

              I praise your name for it is good,
              And sacrifice with ready will,
              For I have seen my foes destroyed;
              You rescued me from every ill.

Doxology: All glory to the Father, Son,
             And to the Holy Spirit be;
             As from the first it was, is now,
             And will be for eternity.

Antiphon: Psalm 54:6–7, NMP
Verses: Psalm 54:3–5, 8–9, Doxology: NMP
© 1986 Christopher Webber

SEVENTEENTH SUNDAY IN ORDINARY TIME

Deus in loco sancto suo: Deus, qui inhabitare facit unanimes in domo:
ipse dabit virtutem et fortitudinem plebi suae. Ps. Exsurgat Deus,
et dissipentur inimici eius: et fugiant, qui oderunt eum, a facie eum.

*God is in his holy dwelling place; the God who causes us to dwell together,
one at heart, in his house; he himself will give power and strength to his
people. V. Let God arise, and let his enemies be scattered; and let those who
hate him flee before his face.*

Meter: LM
Suggested Tune: Old 100th

Antiphon: God in his holy dwelling place
             Assembles those of every race.
             He leads his people home at length,
             Providing them with power and strength.

Verses: Let God arise and scatter those
             Who scorn his law, his ways oppose.
             As fire melts wax and smoke recedes,
             They perish when they see God's face.

             But let the righteous shout with glee,
             Let them exult exceedingly.
             Let your melodious music ring;
             Rejoice in Yahweh, dance and sing!

God helps the orphans, widows, lone;
He gives the desolate a home.
Then prisoners are truly free;
He leads them to prosperity.

Doxology: To God, the Triune One, we raise
Eternal songs of joyful praise,
O Father, Son, and Paraclete,
We praise your name in word and deed.

Antiphon: Psalm 68:36, CT
Verses: Psalm 68:2–7a, Doxology: CT
© 2005 World Library Publications

Eighteenth Sunday in Ordinary Time, Year A

Sitientes venite ad aquas, dicit Dominus: et qui non habetis pretium,
venite, bibite cum laetitia. Ps. Attendite popule meus legem meam:
inclinate aurem vestram in verba oris mei.

*All who are thirsty, come to the waters, says the Lord; and you who have no
money, come, drink in gladness. V. Attend, O my people, to my law; incline
your ears to the words of my mouth.*

First Setting
Meter: LM
Suggested Tune: Tallis' Canon

Antiphon: You thirsty ones, approach, come forth,
Draw near the waters, says the Lord;
And you without the means to spend,
Approach with joyous hearts and drink.

Verses: My people, listen to my word;
In parables deep truths are heard;
The wondrous story must be shown,
Which parents to their young make known.

Instructing them we thus record
The praises and the works of God;
Old wisdoms in this way passed on
Teach generations yet to come.

Thus children learn from history's light
To hope in God, walk in his sight,
His ordinances to obey,
Unlike their ancestors, who strayed.

Doxology: To God, the Triune One, we raise
Eternal songs of joyful praise,
O Father, Son, and Paraclete,
We praise your name in word and deed.

Antiphon: Isaiah 55:1, CT
Verses: Psalm 78:1–8, Doxology: CT
© 2005 World Library Publications

Second Setting
Meter: 10 10 11 11
Suggested Tune: Laudate Dominum

Antiphon: All people who thirst, approach and come forth,
Draw near to the waters, thus says the Lord;
And all those without any money to spend,
Approach with rejoicing and gladness, and drink.

Verses: My people, give ear, attend to my word;
In lessons of old deep truths shall be heard.
The wonderful story by us must be shown,
The story that parents to children made known.

Instructing the young, we gladly record
The praises, the works, the might of the Lord;
He wishes for parents to pass to each child
Ancestral traditions, the mighty and mild.

> Let children thus learn from history's light
> To hope in our God and walk in his sight,
> The God of their parents to fear and obey,
> But unlike their forebears, who turned from his way.

Doxology: Now let us adore the Father and sing
                Our praise to the Son, our Savior and King.
                All praise to the Spirit who loves and remains,
                And was from the first and will be for all days.

Antiphon: Isaiah 55:1, Doxology: CT,
© 2005 World Library Publications
Verses: Psalm 78:1–8, The Psalter alt.

Eighteenth Sunday in Ordinary Time, Year B & C

Deus in adiutorium meum intende: Domine ad adiuvandum me festina: confundantur et revereantur inimici mei, qui quaerunt animam meam. Ps. Avertantur retrorsum et erubescant, qui volunt mihi mala.

O God, come to my assistance; O Lord, make haste to help me; let them be put to confusion and shame, my enemies who seek my life. V. Let them be turned backward and brought to dishonor, who wish me evil.

Meter: SM
Suggested Tune: St. George

Antiphon: O God, come to my aid;
                Make haste to help me, Lord.
                Confound all those who seek my life,
                And put to shame my foes.

Verses: Rebuke those who rejoice
                When people sin and fall.
                Let those who gloat be brought to shame
                And chastised, one and all.

Let all who search for you
Rejoice and sing your praise.
Let those who love your saving power
Proclaim, "Our God is great!"

But I am destitute;
O hasten, Lord, today.
My helper and deliverer,
O Lord, do not delay!

Doxology: Give glory to our God,
              The Father, and the Son,
              And also to the Paraclete,
              Eternal Three-in-One.

Antiphon: Psalm 70:2–3a, CT
Verses: Psalm 70:3b–6, Doxology: CT
© 2005 World Library Publications

Nineteenth Sunday in Ordinary Time

Respice, Domine, in testamentum tuum, et animas pauperum tuorum
ne derelinquas in finem: exsurge, Domine, et iudica causam tuam:
et ne obliviscaris voces quaerentium te. Ps. Ut quid Deus repulisti in
finem: iratus est furor tuus super oves pascuae tuae?

*Remember, O Lord, your covenant, and do not abandon for ever the souls
of your poor; arise, O Lord, and judge your own cause; forget not the
cries of those who seek you. V. O God, why have you cast us off unto the end;
why is your wrath enkindled against the sheep of your pasture?*

First Setting
Meter: 86 886
Suggested Tune: Repton

Antiphon: Remember, Lord, your covenant,
              Do not forsake the poor;

Arise, O Lord, and judge your cause;
Do not forget the cries of those
Whose search for you endures.

Verses: O God, why do you cast us off?
Why does your anger smoke
Against the sheep of your dear flock.
Remember your own people, Lord,
Adopted long ago.

Remember Zion, where you dwelt,
Direct your steps, and see
The endless desolation of
Your temple, wasted by your foes,
Now ruined utterly.

Yet God, my King, you are of old;
Work your salvation soon.
You cleaved the sea with your great might,
Yours is the day, yours is the night,
You made the sun and moon.

Doxology: Give glory to our loving God,
The Father and the Son,
The Holy Spirit equally,
The God who rules eternally,
For ever Three-in-One.

Antiphon: Psalm 74:20a, 19b, 22a, 23b, CT
Verses: Psalm 74:1–3, 12–13a, 16, Doxology: CT
© 2005 World Library Publications

Second Setting
Meter: LM
Suggested Tune: Erhalt uns, Herr

Antiphon: O Lord, recall your covenant,
             Do not forsake the meek and poor.
             Arise, O Lord, and judge your cause;
             Remember those whose search endures.

Verses: O God, why do you cast us off?
             Why does your anger blaze and smoke
             Against the sheep of your dear flock,
             Your own, adopted long ago?

             Remember Zion, where you dwelt.
             Direct your steps; behold and see
             The desolation by your foes,
             Your temple, ruined utterly.

             Yet God, my King, you are of old;
             You made the sun, you made the moon,
             You cleaved the sea with your great might.
             Come and work your salvation soon.

Doxology: Give God the Father endless praise,
             And praise to Jesus Christ, his Son,
             And to the Spirit equal praise,
             Eternal God, the Three-in-One.

Antiphon: Psalm 74:20a, 19b, 22a, 23b, CT
Verses: Psalm 74:1–3, 12–13a, 16, Doxology: CT
© 2005 World Library Publications

Twentieth Sunday in Ordinary Time

Protector noster aspice, Deus, et respice in faciem Christi tui: quia
melior est dies una in atriis tuis super millia. Ps. Quam dilecta
tabernacula tua, Domine virtutum! concupiscit, et deficit anima mea
in atria Domini.

Behold, O God our protector, and consider the face of your Anointed; for
one day in your house is better than a thousand elsewhere. V. How lovely

is your tabernacle, O Lord of hosts! My soul longs and pines after the courts of the Lord.

Meter: LM
Suggested Tune: Duke Street

Antiphon: Behold, O God, and see the face
                   Of your Anointed, filled with grace.
                   For better one day in your house
                   Than thousands elsewhere, far or close.

Verses: How lovely is your dwelling place,
                   O Lord of hosts and God of grace!
                   My soul, O Lord, longs for your courts;
                   In you rejoice my flesh and heart.

                   Even the sparrow finds a home,
                   Swallows build nests to lay their young;
                   Your altars, Lord above the sky,
                   Are their abode, my King on high.

                   Happy are those of every race
                   Who dwell in your most splendid place,
                   They sing forever to your name;
                   Your might, your glory all proclaim.

Doxology: To God, the Triune One, we raise
                   Eternal songs of joyful praise,
                   O Father, Son, and Paraclete,
                   We praise your name in word and deed.

Antiphon: Psalm 84:10–11a, CT
Verses: Psalm 84:2–5, Doxology: CT
© 2005 World Library Publications

Twenty-first Sunday in Ordinary Time

Inclina, Domine, aurem tuam ad me, et exaudi me: salvum fac servum tuum, Deus meus, sperantem in te: miserere mihi, Domine, quoniam ad te clamavi tota die. Ps. Laetifica animam servi tui: quoniam ad te, Domine, animam meam levavi.

Incline your ear to me, O Lord, and hear me; O God, save your servant who trusts in you; have mercy on me, O Lord, for unto you do I cry all the day. V. Gladden the soul of your servant, for unto you, O Lord, have I lifted up my soul.

First Setting
Meter: 66 66 88
Suggested Tune: Rhosymedre

Antiphon: Incline your ear, O Lord,
And listen when I pray.
Preserve your servant who
Confides in you all day.
Have mercy, Lord, and hear my plight,
My soul cries out by day and night.

Verses: Lord, make my soul rejoice,
I lift it up to you;
For you are full of kindness
And of mercy true.
With tender heart you treat the same
Who call on your immortal name.

Give answer to my prayer,
And listen to my plight.
When I am ill distressed
I call you day and night,
Because I know with certainty
That you will always answer me.

Doxology: Give God the Father praise,
And glory to the Son,
And to the Holy Spirit
Equal praise be done.
The God who was and is to be
For us into eternity.

Antiphon: Psalm 86:1a, 2b, 3, CT
Verses: Psalm 86:4–7, Doxology: CT
© 2005 World Library Publications

Second Setting
Meter: 86 886
Suggested Tune: Repton

Antiphon: Incline your ear to me, O Lord,
And listen when I pray.
Preserve your servant who confides
In you; be merciful, for I
Implore your name all day.

Verses: "Delight my soul," your servant says,
"I lift it up anew;
For you, O Lord, are good and just,
Forgiving, pouring steadfast love
On all who call on you."

"Give answer to my humble prayer,
O Lord, when I implore.
In days of my distress I plead,
Because you always answer me.
Whose deeds compare to yours?"

"Show me the favor which will prove
That you are God indeed,
That friends and enemies will see
That you, Lord, help and rescue me
And my poor soul will feed."

Doxology: Give glory to our loving God,
             The Father, and the Son,
             The Holy Spirit equally,
             The God who rules eternally,
             For ever Three-in-One.

Antiphon: Psalm 86:1a, 2b, 3, CT
Verses: Psalm 86:4–7, Doxology: CT
© 2005 World Library Publications

TWENTY-SECOND SUNDAY IN ORDINARY TIME

Miserere mihi, Domine, quoniam ad te clamavi tota die: quia tu,
Domine, suavis ac mitis es, et copiosus in misericordia omnibus
invocantibus te. Ps. Inclina, Domine, aurem tuam et exaudi me:
quoniam inops et pauper sum ego.

*Have mercy on me, O Lord, for I have called out to you all the day; for you,
O Lord, are good and forgiving and plenteous in mercy to all who call upon
you. V. Incline your ear, O Lord, and hear me, for I am needy and poor.*

First Setting
Meter: 86 886
Suggested Tune: Repton

Antiphon: Have mercy on me, O my Lord,
             I cry all day to you.
             For you, O Lord, are good and just,
             Forgiving, pouring steadfast love
             On all who call on you.

Verses: Incline your ear to me, O Lord,
             Despondent and in need.
             Sustain me for I trust in you,
             And save your faithful servant, who
             Depends on you indeed.

Give answer to my humble prayer,
O Lord, when I implore.
In days of my distress I plead,
Because you always answer me.
Whose deeds compare to yours?

Show me your favor, which will prove
That you are God indeed,
That friends and enemies will see
That you, Lord, help and rescue me
And my poor soul will feed.

Doxology: Give glory to our loving God,
The Father, and the Son,
The Holy Spirit equally,
The God who rules eternally,
For ever Three-in-One.

Antiphon: Psalm 86:3, 5, CT
Verses: Psalm 86:1–2, 6–7, 17, Doxology: CT
© 2005 World Library Publications

Second Setting
Meter: 66 66 88
Suggested Tune: Rhosymedre

Antiphon: Take pity on me, Lord,
I cry all day to you.
Lord, make my soul rejoice,
I lift it up anew;
For you impart your faithful love
To those who place in you their trust.

Verses: Incline your ear, O Lord,
And listen when I pray.
Preserve your servant who
Confides in you all day.
Have mercy, Lord, and hear my plight;
My soul cries to you day and night.

Lord, make my soul rejoice,
I lift it up to you;
For you are full of kindness
And of mercy true.
With tender heart you treat the same
Who call on your immortal name.

Give answer to my prayer
And listen to my plight.
When I am ill distressed
I call you day and night,
Because I know with certainty
That you will always answer me.

Doxology: Give God the Father praise,
And glory to the Son,
And to the Holy Spirit
Equal praise be done.
The God who was and is to be
For us into eternity.

Antiphon: Psalm 86:3, 5, CT
Verses: Psalm 86:1–2, 4–5, 6–7, Doxology: CT
© 2005 World Library Publications

Twenty-third Sunday in Ordinary Time

Iustus es, Domine, et rectum iudicium tuum: fac cum servo
tuo secundum misericordiam tuam. Ps. Beati immaculati in via:
qui ambulant in lege Domini.

*You are righteous, O Lord, and right is your judgment; deal with this
servant of yours according to your mercy. V. Blessed are those whose way
is blameless, who walk in the law of the Lord.*

Meter: LM
Suggested Tune: Old 100th

Antiphon: O Lord, my good and gracious God,
               Your judgments are in rightness wrought;
               Now treat me as the child you love
               With truth and mercy from above.

Verses: Happy are those with blameless soul,
               Who follow God and love his law;
               And happy who observe his will
               And with their whole heart seek him still.

               And blest are also those who do
               No wrong and walk in God's ways, too.
               The Lord established his commands
               To be obeyed with diligence.

               Assist me, Lord, and help me keep
               My pathways straight on steady feet.
               I shall not be ashamed at all,
               Keeping my eyes fixed on your law.

               With upright heart I give you thanks
               For teaching me your ordinance.
               I will obey your statutes, Lord;
               Do not forsake me, gracious God.

Doxology: To God, the Triune One, we raise
               Eternal hymns of endless praise.
               O Father, Son, and Paraclete,
               We praise your name in word and deed.

Antiphon: Psalm 119:137, 124, CT
Verses: Psalm 119:1–8, Doxology: CT
© 2005 World Library Publications

Twenty-fourth Sunday in Ordinary Time

Da pacem, Domine, sustinentibus te, ut prophetae tui fideles inveniantur: exaudi preces servi tui, et plebis tuae Israel. Ps. Laetatus sum in his quae dicta sunt mihi: in domum Domini ibimus.

Grant peace to those who are waiting for you, O Lord, so that your prophets may be proved trustworthy; hear the prayers of your servant and of your people Israel. V. I rejoiced when it was said unto me: "Let us go to the house of the Lord."

Meter LM
Suggested Tune: Breslau

Antiphon:
Grant peace to those who wait for you,
And prove your prophets worthy still.
O gracious God, attend my prayer
And hear your people Israel.

Verses:
Jerusalem: with what great joy
I heard them say, "Let us go there!"
And now at last we take our stand
Within her gates to make our prayer.

Jerusalem: a city built
To be a place of unity;
The tribes go up, the tribes of God,
To praise God's name eternally.

Jerusalem: within your walls
The thrones of justice serve God's will;
The ancient thrones of David's house
Stand and unite God's people still.

Jerusalem: pray for her peace:
"May all who love you find success;
Peace be to all within your walls
And in your towers quietness."

Jerusalem: for comrades' sake
My prayers for you will never cease;
Because God's house is standing here,
I pray forever for your peace.

Doxology: All glory to the Father, Son,
And to the Holy Spirit be;
As from the first it was, is now,
And will be for eternity.

Antiphon: Sirach 36:18, CT, © 2005 World Library Publications
Verses: Psalm 122, Doxology: NMP
© 1986 Christopher Webber

Twenty-fifth Sunday in Ordinary Time

Salus populi ego sum, dicit Dominus: de quacumque tribulatione
clamaverint ad me, exaudiam eos: et ero illorum Dominus in
perpetuum. Ps. Attendite popule meus legem meam: inclinate aurem
vestram in verba oris mei.

*I am the salvation of the people, says the Lord; from whatever tribulations
they cry out to me, I will give heed to them; and I will be their Lord
for ever. V. Attend, O my people, to my law; incline your ear to the words
of my mouth.*

First Setting
Meter: 10 10 11 11
Suggested Tune: Laudate Dominum

Antiphon: I am the salvation of my own sheep;
When from tribulation they cry to me
I will hear their pleading and answer their call,
And be their good Lord and the Savior of all.

Verses: My people, give ear, attend to my word;
In lessons of old deep truths shall be heard;
The wonderful story by us must be shown,
The story that parents to children made known.

Instructing the young, we gladly record
The praises, the works, the might of the Lord;
He wishes for parents to pass to each child
Ancestral traditions, the mighty and mild.

Let children thus learn from history's light
To hope in our God and walk in his sight,
The God of their parents to fear and obey,
But unlike their forebears, who turned from his way.

Doxology: Now let us adore the Father and sing
Our praise to the Son, our Savior and King.
All praise to the Spirit who loves and remains,
And was from the first and will be for all days.

Antiphon: Psalm 37:39, 40, 28, Doxology: CT
© 2005 World Library Publications
Verses: Psalm 78:1–8, *The Psalter*, Philadelphia, 1912, alt.

Second Setting
Meter: LM
Suggested Tune: Duke Street

Antiphon: I am the Savior of my sheep,
Who in their trouble cry to me.
I hear their pleading and their prayer
And will remain their Lord for e'er.

Verses: My people, listen to my word;
In parables deep truths are heard;
The wondrous story must be shown,
Which parents to their young make known.

Instructing them we thus record
The praises and the works of God;
Old wisdoms in this way passed on
Teach generations yet to come.

Thus children learn from history's light
To hope in God, walk in his sight,
His ordinances to obey,
Unlike their ancestors, who strayed.

Doxology: To God, the Triune One, we raise
Eternal songs of joyful praise,
O Father, Son, and Paraclete,
We praise your name in word and deed.

Antiphon: Psalm 37:39, 40, CT
Verses: Psalm 78:1–8, Doxology: CT
© 2005 World Library Publications

Twenty-sixth Sunday in Ordinary Time, Year A

In nomine Domini omne genu flectatur, caelestium, terrestrium et infernorum: quia Dominus factus obediens usque ad mortem, mortem autem crucis: ideo Dominus Iesus Christus in gloria est Dei Patris. Ps. Domine exaudi orationem meam: et clamor meus ad te veniat.

At the name of the Lord let every knee bend, in heaven, on earth, and under the earth; for the Lord became obedient unto death, even death on the Cross; that is why Jesus Christ is the Lord, to the glory of God the Father. V. O Lord, hear my prayer, and let my cry come unto you.

Meter: 88 88 88
Suggested Tune: St. Catherine

Antiphon: On earth, in heaven, down below,
At Jesus' name all bend their knee;
For he became obedient
Unto his death upon the Tree.
Let us acclaim our Lord as King;
In hymns and psalms let praises ring.

Verses: Lord, hear my prayer, and let my cry
Have ready access to your throne;

Do not conceal your face from me
When I am troubled and alone.
Attend, O Lord, to my desire,
And hasten quickly when I cry.

For all my days go up in smoke.
My bones are burnt as if by flame,
My heart is withered like the grass,
My daily bread I don't obtain;
By all appearance I am spent,
Crying to you, Lord, without end.

But you, O Lord, enthroned on high,
Your name endures from age to age.
You pity Zion's holy stones
And show her mercy, show her grace.
All kings shall fear your holy name
When you rebuild her walls again.

Doxology: Then let us praise the Triune God,
The Father, Son, and Paraclete,
Who was before the world began,
And lives and reigns eternally.
God's holy name be blessed and praised,
As thankful songs are boldly raised.

Antiphon: Philippians 2:10, 8, 11, CT
Verses: Psalm 102:2–6, 13–14a, 16–17a, Doxology: CT
© 2005 World Library Publications

Twenty-sixth Sunday in Ordinary Time, Year B & C

Omnia quae fecisti nobis, Domine, in vero iudicio fecisti, quia peccavimus tibi, et mandatis tuis non obedivimus: sed da gloriam nomini tuo, et fac nobiscum secundum multitudinem misericordiae tuae. Ps. Beati immaculati in via: qui ambulant in lege Domini.

All that you have inflicted upon us, O Lord, has been dealt out in true justice, for we have sinned against you, and we have failed to obey your commandments; but give glory to your name, and deal with us according to the abundance of your mercy. V. Blessed are those whose way is blameless, who walk in the law of the Lord.

Meter: 77 77 D
Suggested Tune: Aberystwyth

Antiphon: Lord, we have deserved the pain
               That afflicted us again;
               Justly you have dealt with those
               Who have disobeyed your laws.
               But give glory to your name,
               That we may be whole again;
               And, O Lord, show us your way
               And your mercy every day.

Verses: Happy those with blameless heart,
               Following the way of God;
               Happy those who do his will
               And with whole hearts seek him still;
               Blest are also those whose ways
               Are God-fearing nights and days.
               God established his commands
               To be kept with diligence.

               Help me, Lord, that I may keep
               Your commands; make my ways straight.
               I shall not be shamed at all,
               With my eyes fixed on your law.
               With glad heart I give you thanks
               That you teach your ordinance.
               I shall follow in your way,
               Worship you, profess, and pray.

Doxology: To the Triune One we raise
               Glorious hymns of endless praise,

Praise the Father, praise the Son,
Praise the Spirit, with them One.
As it was before all days,
It is now, will be always.
Grateful anthems we present,
Giving glory without end.

Antiphon: Daniel 3:31, 29, 30, 43, CT
Verses: Psalm 119:1–8, Doxology: CT
© 2005 World Library Publications

Twenty-seventh Sunday in Ordinary Time

In voluntate tua, Domine, universa sunt posita, et non est qui possit
resistere voluntati tuae: tu enim fecisti omnia, caelum et terram, et
universa quae caeli ambitu continentur: Dominus universorum tu es.
Ps. Beati immaculati in via: qui ambulant in lege Domini.

All things are submitted to your will, O Lord, and no one can resist your
decisions; you have made all things, heaven and earth, and all that is
contained under the vault of the sky; you are the master of the universe.
V. Blessed are those whose way is blameless, who walk in the law of the Lord.

Meter: 77 77 D
Suggested Tune: Salzburg

Antiphon: Lord, all things are guided still
              By your truth and by your will.
              You made all: the lofty home
              And what is beneath its dome,
              Earth and sea and everything.
              Let creation rise and sing
              Praise to you with mighty verse,
              Master of the Universe.

Verses: Happy those with blameless heart,
              Following the way of God;
              Happy those who do his will

And with whole hearts seek him still.
Blest are also those whose ways
Are God-fearing nights and days.
God established his commands
To be kept with diligence.

Help me, Lord, that I may keep
Your commands; make my ways straight.
I shall not be shamed at all,
With my eyes fixed on your law.
With glad heart I give you thanks
That you teach your ordinance.
I shall follow in your way,
Worship you, profess, and pray.

Doxology: To the Triune One we raise
Glorious hymns of endless praise,
Praise the Father, praise the Son,
Praise the Spirit, with them One.
As it was before all days,
It is now, will be always.
Grateful anthems we present,
Giving glory without end.

Antiphon: Esther 13:9–11, CT
Verses: Psalm 119:1–8, Doxology: CT
© 2005 World Library Publications

Twenty-eighth Sunday in Ordinary Time

Si iniquitates observaveris, Domine, Domine, quis sustinebit? Quia apud te propitiatio est, Deus Israel. Ps. De profundis clamavi ad te, Domine: Domine, exaudi vocem meam.

O Lord, if you were to take into account our iniquities, who would withstand the test? But forgiveness abides with you, O God of Israel. V. Out of the depths have I cried to you, O Lord; Lord, hear my voice.

Meter: LM
Suggested Tune: Erhalt uns, Herr

Antiphon: If you should count each sinful deed,
             Lord, who could stand when you appeared?
             But with you is forgiveness found,
             And therefore, Lord, you shall be feared.

Verses: Out of the depths I call to you,
             Lord, hear my voice and heed my prayer.
             Look with compassion on my plea;
             Weigh my petition, Lord, with care.

             More certainly than watchmen wait
             To see the daylight first appear,
             Does my soul wait upon the Lord;
             I wait in trust and holy fear.

             O Israel, wait upon the Lord
             With whom mercy is always found,
             Who pardons us from all our sin,
             And in whom liberty abounds.

Doxology: All glory to the Father, Son,
             And to the Holy Spirit be;
             As from the first it was, is now,
             And will be for eternity.

Antiphon: Psalm 130:3–4, NMP
Verses: Psalm 130:1–2, 5–6, 7–8, Doxology: NMP alt.
© 1986 Christopher Webber

TWENTY-NINTH SUNDAY IN ORDINARY TIME

Ego clamavi, quoniam exaudisti me, Deus: inclina aurem tuam, et
exaudi verba mea: custodi me, Domine, ut pupillam oculi: sub umbra
alarum tuarum protege me. Ps. Exaudi, Domine, iustitiam meam:
intende deprecationem meam.

I have called out, because you answer me, O God: incline your ear and hear my words; keep me, O Lord, like the apple of your eye; protect me under the shadow of your wings. V. Hear my just cause, O Lord; attend to my supplication.

Meter: SMD
Suggested Tune: Diademata

Antiphon: I call upon you, Lord,
             For you will answer me.
             I pray that you will hear my words;
             Give ear, Lord, to my plea.
             My Savior, keep me as
             The apple of your eye;
             Beneath the shadow of your wings
             In safety let me lie.

Verses: I plead my innocence;
             Give heed, Lord, to my cry,
             And listen to my prayer, which comes
             From lips that do not lie.
             Lord, vindicate me soon,
             That you may see the right;
             I pray you, try and weigh my heart,
             And search my soul at night.

             Melt down my soul and see
             There is no wickedness;
             I heed the words you speak, O Lord,
             That I may not transgress.
             I follow step by step
             The way that you command,
             And in the pathway that I walk
             You guide me by your hand.

Doxology: Give glory to our God,
                The Father, and the Son,
                The Holy Spirit equally,
                Eternal Triune One:
                It was before all time,
                And so it is today,
                And will be for eternity,
                From age to age always.

Antiphon: Psalm 17:6, 8, NMP alt.
Verses: Psalm 17:1–5, NMP alt., © 1986 Christopher Webber
Doxology: CT, © 2005 World Library Publications

THIRTIETH SUNDAY IN ORDINARY TIME

Laetetur cor quaerentium Dominum: quaerite Dominum, et
confirmamini: quaerite faciem eius semper. Ps. Confitemini Domino,
et invocate nomen eius: annuntiate inter gentes opera eius.

*Let the hearts of those who seek the Lord rejoice; seek the Lord and be
strengthened; seek his face for evermore. V. Give thanks to the Lord and call
upon his name; declare his deeds among the gentiles.*

First Setting
Meter: 10 10 10 10
Suggested Tune: Toulon

Antiphon: Let every heart who seeks the Lord rejoice;
                Come, glorify his everlasting name.
                Hope in the Lord, and find your strength in him;
                Desire with him forever to remain.

Verses: Give thanks to God, invoke his holy name.
                Proclaim his wondrous deeds to all the earth.
                Sing praises to the Lord, lift up your voice;
                Make melody, recount his marvelous works.

Recall the wondrous deeds the Lord performed,
His miracles and judgments he made known,
O offspring of his servant Abraham,
Children of Jacob, chosen as his own.

He is the Lord our God eternally,
Remembering his faithful covenant;
His judgments are in all the earth proclaimed,
And what he promised will forever stand.

Doxology: Give praise to God the Father, God the Son,
And God the Spirit, ever Three-in-One,
Who was from the beginning without end,
Is now, and shall be evermore. Amen.

Antiphon: Psalm 105:3–4, CT
Verses: Psalm 105:1–2, 5–6, 7–8, Doxology: CT
© 2005 World Library Publications

Second Setting
Meter: LM
Suggested Tune: Tallis' Canon

Antiphon: Let searching hearts rejoice in God:
Come, glory in his holy name.
Hope in the Lord to find your strength
And in his presence to remain.

Verses: Give thanks to God, invoke his name;
Proclaim his deeds throughout the earth.
Sing praises, lifting up your voice;
Make melody, recount his works.

Recall the deeds the Lord performed,
The miracles that he made known,
O family of Abraham
And Jacob, chosen as his own.

He is our God eternally,
Remembering his covenant;
His judgments are by all proclaimed,
And what he promised us will stand.

Doxology: To God, the Triune One, we raise
Eternal hymns of endless praise.
O Father, Son, and Paraclete,
We praise your name in word and deed.

Antiphon: Psalm 105:3–4, CT
Verses: Psalm 105:1–2, 5–6, 7–8, Doxology: CT
© 2005 World Library Publications

Thirty-first Sunday in Ordinary Time, Year A & B

Ne derelinquas me, Domine, Deus meus, ne discedas a me: intende
in adiutorium meum, Domine, virtus salutis meae. Ps. Domine,
ne in furore tuo arguas me: neque in ira tua corripias me.

*Abandon me not, O Lord my God, do not depart from me; come to my
assistance, O Lord, mainstay of my deliverance. V. O Lord, do not rebuke
me in your anger; chastise me not in your wrath.*

Meter: CM
Suggested Tune: McKee

Antiphon: Forsake me not, my Lord and God,
Do not depart from me.
Come to my refuge, saving Lord,
My friend in time of need.

Verses: Do not rebuke me in your wrath
Or chastise angrily;
Your arrows sink into my heart,
Your hand comes down on me.

> Lord, my desires are known to you,
> You know my moans and sighs;
> My heart throbs, and my strength is spent,
> The light fades from my eyes.
>
> You are my confidence, O Lord,
> You answer plenteously.
> If I transgress, do not allow
> My foes to laugh at me.

Doxology: Give glory to our loving God,
                        The Father, and the Son,
                        And also to the Paraclete,
                        Eternal Three-in-One.

Antiphon: Psalm 38:22–23, CT
Verses: Psalm 38:2–3, 10–11, 16–17, Doxology: CT
© 2005 World Library Publications

Thirty-first Sunday in Ordinary Time, Year C

Misereris omnium, Domine, et nihil odisti eorum quae fecisti, dissimulans peccata hominum propter paenitentiam, et parcens illis: quia tu es Dominus Deus noster. Ps. Miserere mei Deus, miserere mei: quoniam in te confidit anima mea.

Your mercy extends to all things, O Lord, and you despise none of the things you have made. You overlook human sins for the sake of repentance. You grant them your pardon, because you are the Lord our God. V. Be merciful to me, O God, be merciful to me, for my soul confides in you.

Meter: LM
Suggested Tune: Erhalt uns, Herr

Antiphon: O Lord, your mercy does extend
                        To everything formed by your hand.
                        You set repentant sinners free;
                        O Lord our God, now pardon me.

Verses: Be merciful, O Lord, to me,
My soul to you for refuge flees;
In shadows of your wings I'll lie,
Until destroying storms pass by.

I cry to you, O Majesty!
Fulfill your promises to me.
Descend from heaven with constancy,
That none may hurt or harry me.

Though I am caught in lions' jaws,
Their teeth like arrows, tongues like swords,
I praise you, Lord above the sky,
Let not your glory pass me by.

My heart is steadfast, God and King,
I will make melody and sing.
With harp and lyre in gratitude,
I'll wake the dawn, for it is good.

Doxology: To God, the Triune One, we raise
Eternal hymns of endless praise.
O Father, Son, and Paraclete,
We praise your name in word and deed.

Antiphon: Wisdom 11:24–25, 27, CT
Verses: Psalm 57:2–6, 8–9, Doxology: CT
© 2005 World Library Publications

THIRTY-SECOND SUNDAY IN ORDINARY TIME

Intret oratio mea in conspectu tuo: inclina aurem tuam ad precem meam, Domine. Ps. Domine, Deus salutis meam: in die clamavi, et nocte coram te.

Let my prayer enter into your presence; incline your ear to my supplication, O Lord. V. O Lord, God of my salvation, day and night have I cried before you.

Meter: SM
Suggested Tune: St. Bride

Antiphon: Allow my prayer and plea
              To come into your courts;
              Incline your ear to my complaint
              And help me, gracious Lord.

Verses: O Lord, my saving God,
              I cry for you by night;
              Allow my prayer to reach your ears
              And listen to my plight.

              For troubles fill my soul
              And I am near the end.
              They count me with the fallen ones;
              My strength is fully spent.

              I am deprived of friends;
              You made them shun my sight.
              Imprisoned, I cannot escape;
              My eyes are dim with plight.

Doxology: Give glory to our God,
              The Father, and the Son,
              And also to the Paraclete,
              Eternal Three-in-One.

Antiphon: Psalm 88:3, CT
Verses: Psalm 88:2–5, 9–10a, Doxology: CT
© 2005 World Library Publications

Thirty-third Sunday in Ordinary Time

Dicit Dominus: Ego cogito cogitationes pacis, et non afflictionis: invocabitis me, et ego exaudiam vos: et reducam captivitatem vestram de cunctis locis. Ps. Benedixisti, Domine, terram tuam: avertisti captivitatem Iacob.

The Lord says: "I am pondering thoughts of peace and not of affliction; you shall call upon me, and I will hear you; and I will bring you back from all the lands where you are held captive." V. O Lord, you have blessed your land; you have put an end to Jacob's captivity.

Meter: 76 76 D
Suggested Tune: Gaudeamus pariter

Antiphon:	God proclaims for all to hear:
	"Listen to my wisdom:
	I consider peace for you
	And not your affliction.
	When you call upon my name,
	I will hear and help you.
	I will bring you home from lands
	Where your captors held you."
Verses:	Lord, you favored once your land,
	Brought back Jacob's fortunes
	And forgave your people's sins,
	Pardoned their transgressions.
	You withdrew from them your wrath,
	Turning from your hot anger.
	Now restore us, saving God;
	Let your rage not linger.
	Mercy, love, and faithfulness
	Have met in God's presence;
	Peace and justice have embraced,
	Have become one essence.
	Faithfulness springs from the earth;
	Justice rains profusely
	And shall walk before our God;
	Peace shall follow closely.
Doxology:	Glory to the Triune God:
	Praises to the Father;
	Praises also to the Son,

Who became our brother;
Sing the Holy Spirit's praise,
Peaceful dove, descending;
As at first is was, is now,
And will be unending.

Antiphon: Jeremiah 29:11, 12, 14, CT
Verses: Psalm 85:2–5, 11–12, 14, Doxology: CT
© 2005 World Library Publications

LAST SUNDAY IN ORDINARY TIME

Our Lord Jesus Christ the King

Thirty-fourth Sunday in Ordinary Time

Dignus est Agnus, qui occisus est, accipere virtutem, et divinitatem,
et sapientiam, et fortitudinem, et honorem. Ipsi gloria et imperium
in saecula saeculorum. Ps. Deus, iudicium tuum Regi da: et iustitiam
tuam Filio Regis.

The Lamb who was slain is worthy to receive power and divinity and
wisdom and strength and honor; let glory and dominion be his for ever and
ever. V. Endow the King with your judgment, O God, and the King's son
with your righteousness.

First Setting
Meter: LM
Suggested Tunes: Duke Street

Antiphon: Worthy the Lamb who died for us,
               Worthy of all divinity,
               And wisdom, holiness, and might,
               Whose rule shall last eternally.

Verses: Teach righteous judgment to the king
               And to his only son, that he
               May judge the people in your truth,
               The poor in fairest equity.

Let every mountain, every hill
Bring peace on earth eternally.
With justice he will save the poor,
Crush their oppressors' savagery.

As long as sun and moon endure,
Let him, O God, rule over us.
He will descend like gentle showers,
Like tender rain upon the grass.

Justice shall flourish in his days,
And peace until the moon shall cease.
His rule extend to farthest earth,
And stretch from sea to shining sea.

Doxology: To God the Father, God the Son,
And God the Spirit praises be,
Who was before the world began,
Is now and in eternity.

Antiphon: Revelation 5:12; 1:6, CT
Verses: Psalm 72:1–8, Doxology: CT
© 2005 World Library Publications

Second Setting
Meter: 87 87 887
Suggested Tunes: Mit Freuden zart

Antiphon: Worthy the Lamb who died for us,
Worthy of reign and power,
Worthy of all divinity
And wisdom, strength, and honor.
Let glory and dominion be
With him into eternity
In songs of awe and wonder.

Verses:

Endow the king with justice, Lord,
His son with righteous judgment,
That he rule fairly o'er your own
And show the poor fair judgment.
Let every mountain, every hill
Bring peace, and save from every ill
The needy and despondent.

As long as sun and moon endure,
Let him, O God, rule ever.
He will descend on hill and plain
Like showers the rains deliver.
Justice shall flower in his days,
And peace, until the moon shall cease.
His kingdom fails us never.

Doxology:

To Father, Son, all glory be
And to the Holy Spirit,
Who was before the light of day,
Is now, and without limit.
Our songs and anthems now we raise
In highest ecstasy and praise.
With heart and soul we sing it.

Antiphon: Revelation 5:12; 1:6, CT
Verses: Psalm 72:1–8, Doxology: CT

Chapter 14

Sanctorale
Solemnities of the Lord
during Ordinary Time

Presentation of the Lord

Februrary 2

Suscepimus, Deus, misericodiam tuam in medio templi tui: secundum nomen tuum Deus, ita et laus tua in fines terrae: iustitia plena est dextera tua. Ps. Magnus Dominus et laudabilis nimis: in civitate Dei nostri, in monte sancto eius.

We have received your mercy, O God, in the midst of your temple; even as your name, so also does your praise extend to the ends of the earth; your right hand is filled with righteousness. V. Great is the Lord and worthy of all praise, in the city of our God, on his holy mountain.

Meter: LM
Suggested Tune: Winchester New

Antiphon: Within your temple, mighty Lord,
             We ponder and receive your love.
             Your name and praise surround the earth,
             And your right hand does what is just.

Verses: Great is the Lord and to be praised
             In his most awesome holy place;
             His sacred mountain is the joy
             Of every land and every race.

Mount Zion, center of the earth,
On you shall royalty endure.
Within your citadels is God;
Our stronghold and defense is sure.

Doxology: All glory to the Father, Son,
And to the Holy Spirit be;
As from the first it was, is now,
And will be for eternity.

Antiphon: Psalm 48:10–11, CT
Verses: Psalm 48:2–4, Doxology: CT
© 2005 World Library Publications

Saint Joseph

March 19

Iustus ut palma florebit: sicut cedrus Libani multiplicabitur: plantatus in domo Domini, in atriis domus Dei nostri. Ps. Bonum est confiteri Domino: et psallere nomini tuo, Altissime.

The righteous shall flourish like the palm tree; they shall grow up like the cedar of Lebanon; for they are planted in the house of the Lord, in the courts of our God. V. It is good to give praise to the Lord; and to sing in honor of your name, O Most High.

First Setting
Meter: 10 10 10 10
Suggested Tune: Woodlands

Antiphon: The upright thrive and flourish like the palm;
They shall grow strong like cedars from the North,
For they are planted in the house of God
And find repose within its inner courts.

Verses: How good it is to thank and praise the Lord,
Make music to your name, O God of Might,
To tell your faithful love at dawn of day
And your great constancy all through the night.

The upright thrive and flourish like the palm;
Advanced in age, remaining fresh and green,
Still bearing fruit to tell of Yahweh's love,
My rock, in whom no fault is ever seen.

Doxology: Give praise to God the Father, God the Son,
And God the Spirit, ever Three-in-One,
Who was from the beginning without end,
Is now, and shall be evermore. Amen.

Antiphon: Psalm 92:13–14, CT
Verses: Psalm 92:2–3, 13a, 15–16, Doxology: CT
© 2005 World Library Publications

Second Setting
Meter: LM
Suggested Tune: Truro

Antiphon: The upright flourish like the palm,
And grow like cedars from the North,
For planted in the house of God,
They find repose within its courts.

Verses: How good it is to thank you, Lord,
And sing your name, O God of Might,
To tell your faithful love at dawn,
Your constancy all through the night.

The upright flourish like the palm,
Advanced in age, remaining green,
Still bearing fruit to tell God's love,
My rock, in whom no fault is seen.

Doxology: To God the Father, God the Son,
And God the Spirit praises be,
Who was before the world began,
Is now and in eternity.

Antiphon: Psalm 92:13–14, CT
Verses: Psalm 92:2–3, 13a, 15–16, Doxology: CT
© 2005 World Library Publications

The Annunciation of the Lord

March 25

Rorate caeli desuper, et nubes pluant iustum: aperiatur terra, et
germinet Salvatorem. Ps. Caeli enarrant gloriam Dei: et opera
manuum eius annuntiat firmamentum.

*Skies, let the Just One come forth like the dew, let him descend from the
clouds like the rain. The earth will open up and give birth to our Savior.
V. The heavens declare the glory of God, and the firmament proclaims
the work of his hands.*

Meter: CM
Suggested Tune: Winchester Old

Antiphon: O heavens, let the Just One come
             Like rain from clouds above.
             The earth will be unsealed and yield
             Our Lord who saves and loves.

Verses: The heavens declare your glory, Lord,
             The work your hands have made;
             Day after day your power is shown
             And night by night displayed.

             There is no utterance or speech,
             No voice is ever heard,
             Yet to all nations comes the sound,
             To every place their word.

             Forth like a bridegroom comes the sun
             From its appointed place,
             And like a hero on his course
             Rejoices in the race.

It runs from East to farthest West
To make its course complete,
And nothing in the world beneath
Escapes its scorching heat.

Doxology: Give glory to the Father, Son,
And Spirit equally,
As from the first it was, is now,
And evermore shall be.

Antiphon: Isaiah 45:8, CT, © 2005 World Library Publications
Verses: Psalm 19:2–7, Doxology: NMP
© 1986 Christopher Webber

NATIVITY OF SAINT JOHN THE BAPTIST: VIGIL MASS

June 24

Ne timeas, Zacharia, exaudita est oratio tua: et Elisabeth uxor tua
pariet tibi filium, et vocabis nomen eius Ioannem: et erit magnus
coram Domino: et Spiritu Sancto replebitur adhuc ex utero matris
suae: et multi in nativitate eius gaudebunt. Ps. Domine, in virtute tua
laetabitur rex: et super salutare tuum exsultabit vehementer.

Fear not, Zechariah, your prayer has been answered; Elizabeth, your wife,
will bear you a son, and you shall call his name John. He will be great before
the Lord, and he will be filled with the Holy Spirit even from his mother's
womb; and many will rejoice at his birth. V. In your strength shall the king
rejoice, O Lord, and in your salvation shall he greatly exult.

First Setting
Meter: 77 77 D
Sugested Tunes: Salzburg

Antiphon: Zechariah, do not fear,
The response you sought is here:
Your dear wife will bear a son;
Great before the Lord is John.

Even from his mother's womb,
God the Spirit fills him soon.
Let all nations, filled with mirth,
Welcome John the Baptist's birth.

Verses:

Lord, the king admires your might;
Your great deeds give him delight.
You have granted his request,
Satisfied his lips' behest.
Lord, you bless and favor him
With the markings of a king,
Promised that his life shall be
Long and glad eternally.

When your foes devise their schemes,
They are doomed, will not succeed,
They retreat, from you depart,
As your arrows strike their mark.
Rise, O Yahweh, in your might,
We praise you by day and night,
Making music every hour
To the glory of your power.

Doxology:

To the Triune One we raise
Glorious hymns of endless praise,
Praise the Father, praise the Son,
Praise the Spirit, with them One.
As it was before all days,
It is now, will be always.
Grateful anthems we present,
Giving glory without end.

Antiphon: Luke 1:13, 15, 14, CT
Verses: Psalm 21:2–5, 12–14, Doxology: CT

Second Setting
Meter: 87 87 887
Sugested Tunes: Mit Freuden zart

Antiphon: O Zechariah, do not fear,
                 Your prayer was answered boldly:
                 Your wife will bear a son for you;
                 John will be great and holy.
                 The Holy Spirit fills him soon,
                 E'en from his blessed mother's womb;
                 Let all rejoice his coming.

Verses: The king rejoices in your power,
                 He ponders your salvation.
                 You granted him his heart's desire,
                 Denying no oration.
                 Lord, how you bless and favor him,
                 Bestow the markings of a king,
                 Give length of days forever.

                 When enemies have laid their traps
                 And plotted, they have faltered.
                 You make them turn and sound retreat,
                 Your arrows strike their targets.
                 Arise, O Lord, in your great might,
                 We sing to you by day and night,
                 Make music in your honor.

Doxology: To Father, Son, all glory be
                 And to the Holy Spirit,
                 Who was before the light of day,
                 Is now, and without limit.
                 Our songs and anthems now we raise
                 In highest ecstasy and praise.
                 With heart and soul we sing it.

Antiphon: Luke 1:13, 15, 14, CT
Verses: Psalm 21:2–5, 12–14, Doxology: CT
© 2005 World Library Publications

NATIVITY OF SAINT JOHN THE BAPTIST: MASS DURING THE DAY

June 24

De ventre matris meae vocavit me Dominus nomine meo: et posuit os meum ut gladium acutum: sub tegumento manus suae protexit me, posuit me quasi sagitam electam. Ps. Bonum est confiteri Domino: et psallere nomini tuo, Altissime.

From my mother's womb the Lord called me by my name; and he made my mouth like unto a sharp sword; he protected me in the shadow of his hand, and he made me as his chosen arrow. V. It is good to give praise to the Lord; and to sing in honor of your name, O Most High.

First Setting
Meter: 10 10 10 10
Suggested Tune: Woodlands

Antiphon: Called by my name since in my mother's womb,
My mouth was fashioned like the sharpest sword;
And resting in the shadow of God's hand,
He made of me the arrow of the Lord.

Verses: How good it is to thank and praise the Lord,
Make music to your name, O God of Might,
To tell your faithful love at dawn of day
And your great constancy all through the night.

The upright thrive and flourish like the palm;
Advanced in age, remaining fresh and green,
Still bearing fruit to tell of Yahweh's love,
My rock, in whom no fault is ever seen.

Doxology: Give praise to God the Father, God the Son,
And God the Spirit, ever Three-in-One,
Who was from the beginning without end,
Is now, and shall be evermore. Amen.

Antiphon: Isaiah 49:1–2, CT
Verses: Psalm 92:2–3, 13a, 15–16, Doxology: CT
© 2005 World Library Publications

Second Setting
Meter: LM
Suggested Tune: Tallis' Canon

Antiphon: Called from my mother's womb by name,
                 My mouth was fashioned like a sword;
                 By God's own hand I have become
                 The chosen arrow of the Lord.

Verses: How good it is to thank you, Lord,
                 And sing your name, O God of Might,
                 To tell your faithful love at dawn,
                 Your constancy all through the night.

                 The upright flourish like the palm,
                 Advanced in age, remaining green,
                 Still bearing fruit to tell God's love,
                 My rock, in whom no fault is seen.

Doxology: To God the Father, God the Son,
                 And God the Spirit praises be,
                 Who was before the world began,
                 Is now and in eternity.

Antiphon: Isaiah 49:1–2, CT
Verses: Psalm 92:2–3, 13a, 15–16, Doxology: CT
© 2005 World Library Publications

SAINTS PETER AND PAUL: VIGIL MASS

June 29

Dicit Dominus Petro: Cum esse iunior, cingebas te, et ambulabas ubi
volebas: cum autem senueris, extendes manus tuas, et alius te cinget,
et ducet quo tu non vis: hoc autem dixit, significans qua morte

clarificaturus esset Deum. Ps. Caeli enarrant gloriam Dei: et opera manuum eius annuntiat firmamentum.

The Lord said unto Peter: "When you were young, you girded yourself and walked where you would; but when you are old, you will stretch forth your hands, and another will gird you and lead you where you do not wish to go." This he said to signify by what death he was to glorify God. V. The heavens declare the glory of God; and the firmament proclaims the work of his hands.

Meter: CMD
Suggested Tune: Kingsfold

Antiphon:
The Lord declared: "When you were young,
You walked where you would go;
But soon you will stretch forth your hands,
When you are wise and old,
And others gird and lead you where
You do not wish to go."
The glorious death that Peter would
Endure was thus foretold.

Verses:
The heavens above declare God's praise,
The work his hands have made;
Day after day his power is shown
And night by night displayed.
God's law is perfect and gives life,
Revives the weary soul;
His testimonies all are sure,
Wisdom for all to hold.

And even more to be desired
Than gold, the finest gold,
And sweeter than the honeycomb,
The words God spoke of old.
Your servant finds enlightenment
By means of them, O Lord;
And in the keeping of your law,
There is a great reward.

Doxology: All glory be to God on high
               And on the earth, the Lord
               In Triune Godhead be proclaimed
               And evermore adored.
               Give glory to the Father, Son,
               And Spirit equally;
               As from the first it was, is now,
               And evermore shall be.

Antiphon: John 21:18, 19, CT, © 2005 World Library Publications
Verses: Psalm 19:2–3 8, 11–13, NMP, © 1986 Christopher Webber
Doxology: CT, NMP

SAINTS PETER AND PAUL: MASS DURING THE DAY
June 29

Nunc scio vere, quia misit Dominus Angelum suum: et eripuit me
de manu Herodis, et de omni exspectatione plebis Iudaeorum.
Ps. Domine probasti me, et cognovisti me: tu cognovisti sessionem
meam, et resurrectionem meam.

*Now I know that the Lord really has sent his Angel and has delivered me
out of the hands of Herod and from all that the Jewish people were expecting.
V. O Lord, you have searched me and know me; you know when I sit down
and when I rise up.*

Meter: 87 87 87
Suggested Tune: Lauda anima

Antiphon: Now I know my Lord and Savior
               Sent his Angel to my side
               And delivered me to safety
               From a poor and hopeless plight;
               Saved me from a wicked people
               Out of darkness into light.

Verses:　　Alleluia! Lord, you search me,
　　　　　And you know my every way,
　　　　　Know my sitting, know my rising,
　　　　　Know my thoughts from far away,
　　　　　Know my walking, know my sleeping
　　　　　Through the night and all the day.

　　　　　Lord, you know the words I'm speaking
　　　　　Long before they are proclaimed.
　　　　　Lord, you are before, behind me,
　　　　　Blessing me by your own hand.
　　　　　Such great knowledge is too lofty
　　　　　For my soul to understand.

　　　　　Lord, where could I flee your Spirit?
　　　　　Where could I abandon you?
　　　　　If I scale the highest heavens,
　　　　　Lands of death, deep oceans, too,
　　　　　Even there your hand will guide me;
　　　　　Your right hand draws me to you.

Doxology:　　Glory be to God the Father,
　　　　　And to Jesus Christ, his Son,
　　　　　Glory to the Holy Spirit,
　　　　　Triune God, the Three in One.
　　　　　As it was in the beginning,
　　　　　It endures as ages run.

Antiphon: Acts 12:11, CT
Verses: Psalm 139:1–10, Doxology: CT
© 2005 World Library Publications

THE TRANSFIGURATION OF THE LORD

August 6

Tibi dixit cor meum, quaesivi vultum tuum, vultum tuum, Domine, requiram: ne avertas faciem tuam a me. Ps. Dominus illuminatio mea, et salus mea: quem timebo?

My heart declared to you: "Your countenance have I thought; I shall ever seek your countenance, O Lord; do not turn your face from me." V. The Lord is my light and my salvation; whom shall I fear?

Meter: LM
Suggested Tune: Duke Street

Antiphon: My heart declared to you, O Lord:
               "Your countenance my soul has sought;
               My heart shall ever seek your face;
               Do not reject me, O my God."

Verses: My light, my Savior is the Lord,
               Of whom should I have any fear?
               He is the stronghold of my life;
               Whom should I dread if he is near?

               When evildoers seek my life
               And in their malice draw around,
               My adversaries and my foes
               Will stumble and fall to the ground.

               Though hostile tents encircle me,
               My heart will never be dismayed;
               Though war rise up against my life,
               I will trust God, not be afraid.

               One thing alone I ask of God:
               To dwell in his most holy place,
               To seek him in his holy court
               And see his beauty face to face.

Doxology: All glory to the Father, Son,
               And to the Holy Spirit be;
               As from the first it was, is now,
               And will be for eternity.

Antiphon: Psalm 27:8, 9, CT, © 2005 World Library Publications
Verses: Psalm 27:1–4, Doxology: NMP
© 1986 Christopher Webber

THE ASSUMPTION OF THE BLESSED VIRGIN MARY: VIGIL MASS

August 15

Vultum tuum deprecabuntur omnes divites plebis: adducantur regi virgines post eam: proximae eius adduncentur tibi in laetitia et exsulatione. Ps. Eructavit cor meum verbum bonum: dico ego opera mea regi.

All the rich among the people will implore your countenance. Virgins will be brought to the king in her retinue; her companions will be taken to you in gladness and rejoicing. V. My heart overflows with a goodly theme; I address my works to the King.

First Setting
Meter: 10 10.12 10
Tune: Gabriel's Message

Antiphon: The rich and noble come to seek her face,
             And virgins will be brought to see his grace.
             Her followers will come with joy before the Lord.
             Most highly favored Lady. Gloria!

Verses: My heart is overcome by noble themes,
             My song of songs is only for the king!
             And as a writer's nimble pen, my soul may sing:
             Most highly favored Lady. Gloria!

             O hearken, daughter, fair and lovely one,
             Forget the people of your land and home,
             Leave father, mother, brothers, sisters all behind.
             Most highly favored Lady. Gloria!

With golden robes you are bedecked today,
And by the king adored, in rich array.
Your followers will come with joy before the Lord.
Most highly favored Lady. Gloria!

Doxology: Give glory to the Father and the Son,
The Spirit equally, the Three-in-One,
For as it was in the beginning and is now,
It will be for all ages. Gloria!

Antiphon: Psalm 45:13b, 15b, 16, CT
Verses: Psalm 45:2, 11–12a, 14–16, Doxology: CT
© 2005 World Library Publications

Second Setting
Meter: CM
Suggested Tune: Winchester Old

Antiphon: The rich will come to seek her face;
Her friends will see the Lord.
And those who follow her will come
With joy into his court.

Verses: My heart is stirred by noble themes,
My song is for the king!
And as a writer's nimble pen
May my soul freely sing.

O hearken, daughter, listen well,
O fair and lovely one,
Forget the people of your land
And leave your father's home.

With golden robes you are bedecked
And by the king adored,
And those who follow you will come
With joy before the Lord.

Doxology: Give glory to our loving God,
                 The Father, and the Son,
                 And also to the Paraclete,
                 Eternal Three-in-One.

Antiphon: Psalm 45:13b, 15b, 16, CT
Verses: Psalm 45:2, 11–12a, 14–16, Doxology: CT
© 2005 World Library Publications

The Assumption of the Blessed Virgin Mary: Mass during the Day

August 15

Signum magnum apparuit in caelo: mulier amicta sole, et luna sub pedibus eius, et in capite eius corona stellarum duodecim. Ps. Salvavit sibi dextera eius: et brachium sanctum eius.

A great sign appeared in heaven: a woman clothed with the sun, and the moon under her feet; and on her head a crown of twelve stars. V. Sing unto the Lord a new song, for he has accomplished wondrous deeds.

Meter: CM
Suggested Tune: Graefenberg, St. Magnus

Antiphon: Behold! In heaven, clothed with the sun,
                 A woman has appeared,
                 A crown of twelve stars on her head,
                 The moon beneath her feet.

Verses: O sing a new song to the Lord,
                 He has done wondrous deeds.
                 His right hand and his holy arm
                 Have gained the victory.

                 The Lord displayed his saving power
                 And truth and constancy;
                 He has revealed his justice and
                 His strength for all to see.

To Israel's house God has recalled
His faithfulness and love.
The farthest ends of earth have seen
The victory from above.

Make joyful noises to the Lord,
Break forth in harmony.
Sing praises to the Lord our God
With lyre and melody.

Let oceans thunder, and the waves,
The world and all therein;
You rivers, clap your mighty hands,
You mountains, shout and sing.

Doxology: Give glory to our loving God,
The Father, and the Son,
And also to the Paraclete,
Eternal Three-in-One.

Antiphon: Revelation 12:1, CT
Verses: Psalm 98:1–5, 7–8, Doxology: CT
© 2005 World Library Publications

The Exaltation of the Holy Cross

September 14

Nos autem gloriari oportet, in cruce Domini nostri Iesu Christi: in quo est salus, vita, et resurrectio nostra: per quem salvati, et liberati sumus. Ps. Deus misereatur nostri, et benedicat nobis: illuminet vultum suum super nos, et misereatur nostri.

Let our glory be in the cross of our Lord Jesus Christ; in him we have salvation, life, and resurrection; through him we are rescued and set free. V. May God have mercy on us and bless us; may he cause his face to shine upon us, and may he have mercy on us.

Meter: LM
Suggested Tune: Melcombe

Antiphon:	Then let us glory in the cross Of Jesus Christ, who sets us free; He rescues us and gives us life That we may sing eternally.
Verses:	My God be merciful to us, Bless us, shine on us from above; Let all earth's people know your ways, All nations know your saving love.
	Let all the nations praise you, Lord, Let them praise you, be glad, and sing, You judge with equity all lands And rule the nations as their king.
	Let all the nations praise you, Lord, And may the earth yield its increase; Then God, our God, will bless our land And nations worship him in peace.
Doxology:	Then praise the Father, praise the Son, And praise the Spirit equally, Who was before the light of day, Is now, and reigns eternally.

Antiphon: Galatians 6:14, CT, © 2005 World Library Publications
Verses: Psalm 67:1, Doxology: CT
© 1986 Christopher Webber

ALL SAINTS

November 1

Gaudeamus omnes in Domino, diem festum celebrantes sub honore
Sanctorum omnium: de quorum solemnitate gaudent angeli, et collau-
dant Filii Dei. Ps. Exsultate iusti in Domino: rectos decet collaudatio.

Let us all rejoice in the Lord, as we celebrate this feast day in honor of all the saints; it is a solemnity which causes the Angels to rejoice and to praise together the Son of God. V. Rejoice in the Lord, O you righteous! Praising befits those who are upright.

Meter: SM
Suggested Tune: Festal Song

Antiphon: In honor of all saints,
Let us rejoice and sing.
The Angels join us in the feast
To praise our Lord and King.

Verses: You upright in the Lord,
Rejoice, let praises ring.
Give thanks to Yahweh with the lyre,
Make melody and sing.

Compose a song to God,
Play strings with great finesse.
His word is honest, and he works
His deeds in uprightness.

Let all the earth fear God,
Let everyone admire;
For when he spoke, the earth was made
And stood at his desire.

Doxology: Give glory to our God,
The Father, and the Son,
And also to the Paraclete,
Eternal Three-in-One.

Antiphon: CT
Verses: Psalm 33:1–4, 8–9, Doxology: CT
© 2005 World Library Publications

THE DEDICATION OF THE LATERAN BASILICA

November 9

Deus in loco sancto suo: Deus, qui inhabitare facit unanimes in domo: ipse dabit virtutem et fortitudinem plebi suae. Ps. Exsurgat Deus, et dissipentur inimici eius: et fugiant qui oderunt eum, a facie eius.

God is in his holy dwelling place; the God who causes us to dwell together, one at heart, in his house; he himself will give power and strength to his people. V. Let God arise, and let all enemies be scattered; and let those who hate him flee before his face.

Meter CMD
Suggested Tune: Kingsfold

Antiphon: Our God dwells in his holy place,
The God who wills that we
Should live together, one in heart,
In love and harmony.
He gives his people power and strength
And confidence and might;
They glorify his holy name
And worship day and night.

Verses: Let God arise and strike his foes;
Let those who hate him flee;
Let them, like smoke the wind blows off,
All vanish speedily.
Before God let the wicked melt
As wax does in the flame,
But let the righteous dance for joy
And offer God acclaim.

God scatters kings like falling snow
On Zalmon's lofty crown.
O mighty Bashan, why are you
So envious looking down?

This is the hill where God will dwell,
On which he chose to rest;
With twenty thousand chariots
He comes in holiness.

Doxology: All glory be to God on high
And on the earth, the Lord
In Triune Godhead be proclaimed
And evermore adored.
Give glory to the Father, Son,
And Spirit equally;
As from the first it was, is now,
And evermore shall be.

Antiphon: Psalm 68:6, 7, 36, CT, © 2005 World Library Publications
Verses: Psalm 68:2–4, 15–18, NMP, © 1986 Christopher Webber
Doxology: CT, NMP

The Immaculate Conception of the Blessed Virgin Mary

December 8

Gaudens gaudebo in Domino et exsultabit anima mea in Deo meo:
quia induit me vestimentis salutis, et indumento iustitiae circumdedit
me, quasi sponsam ornatam monilibus suis. Ps. Exaltabo te, Domine,
quoniam suscepisti me: nec delectasti inimicos meos super me.

*I will rejoice in the Lord, and my soul shall be joyful in my God; for he has
clothed me with the garments of salvation; and with the robe of righteousness he has covered me, as a bridegroom decked with a crown, and as
a bride adorned with her jewels. V. I will extol you, O Lord, for you have
lifted me up, and have not let my foes rejoice over me.*

Meter: SM
Suggested Tune: Swabia

Antiphon: In God I will rejoice,
             For I am clothed and robed
             In his salvation, as a bride
             And bridegroom are adorned.

Verses: I will extol you, Lord,
             For you have lifted me
             And have not let my foes rejoice
             Or gain the victory.

             Lord God, I cried to you
             And you have made me whole;
             You brought me up, O Lord, from death,
             Restoring mind and soul.

             You servants of the Lord,
             Approach, let music ring;
             Remembering his holiness,
             Give thanks to God our King.

Doxology: Give glory to our God,
             The Father, and the Son,
             And also to the Paraclete,
             Eternal Three-in-One.

Antiphon: Isaiah 61:10, CT
Verses: Psalm 30:2–5, Doxology: CT
© 2005 World Library Publications

Appendixes

Appendix 1

Ordines Romani

The Ordines Romani are directories for the celebration of pontifical liturgical rites. All surviving copies are of Frankish and German origin. Ordo I, the only purely Roman ordo, was already widely known in the Frankish empire around 750.

When reading these ordines for the purpose of gaining insights into musical performance of the introits, we must keep in mind that they are primarily liturgical documents. Music is only mentioned as incidental to the liturgical action. Very often, not all the particular expected parts of the introit are mentioned, and we have to piece the elements together from other sources. Thus, in our discussion below, if a particular element seems to be missing, it does not automatically mean that this omission was a practice at that time in that place.

In the ninth century, the ordines no longer fulfilled the role of liturgical books but served as reference works for the instruction of the clergy. Various ordines were then combined with Sacramentaries to form the Romano-German Pontifical, which was widely copied, and parts of which are used to this day.[1]

ORDO I, 692–731, ROMAN

Ordo I describes the papal stational Mass, which was imitated throughout the region and to a certain extent in the rest of the Western Church.[2] Froger argues that it reflects the Roman rite under Gregory III (731–741).[3] The first full description of Eucharistic worship in Rome, it contains some information about Church hierarchy within the liturgy, which resembles the status of the late seventh century. There are two recensions of this document, both of which are copies of a Roman original. Ordo I passed into Gaul between 700 and 750.

It refers to stational Masses in a "diaconia," and thus could hardly have been before Gregory II (715–731). It also refers to the Lateran Palace as "patriarchum," which was a term first introduced by Sergius I (687–701).[4] Ordo I mentions the Agnus Dei, which was introduced into the Mass in 692 by Pope Sergius (687–701), according to the *Liber pontificalis*. It was widely known in the Frankish empire around 750. Therefore, the span of its composition would most likely be 692–730.[5]

Ordo ecclesiastica Romanae ecclesiae sanctae, qualiter missa caelebratur

5. Cum vero ecclesiam introierit pontifex, non ascendit continuo ad altare, set prius intrat in sacrarium sustenatus a diaconibus.

7. Deinde subdiaconus regionarius, tenens mappulam pontificis in sinistro brachio super planetam revolutam, exigens ad regiam secretarii dicit: Scola! Respondet: Adsum. Et ille: Quis psallet? Respondet: Ille et ille. Et rediens ad pontificem subdiaconus porrigit ei mappulam, inclinans se ad genua pontificis et dicens: Servi tui, domini mei, talis subdiaconus regionarius legit apostolum, et talis ac talis cantant. Et iam non licet alterum mutare in locum lectoris vel cantoris; quod si factum fuerit, archiparafonista a pontifice excommunicabitur, i.e. quartus scolae, qui semper pontifici nuntiat de cantoribus. Quod cum subdiaconum adstans ante faciem pontificis, usque dum ei annuat pontifex, ut psallant. Qui dum annuerit, statim egreditur ante fores secretarii, dicens: Incendite! Qui dum incenderint, statim subdiaconus sequens tenens tymiaterium aureum pro foribus ponat incensum, ut pergat ante pontificem. Et illi quartus scolae pervenit in presbyterio ad priorem scolae vel secundum sive tertium, [et] inclinato capite dicit: Domni, iubete!

8. Tunc illi elevantes se per ordinem vadunt ante altare; statuuntur acies duae tantum iuxta ordinem, parafonista quidem hinc inde a foris, infantes ab utroque latere infra per ordinem. Et mox incipit prior scolae antiphonam ad introitum. Quorum vocem diaconi dum audierint, continuo intrant ad pontificem in secretarium. Et tunc pontifex elevans se dat manum dextram archidiacono et sinistram secundo vel qui fuerit in ordine. Et illi osculatis manibus ipsius procedunt cum ipso sustentantes eum. Tunc subdiaconus cum tymiaterio praecedit ante ipsum mittens incensum, et VII acolyti illius [regionis], cuius domus vel dies fuerit, portantes septem cereostata accenso, praecedunt ante pontificem usque ante altare. Set priusquam vcniant ante altare, diacones in presbyterio exuuntur planetis, et suscipit eas subdiaconus regionarius et porrigit illas ad acolytos regionis, cuius fuerint diaconi. Et tunc duo acolyti tenent capsas cum Sancta apertas et subdiaconus sequens cum ipsis tenens manum suam in ore capsae ostendit Sancta pontifici vel diacono, qui praecesserit. Tunc inclinato

capite pontifex vel diaconus salutat Sancta et contemplatur, ut, si fuerit
superabundans, praecipiat, ut ponatur in conditorio. Tunc antequem
praecedens veniat ad scolam, dividuntur VII cereostata, IV ad dextram
et III at sinistram, et pertransit pontifex in caput scolae et inclinat caput
ad altare, surgens et orans et faciens crucem in fronte sua, et dat pacem
uni episcopo de hebdomadariis et archipresbytero et diaconibus omnibus.
Et respiciens ad priorem scolae annuit ei, ut dicat Gloriam. Et prior scolae
inclinat se pontifici et imponit. Quartus vero scolae praecedit ante pontificem, ut ponat oratorium ante altare. Et accedens pontifex orat super
ipsum usque ad repetitionem versus. Nam diaconi surgunt, quando dicitur:
Sicut erat in principio et reliqua, ut salutent altari latera, prius duo et duo
vicissim, redeuntes ad pontificem. Et surgens pontifex osculat evangelia et
altare et accedit ad sedem suam et stat versus ad orientem.

The introit is directly followed by the Kyrie. Then the pope
intones the Gloria, if there is time ("si tempus fuerit" could also
mean if it is the season; however, this can be eliminated as a meaning
because of what follows). After the first reading, "cantor cum can-
tatorio dicit Responsorium" (Gradual), then, if there is time ("si tempus
fuerit"), the Alleluia or the tract—if not, only the Responsorium
gradale. The next musical number is the offertory antiphon and several
verses of the psalm, the Sanctus, and Agnus Dei. As soon as the
pope communes, the "antiphona ad communionem" is begun. At the
end of communion, the pope gives the prior scolae a sign to begin
the Gloria Patri, which is followed by the antiphon ("et tunc repetito
versu quiescunt").

The term "versu" at the end of the communio clearly refers
to the antiphon. The same wording is applied to the introit, when
the document mentions "usque ad repetitionem versus." The words
"sicut erat" are preceded by "nam" (meanwhile), indicating that the
deacons' action during the singing of "sicut erat" would have occurred
before the repeat of the antiphon, and not after,[6] and therefore the
Gloria Patri is not split in two parts, as in Ordo XV.

Thus we arrive at this outline:

Antiphon
Several psalm verses
Gloria Patri
Antiphon

It is furthermore likely that the psalm verses would have been alternated between the two sides of the schola in antiphonal fashion. McKinnon's claim that Ordo I used solo performance in the psalm verses and that the antiphon was repeated after each verse[7] cannot be substantiated.

Ordo IV, 780–790, Romano-Frankish

This hybrid Romano-Frankish ordo, dependent on Ordo I, was a literary work only, since it was already supplemented by Ordo III by the time it was copied. It contains several modifications for Frankish use (for example, regrouping of the ministers).[8] Transcribed around 800, it is called the Saint Amand ordo.[9]

[Entrance, Introit]

14. Et transit pontifex cum diaconis per mediam scolam et annuit primum scolae, ut dicatur Gloria . . .

17. Dum dixerit scola: Sicut erat in principio, erigunt se diaconi ab oratione et osculunt altare hinc et inde.

18. Et dum dixerit scola versum ad repetendum, surgit pontifex ab oratione . . .

20. Et dum compleverit scola antiphonam, annuit pontifex ut dicatur Kyrie eleison.

In paragraph 18, the pope rises from his prayer during the singing of the versus ad repetendum. In Ordo I, the pope's rise from prayer coincides with "repetitionem versus," which is interpreted to mean the antiphon. Could the author of Ordo IV have misread or misinterpreted Ordo I?

Also, it is not clear from the document whether the antiphon is repeated before the versus ad repetendum or whether the Gloria Patri is split by the insertion of an antiphon, as indicated by the almost contemporary Ordo XV.

Antiphon
Psalm verse(s)
Gloria Patri
One or several versus ad repetendum
Antiphon

Ordo V, 850–900, Romano-German (Rhineland)

This Ordo uses Amalar of Metz's "Liber officialis" and "De ordine romano" and diverges widely from Ordo I.[10]

> 14. Et mox incipit prior scolae antiphonam ad introitum . . .
> 18. Et respiciens ad priorem scolae innuit ei ut dicat Gloria patri. Et prior scolae inclinans se pontifici dat gloriam trinitati . . .
> 21. Diaconi vero sicut superius, prius stantes retro episcopum inclinati, quando dicitur: Sicut erat in principio, surgunt . . .
> 22. Scola vero ad nutum diaconi imponit letaniam Kyrieleyson.[11]

Again, we can get little information about the performance practice of the introit from this document. However, Ordo VI, which is otherwise an exact copy of Ordo V, mentions a repeat of the introit antiphon after the Gloria Patri.

Antiphon
Psalm verse(s)
Gloria Patri
(Antiphon)

Ordo XV, 775–787, Romano-Frankish

Besides Ordo I, this is the most explicit of the Ordines Romani regarding performance of the introit. A directory designed for all ecclesiastics, secular and regular, it takes the form of a "Capitulare" ("Capitulare ecclesiastici ordinis"). The extant copy is Saint Gall 349, late eighth century.[12] Ordo XV was probably written by a Frankish monk who had a great admiration of Rome but little or no experience with the city or its liturgical peculiarities. Probably composed in Austrasia or Burgundy a little before 787, it used the Gallicanized version of Ordo I in Ordo XIX as a model.[13]

[Christmas Dawn]
> 10. Et mox ut gallus cantaverit, dominus apostolicus cum omni ordine sacerdotum ad missas ingrediuntur.
> 13. Deinde, post modicum spacium, cantantibus antephonam ad introitum clericis . . .

15. Inde peraccedit ad altare et, prostrato omni corpore in terra, facit orationem usquedum clerici antephonam ad introitum cum psalmo et Gloria et repetito verso dixerint.

16. Surgens autem ab orationem, transit post altare ad sedem suam et usquedum Kyriaeleison novem vicibus . . .[14]

[Order of Mass]

121. . . . observare debit, ut semper ad introitum antephona cum psalmo et Gloria adiungat.

122. Si autem ipsa antephona de psalmo fuerit, pre ipsa verso primo de ipso psalmo debit dicere et p[re] verso ipsa canit et p[re] antephona subsequitur Gloria patri et filio et spiritui sancto; et iterum antephona est canenda, et p[re] ipsa adiungit: Sicut erat in principio et nunc et semper et in secula seculorum. Amen. et iterum canit ipsa antephona et item postea dicit alio verso de ipso psalmo et iterum cantat ipsa antephona.

Andrieu footnotes the use of the word "pre" in paragraph 122.[15] The first time, it is written out; the other times, it is abbreviated with the symbol "p" for "pre." In other locations, the writer used a different form of "p" meaning "post," which is clearly the intent here. Because the text only makes sense if "post" is read throughout, this was clearly a copyist's mistake.

When we read paragraph 122, substituting "post" for all occurrences of "pre," we get the clearest indication yet of the Frankish versus ad repetendum:

122. If, however, this antiphon is from the psalm, then after it [the schola] must sing the first verse of that psalm, and after the verse [the schola] sings it [the antiphon], and after the antiphon follows "Gloria patri et filio et spiritui sancto"; and again the antiphon is sung, and after it [the schola] adds: "Sicut erat in principio et nunc et semper et in secula seculorum. Amen." And again [the schola] sings the antiphon and also thereafter sings another verse of this psalm and again sings this antiphon.

We arrive at this practice:
Antiphon
First Psalm verse
Antiphon
Gloria Patri (first half)
Antiphon
Sicut erat
Antiphon

Versus ad repetendum

Antiphon

The use of the term "clerici" in conjunction with the schola is notable. These could be either priests or seminarians or other ordained ministers. The ordination rite in the Romano-Germanic Pontifical contains a section for the ordination of a psalmist or cantor who sings the gradual. This could have been the prior schola or another member of the schola.

In the description of the communion antiphon later in the document, we discover that the whole psalm was performed (151. . . . "totum psalmum con antephona . . ."), then the Gloria Patri, more verses, and finally a repeat of the antiphon. In this case, as would be the case of the versus ad repetendum of the introit, the psalm verses added after the doxology would have had the purpose of extending the composition to cover the liturgical action.

Ordo XVII, 780–790, Romano-Frankish

This Ordo borrowed material from Ordos XV and XVI and used Ordo I only by the way of Ordo XV.[16]

[Christmas and all high feast days]

18. Et incipiunt clerici antifonam ad introitum de ipso die pertinentem.

19. Cum autem primo verso psalmo incipiunt, procedant sacerdotes de sacrario . . .

25. Inde prope accedat ad altare et, prostrato omni corpore in terra, fundens orationem pro se vel pro peccata populi, usquedum antiphona ad introitum cum psalmo et Gloria cum versus ad repetendum dixerint.

28. Expleta autem antiphona ad introitum cum Kirieleison . . .[17]

Paragraphs 19 and 25 imply that several verses of the psalm would have been sung. The procession began after the antiphon, with the first verse of the psalm. If the Gloria Patri began as the bishop ascended the altar steps, several verses would have been necessary, even if the aisle was short or the procession did not use the whole aisle.

Antiphon

Psalm verses

Gloria Patri

One or several versus ad repetendum

Antiphon

ORDO XXXV, 975–1010, ROMANO-GERMAN

Assembled probably in Mainz, this ordo used parts of eighth-century ordines.[18]

Ordinatio Episcopi:

1. . . . . Procedens ante altare, innuit primo scolae, qui mox inchoat antiphonam ad introitum: Benedixit te hodie Deus, cum psalmo Deus deorum dominus et Gloria.[19]

Interpretation:
Antiphon
Psalm verse(s)
Gloria Patri
(Antiphon)

Appendix 2

Pontificals

Pontificals grew out of collections of ordines and tried to decree correct liturgical usage in a more universal way. For our discussion of the introit, it becomes clear that the pontificals are either rather vague or that the introit had indeed simplified. The pontificals were copied by hand, and many sources are corrupt and in places illegible. Where the latter occurs, the editors placed dots or ellipses on the manuscripts.

ROMANO-GERMAN PONTIFICAL, 950–963, MAINZ

The RGP displays uniform editorship and was probably assembled in Mainz, the spiritual center of Germany at the time. Some elements survive to this day. This was a supervised work by several people, probably under Archbishop William of Mainz (954–968), and its intrinsic value caused its quick dissemination and popularity, which is demonstrated by some 50 extant copies. It arrived in Rome between 951 and 972 and became a major tool of liturgical reform in Rome and Italy.[1]

> XV. Ordo qualiter in romana aecclesia sacri ordines fiunt [Ordinatio psalmistae, estiarii, lectoris, exorcisme, acolyti].[2]
> 8. Psalmistae, id est cantores, possunt absque scientia episcopi sola iussione presbiteri officium suscipere cantandi, donante ei presbitero vel potius episcopo antiphonarium in manus et dicendo sibi: Videte ut quod ore cantabis corde credatis et quod corde creditis operibus probetis.
> XCII. Ordo processionis ad ecclesiam sive missam secundum Romanos. [Order of Mass same as Ordo V]
> XCIV. Incipit expositio totius missae ex concordia scriptuarum divinarum.
> 2. Versus, qui cantatur ad recipiendum introitum, per priorem Christi adventum significat prophetiam.
> XCV. Item alia expositio totius missae ex c . . .

1. Introitus missae quare dicitur? R. Eo quod per eum introitur ad eius officium. Int. Versus eius quare cantatur? R. Eo quod per eum revertitur ad introitum. Int. Gloria cur cantatur? R. Ut ostendatur habere patrem et filium et spiritum sanctum aequalem gloriam, coeternam maiestatem, in principo et nunc et semper et in secula seculorum, id est in praeterito et praesenti et futuro tempore.

XCVIII. Ordo processionis, si quando episcopus festivis diebus missam celebrare voluerit, ita ut ab antiquis patribus occidentalium institutione est constitutus, hic adesse cernitur scriptus. [same as Ordo X, whose sources are V and IX, but not I directly; redactor Frankish or from Mainz, 900–950][3]

7. Dehinc, innuente episcopo, cantetur introitus et pontifex, a custode aecclesiae, qui alba indutus esse debet, incensum accipiens . . .

8. His impletis, cum psalmus cantatur, innuente episcopo, procedant . . .

15. Igitur, his peractis, cum Gloria, innuente episcopo, cantabitur, a sepedicti presbiteris . . .

17. Sed continuo ut episcopus in altiore scandere inceperit, subdiaconis, qui prius iuxta altare stabant, choro Gloria patri canente, ad propria loca revertendum est . . .

18. Quibus ita finitis, item versus a choro cantandus est et pontifex usque in medietatem altaris ducendus . . .

20. Peracto itaque introitu, innuente episcopo, cantandum est Kyrieleyson . . .

XCIX. In Christi nomine incipit ordo catholicorum librorum qui in ecclesia romana ponuntur. [same as Ordo L]

253. Cantor autem et scola, statim ut iussum fuerit, imponat introitu ad missam. Antiphona: Nos autem gloriari oportet [Holy Thursday Chrism Mass], cum psalmo et Gloria et versu et Kyrie eleison . . .[4]

Paragraph 18 mentions another verse or several verses sung after the Gloria Patri, but it is not clear whether this refers to the versus ad repetendum or the repeat of the antiphon, which is not mentioned again.

> Antiphon
> One or several psalm verses
> Gloria Patri
> One or several versus ad repetendum(?)
> Antiphon(?)[5]

Twelfth-century Roman Pontifical

[Holy Thursday, Chrism Mass]

28. Cantor autem et scola, statim ut iussum fuerit, imponat introitum ad missam: Nos autem gloriari cum psalmo et Gloria et Kyrie eleison. Tunc dicat pontifex Gloria in excelsis Deo.[6]

While there is little information here, the standard Roman order of Ordo I is confirmed. Because nothing is mentioned to the contrary, we have to assume that the antiphon is repeated after the Gloria patri.

Antiphon
Psalm verse(s)
Gloria Patri
(Antiphon)

Pontifical of the Roman Curia, Thirteenth Century

[Holy Thursday, Chrism Mass]

9. Interim autem decantetus a cantoribus introitus sine Gloria patri [the Roman custom in the thirteenth century omitted the Gloria patri on Holy Thursday]. Et finitu versu primo repetatur introitus et cantetur Kyrie.[7]

This document makes it clear that only the first verse of the psalm was sung, and that the Gloria Patri would still have been sung on other days, since its omission here is mentioned explicitly as an exception. Also to note is the absence of a versus ad repetendum.

Antiphon
First Psalm Verse
Gloria patri (omitted at Chrism Mass)
Antiphon

Pontifical of Guillaume Durand, about 1285

This pontifical reflects the usage of the papal court in Avignon around 1285.[8]

Primo ordo feria quarta in capite ieiuniorum: [Ash Wednesday] Incipit enim ante altare, scola prosequente, antiphonam Exaudi nos. Require infra, in Titulo Ordo ad concilium vel sinodum celebrandum. Ps. Salvum me fac. Vers. Gloria patri. et repetitur antiphona. Deinde dicit: Dominus vobiscum. Oremus.⁹

In quinta feria cene domini: [Holy Thursday, Chrism Mass]

50. Tunc cantor inchoat introitum Nos autem gloriari. Vers. Deus misereatur nostri.

51. Cumque cantor inceperit Gloria patri, quod tamen ecclesia romana non dicit [it was the Roman custom on Holy Thursday not to sing the Gloria patri], tunc pontifex cum tota premissa processione sollempni et cum cruce . . . procedit ad altare et dicitur Gloria in excelsis Deo. Sed quando crisma non conficitur, nec Gloria in excelsis Deo, nec Ite missa est, nec Credo in unum Deo dicuntur.¹⁰

The model for the late thirteenth century makes no more mention of versus ad repetendum.

Antiphon

Psalm Verse(s)

Gloria Patri

Antiphon

Appendix 3

Liturgical Index

Liturgy	Psalm Verse	Meter	Suggested Tune
Advent 1	25	SM	St. Bride
Advent 2	80	LM	Winchester New
Advent 3	85	7676D	Gaudeamus pariter
Advent 3 alt.	85	LM	Winchester New
Advent 4	19	CM	Winchester Old
Christmas Vigil	24	LM	Puer nobis
Christmas Midnight	2	7777	Nun komm, der Heiden Heiland
Christmas Midnight alt.	2	CMD	Forest Green
Christmas Dawn	93	SM	Festal Song
Christmas Day	98	CMD	Carol
Holy Family	68	CMD	Forest Green
Mary, Mother of God	45	10 10.12 10	Gabriel's Message
Mary, Mother of God alt.	45	CM	Winchester Old
Christmas 2	93	SM	St. George
Epiphany	72	CM	Winchester Old
Baptism of the Lord	45	CM	Coronation
Ash Wednesday	57	LM	Erhalt uns, Herr
Lent 1	91	8787D	In Babilone
Lent 2	27	LM	Breslau
Lent 3	25	SM	St. Bride
Lent 4	122	LM	Truro
Lent 5	43	7676D	Passion Chorale

Liturgy	Psalm Verse	Meter	Suggested Tune
Holy Thursday: Chrism	45	LM	Deus tuorum militum
Holy Thursday: Supper	67	LM	Duguet
Easter	139	878787	Lauda anima
Easter alt.	139	7777 w/All.	Easter Hymn
Easter 2	81	CM	Graefenberg
Easter 3	66	LM w/All.	Lasst uns erfreuen
Easter 4	33	SM	Festal Song
Easter 5	98	LM	St. Magnus
Easter 6	66	LM w/All.	Lasst uns erfreuen
Ascension	47	SM	Swabia
Easter 7	27	LM	Duke Street
Pentecost Vigil	34	LM	Tallis' Canon
Pentecost Day	68	LM w/All.	Lasst uns erfreuen
Trinity AB	8	8787D	Hyfrydol
Trinity C	103	SM	St. Thomas (Williams)
Corpus Christi	81	CM	Azmon
Sacred Heart	33	SM	Festal Song
Ordinary Time 2	66	LM	Duke Street
Ordinary Time 3 AB	19	CM	McKee
Ordinary Time 3 C	97	7777	Luebeck
Ordinary Time 4	105	LM	Old 100th
Ordinary Time 4 alt.	105	10 10.10 10	Toulon
Ordinary Time 5	95	666688	Darwall's 148th
Ordinary Time 5 alt.	95	86886	Repton
Ordinary Time 6	31	CM	St. Anne
Ordinary Time 7	13	SM	Swabia
Ordinary Time 8	18	11 11.11 11	St. Denio
Ordinary Time 9	25	SM	Festal Song
Ordinary Time 10 AC	27	8787D	Hyfrydol
Ordinary Time 10 B	130	LM	Jesu, dulcis memoria

Liturgy	Psalm Verse	Meter	Suggested Tune
Ordinary Time 11	27	LM	Erhalt uns, Herr
Ordinary Time 12	28	11 11.11 11	St. Denio
Ordinary Time 13	47	SM	Festal Song
Ordinary Time 14	48	LM	Winchester New
Ordinary Time 15	55	CMD	Kingsfold
Ordinary Time 16	54	LM	Melcombe
Ordinary Time 17	68	LM	Old 100th
Ordinary Time 18 A	78	10 10.11 11	Laudate Dominum
Ordinary Time 18 A alt.	78	LM	Tallis' Canon
Ordinary Time 18 BC	70	SM	St. George
Ordinary Time 19	74	86886	Repton
Ordinary Time 19 alt.	74	LM	Erhalt uns, Herr
Ordinary Time 20	84	LM	Duke Street
Ordinary Time 21	86	666688	Rhosymedre
Ordinary Time 21 alt.	86	86886	Repton
Ordinary Time 22	86	86886	Repton
Ordinary Time 22 alt.	86	666688	Rhosymedre
Ordinary Time 23	119	LM	Old 100th
Ordinary Time 24	122	LM	Breslau
Ordinary Time 25	78	10 10.11 11	Laudate Dominum
Ordinary Time 25 alt.	78	LM	Duke Street
Ordinary Time 26 A	102	888888	St. Catherine
Ordinary Time 26 BC	119	7777D	Aberystwyth
Ordinary Time 27	119	7777D	Salzburg
Ordinary Time 28	130	LM	Erhalt uns, Herr
Ordinary Time 29	17	SMD	Diademata
Ordinary Time 30	105	10 10.10 10	Toulon
Ordinary Time 30 alt.	105	LM	Old 100th
Ordinary Time 31 AB	38	CM	McKee
Ordinary Time 31 C	57	LM	Erhalt uns, Herr

Liturgy	Psalm Verse	Meter	Suggested Tune
Ordinary Time 32	88	SM	St. Bride
Ordinary Time 33	85	7676D	Gaudeamus pariter
Christ the King	72	LM	Duke Street
Christ the King alt.	72	8787.887	Mit Freuden zart
Presentation	48	LM	Winchester New
St. Joseph	92	10 10.10 10	Woodlands
St. Joseph alt.	92	LM	Truro
Annunciation	19	CM	Winchester Old
St. John Vigil	21	7777D	Salzburg
St. John the Bapt., Vigil alt.	21	8787.887	Mit Freuden zart
St. John the Bapt., Day	92	10 10.10 10	Woodlands
St. John Day alt.	92	LM	Tallis' Canon
Ss. Peter & Paul, Vigil	19	CMD	Kingsfold
Ss. Peter & Paul, Day	139	878787	Lauda anima
Transfiguration	27	LM	Duke Street
Assumption, Vigil	45	10 10.12 10	Gabriel's Message
Assumption, Vigil alt.	45	CM	Winchester Old
Assumption, Day	98	CM	St. Magnus
Triumph of the Cross	67	LM	Melcombe
All Saints	33	SM	Festal Song
Ded. Lateran Basilica	68	CMD	Kingsfold
Immaculate Conception	30	SM	Swabia

Appendix 4

Index of Psalm Verses

Psalm Verse	Liturgy	Meter	Suggested Tune
2	Christmas Midnight	7777	Nun komm, der Heiden Heiland
2	Christmas Midnight alt.	CMD	Forest Green
8	Trinity AB	8787D	Hyfrydol
13	Ordinary Time 7	SM	Swabia
17	Ordinary Time 29	SMD	Diademata
18	Ordinary Time 8	11 11.11 11	St. Denio
19	Advent 4	CM	Winchester Old
19	Ordinary Time 3 AB	CM	McKee
19	Annunciation	CM	Winchester Old
19	Saints Peter and Paul, Vigil	CMD	Kingsfold
21	John the Baptist, Vigil	7777D	Salzburg
21	John the Baptist, Vigil alt.	8787.887	Mit Freuden zart
24	Christmas Vigil	LM	Puer nobis
25	Advent 1	SM	St. Bride
25	Lent 3	SM	St. Bride
25	Ordinary Time 9	SM	Festal Song
27	Lent 2	LM	Breslau
27	Easter 7	LM	Duke Street
27	Ordinary Time 10 AC	8787D	Hyfrydol

Psalm Verse	Liturgy	Meter	Suggested Tune
27	Ordinary Time 11	LM	Erhalt uns, Herr
27	Transfiguration	LM	Duke Street
28	Ordinary Time 12	11 11.11 11	St. Denio
30	Immaculate Conception	SM	Swabia
31	Ordinary Time 6	CM	St. Anne
33	Easter 4	SM	Festal Song
33	Sacred Heart	SM	Festal Song
33	All Saints	SM	Festal Song
34	Pentecost Vigil	LM	Tallis' Canon
38	Ordinary Time 31 AB	CM	McKee
43	Lent 5	7676D	Passion Chorale
45	Mary, Mother of God	10 10.12 10	Gabriel's Message
45	Mary, Mother of God alt.	CM	Winchester Old
45	Baptism of the Lord	CM	Coronation
45	Holy Thursday: Chrism	LM	Deus tuorum militum
45	Assumption, Vigil	10 10.12 10	Gabriel's Message
45	Assumption, Vigil alt.	CM	Winchester Old
47	Ascension	SM	Swabia
47	Ordinary Time 13	SM	Festal Song
48	Ordinary Time 14	LM	Winchester New
48	Presentation	LM	Winchester New
54	Ordinary Time 16	LM	Melcombe
55	Ordinary Time 15	CMD	Kingsfold
57	Ash Wednesday	LM	Erhalt uns, Herr
57	Ordinary Time 31 C	LM	Erhalt uns, Herr
66	Easter 3	LM w/All.	Lasst uns erfreuen
66	Easter 6	LM w/All.	Lasst uns erfreuen
66	Ordinary Time 2	LM	Duke Street
67	Holy Thursday: Supper	LM	Duguet
67	Triumph of the Cross	LM	Melcombe

Psalm Verse	Liturgy	Meter	Suggested Tune
68	Holy Family	CMD	Forest Green
68	Pentecost Day	LM w/All.	Lasst uns erfreuen
68	Ordinary Time 17	LM	Old 100th
68	Dedication of Lateran Basilica	CMD	Kingsfold
70	Ordinary Time 18 BC	SM	St. George
72	Epiphany	CM	Winchester Old
72	Christ the King	LM	Duke Street
72	Christ the King alt.	8787887	Mit Freuden zart
74	Ordinary Time 19	86886	Repton
74	Ordinary Time 19	LM	Erhalt uns, Herr
78	Ordinary Time 18 A	LM	Tallis' Canon
78	Ordinary Time 18 A alt.	10 10.11 11	Laudate Dominum
78	Ordinary Time 25	10 10.11 11	Laudate Dominum
78	Ordinary Time 25 alt.	LM	Duke Street
80	Advent 2	LM	Winchester New
81	Easter 2	CM	Graefenberg
81	Corpus Christi	CM	Azmon
84	Ordinary Time 20	LM	Duke Street
85	Advent 3	7676D	Gaudeamus pariter
85	Advent 3 alt.	LM	Winchester New
85	Ordinary Time 33	7676D	Gaudeamus pariter
86	Ordinary Time 21	666688	Rhosymedre
86	Ordinary Time 21 alt.	86886	Repton
86	Ordinary Time 22	86886	Repton
86	Ordinary Time 22 alt.	666688	Rhosymedre
88	Ordinary Time 32	SM	St. Bride
91	Lent 1	8787D	In Babilone
92	Saint Joseph	10 10.10 10	Woodlands
92	Saint Joseph alt.	LM	Truro

Psalm Verse	Liturgy	Meter	Suggested Tune
92	John the Baptist, Day	10 10.10 10	Woodlands
92	John the Baptist, Day alt.	LM	Tallis' Canon
93	Christmas Dawn	SM	Festal Song
93	Christmas 2	SM	St. George
95	Ordinary Time 5	666688	Darwall's 148th
95	Ordinary Time 5 alt.	86886	Repton
97	Ordinary Time 3 C	7777	Luebeck
98	Christmas Day	CMD	Carol
98	Easter 5	CM	St. Magnus
98	Assumption, Day	CM	St. Magnus
102	Ordinary Time 26 A	888888	St. Catherine
103	Trinity C	SM	St. Thomas (Williams)
105	Ordinary Time 4	LM	Old 100th
105	Ordinary Time 4 alt.	10 10.10 10	Toulon
105	Ordinary Time 30	10 10.10 10	Woodlands
105	Ordinary Time 30 alt.	LM	Old 100th
119	Ordinary Time 23	LM	Old 100th
119	Ordinary Time 26 BC	7777D	Aberystwyth
119	Ordinary Time 27	7777D	Salzburg
122	Lent 4	LM	Truro
122	Ordinary Time 24	LM	Breslau
130	Ordinary Time 28	LM	Erhalt uns, Herr
130	Ordinary Time 10 B	LM	Jesu, dulcis memoria
139	Easter	878787	Lauda anima
139	Easter alt.	7777 w/All.	Easter Hymn
139	Saints Peter and Paul, Day	878787	Lauda anima

Appendix 5

Metrical Index

Meter	Suggested Tune	Liturgy	Psalm Verse
666688	Darwall's 148th	Ordinary Time 5	95
	Rhosymedre	Ordinary Time 21	86
	Rhosymedre	Ordinary Time 22 alt.	86
SM	St. Bride	Advent 1	25
	Festal Song	Christmas Dawn	93
	St. George	Christmas 2	93
	St. Bride	Lent 3	25
	Festal Song	Easter 4	33
	Swabia	Ascension	47
	St. Thomas (Williams)	Trinity C	103
	Festal Song	Sacred Heart	33
	Swabia	Ordinary Time 7	13
	Festal Song	Ordinary Time 9	25
	Festal Song	Ordinary Time 13	47
	St. George	Ordinary Time 18 BC	70
	St. Bride	Ordinary Time 32	88
	Festal Song	All Saints	33
	Swabia	Immaculate Conception	30
6686D	Diademata	Ordinary Time 29	17
7676D	Gaudeamus pariter	Advent 3	85
	Passion Chorale	Lent 5	43
	Gaudeamus pariter	Ordinary Time 33	85

Meter	Suggested Tune	Liturgy	Psalm Verse
7777	Nun komm, der Heiden	Christmas Midnight	2
	Luebeck	Ordinary Time 3 C	97
7777 w/All.	Easter Hymn	Easter alt.	139
7777D	Aberystwyth	Ordinary Time 26 BC	119
	Salzburg	Ordinary Time 27	119
	Salzburg	John the Baptist, Vigil alt.	21
CM	Winchester Old	Advent 4	19
	Winchester Old	Mary, Mother of God alt.	45
	Winchester Old	Epiphany	72
	Coronation	Baptism of the Lord	45
	Graefenberg	Easter 2	81
	St. Magnus	Easter 5	98
	Azmon	Corpus Christi	81
	McKee	Ordinary Time 3 AB	19
	St. Anne	Ordinary Time 6	31
	McKee	Ordinary Time 31 AB	38
	Winchester Old	Annunciation	19
	Winchester Old	Assumption, Vigil alt.	45
	St. Magnus	Assumption, Day	98
CMD	Carol	Christmas Midnight alt.	2
	Forest Green	Christmas Day	98
	Forest Green	Holy Family	68
	Kingsfold	Ordinary Time 15	55
	Kingsfold	Saints Peter and Paul, Vigil	19
	Kingsfold	Dedication of the Lateran Basilica	68
86886	Repton	Ordinary Time 5	95
	Repton	Ordinary Time 19	74
	Repton	Ordinary Time 21	86

Meter	Suggested Tune	Liturgy	Psalm Verse
	Repton	Ordinary Time 22	86
878787	Lauda Anima	Easter	139
	Lauda Anima	Saints Peter and Paul, Day	139
8787D	In Babilone	Lent 1	91
	Hyfrydol	Trinity A & B	8
	Hyfrydol	Ordinary Time 10 AC	27
8787.887	Mit Freuden zart	Christ the King alt.	72
	Mit Freuden zart	John the Baptist, Vigil alt.	21
LM	Winchester New	Advent 2	80
	Winchester New	Advent 3 alt.	85
	Puer nobis	Christmas Vigil	24
	Erhalt uns, Herr	Ash Wednesday	57
	Breslau	Lent 2	27
	Truro	Lent 4	122
	Deus tuorum militum	Holy Thursday: Chrism	45
	Duguet	Holy Thursday: Supper	67
	Duke Street	Easter 7	27
	Tallis' Canon	Pentecost Vigil	34
	Duke Street	Ordinary Time 2	66
	Old 100th	Ordinary Time 4	105
	Jesu, dulcis memoria	Ordinary Time 10 B	130
	Erhalt uns, Herr	Ordinary Time 11	27
	Winchester New	Ordinary Time 14	48
	Melcombe	Ordinary Time 16	54
	Old 100th	Ordinary Time 17	68
	Tallis' Canon	Ordinary Time 18 A	78
	Erhalt uns, Herr	Ordinary Time 19 alt.	74
	Duke Street	Ordinary Time 20	84
	Old 100th	Ordinary Time 23	119
	Breslau	Ordinary Time 24	122

Meter	Suggested Tune	Liturgy	Psalm Verse
	Duke Street	Ordinary Time 25 alt.	78
	Erhalt uns, Herr	Ordinary Time 28	130
	Old 100th	Ordinary Time 30 alt.	105
	Erhalt uns, Herr	Ordinary Time 31 C	57
	Duke Street	Christ the King	72
	Winchester New	Presentation	48
	Truro	Saint Joseph alt.	92
	Tallis' Canon	John the Baptist, Day alt.	92
	Duke Street	Transfiguration	27
	Melcombe	Triumph of the Cross	67
LM w/All.	Lasst uns erfreuen	Easter 3	66
	Lasst uns erfreuen	Easter 6	66
	Lasst uns erfreuen	Pentecost Day	68
888888	St. Catherine	Ordinary Time 26 A	102
10 10.10 10	Toulon	Ordinary Time 4 alt.	105
	Toulon	Ordinary Time 30	105
	Woodlands	Saint Joseph	92
	Woodlands	John the Baptist, Day	92
10 10.11 11	Laudate Dominum	Ordinary Time 18 A	78
	Laudate Dominum	Ordinary Time 25	78
10 10.12 10	Gabriel's Message	Mary, Mother of God	45
	Gabriel's Message	Assumption, Vigil	45
11 11.11 11	St. Denio	Ordinary Time 8	18
	St. Denio	Ordinary Time 12	28

Appendix 6

Index of Suggested Tunes

Tune	Liturgy
Aberystwyth	CT 26 B & C
Azmon	Body and Blood
Breslau	Lent 2, OT 24
Carol	Christmas Day
Coronation	Baptism of the Lord
Darwall's 148th	OT 5
Deus tuorum militum	Holy Thursday: Chrism
Diademata	OT 29
Duguet	Holy Thursday: Supper
Duke Street	Easter 7, OT 20, OT 25 alt., Christ the King, Transfiguration
Easter Hymn	Easter alt.
Erhalt uns, Herr	Ash Wednesday, OT 11, OT 19C, OT 28, OT 31 C
Festal Song	Easter 4, Sacred Heart, OT 9, OT 13, All Saints
Forest Green	Christmas Midnight alt., Holy Family
Gabriel's Message	Mary Mother of God, Assumption Vigil
Gaudeamus pariter	Advent 3, OT 33
Graefenberg	Easter 2
Hyfrydol	Trinity A & B, OT 10 AC
In Babilone	Lent 1
Jesu, dulcis memoria	Ot 10 B
Kingsfold	OT 15, Saints Peter and Paul Vigil, Dedication of the Lateran Basilica

Endnotes

CHAPTER I

1. John F. Baldovin, SJ. *The Urban Character of Christian Worship.* Orientalia Christiana Analecta 228 (Rome: Pont. Institutum Studiorum Orientalium, 1987), 109.

2. Ibid., 113.

3. Ibid., 116.

4. Ibid., 104.

5. Franz Leitner. *Der gottesdienstliche Volksgesang im juedischen und christlichen Altertum* (Freiburg, 1906), vi: "rasche Ausbreitung des christlichen Gesangs, besonders vom 4. Jahrhundert an."

6. James McKinnon. *The Advent Project: The Later-Seventh-Century Creation of the Roman Mass Proper* (Berkeley: University of California Press, 2000), 35.

7. The Epistolary of the Comes of Wuerzburg (about 600), the earliest extant Roman Lectionary, has readings for six Sundays of Advent. The evangelary of the same document, about 50 years later, contains only five Sundays. The present grouping of only four Sundays of Advent must have occurred at an even later date. The Rheinau antiphoner uses five Sundays of Advent, whereas the other earliest Frankish antiphoners use four; the Second through the Fifth Sundays of Advent in Rheinau antiphoner show the same chants as the First through the Fourth in the other antiphoners.

8. Baldovin, 199, the list of martyrs reflects the usage of 336, the list of bishops that of 354.

9. It should be mentioned here that Mass was celebrated on Sundays and special feasts only. The notion of daily Mass would not appear for several centuries.

10. Baldovin, 123: De fermento vero, quod die Dominica per titulos mittimus, superflue nos consulere voluisti, cum omnes ecclesiae nostrae intra civitatem sint constitutae. Quarum prebyteri, quia die ipsa propter plebe sibi creditam nobiscum convenire non possunt; idcirco fermentum a nobis confectum per acolitos accipiunt, ut se a nostra communione, maxima illa die, non judicent separatos. Quod per paroechias fieri debere non puto; quia nec longe portanda sunt sacramento nec nos per coemeteria diversa constitutis presbyteris destinamus et presbyteri eorum conficiendorum jus habeant atque licentiam.

11. Baldovin, 125.

12. McKinnon Advent, 334–336.

13. Aime Georges Martimort. *The Church at Prayer* (Collegeville, Minnesota: The Liturgical Press, 1988), 65.

14. Brad Maiani. "Approaching the Communion Melodies." *JAMS* vol. 53 No. 2 (Summer 2000), 210.

15. Circumdederunt me gemitus mortis, dolores inferni circumdederunt me: et in tribulatione mea invocavi Dominum, et exaudivit de templo sancto suo vocem meam.

CHAPTER 2

1. P. Juan B. Ferreres, SJ. *Historia del Misal Romano* (Barcelona: E. Subriana, 1929), 81: "Las partes salmodicas de la Misa en un prinicipio eran salmos enteros. Unas se cantaban a dos coros y constituian el canto antifonico; tales son el introito, ofertorio y el communio. Otras se cantaban por un solista, al que contestaba el coro, y constituian el canto responsorial; tales son el gradual y el Alleluia." Ferreres is actually wrong about the Offertory, a mistake frequently made by other scholars as well. The Offertory bears no similarity to antiphonal psalmody but belongs into a category by itself, resembling the Great Responsories of Matins.

2. Maiani, 250 ff.

3. Cyrille Vogel, translated by William G. Storey and Niels Krogh Rasmussen, OP. *Medieval Liturgy: An Introduction to the Sources* (Washington, D.C.: Pastoral Press, 1986), 153.

4. J. F. Niedermeyer. *Mediae Latinitatis Lexicon minus* (Leiden: Brill, 1984), "antiphona."

5. Andreas Jungmann, SJ. *Liturgie der christlichen Fruehzeit bis auf Gregor den Grossen* (Freiburg, Switzerland: Universitaetsverlag, 1967), 192.

6. Leitner, 114.

7. Hiley, David. *Western Plainchant—A Handbook* (Oxford: Clarendon Press, 1995), 490.

8. Isidor of Seville, Etymology VI, 19, 7f (ed. Lindsay), as quoted in Anders Ekenberg. *Cur Cantatur?* (Stockholm: Almqvist & Wiksell International, 1987), 35.

9. Even within the differences of the various communion melody types described by Maiani, there is still a certain homogeneity among them, at least as far as the Gregorian repertoire is concerned, and the fact that the communions and introits exhibit antiphonal form and almost unique assignments throughout the yearly cycle makes them compatible. It is in the Old Roman communions that we find more divergent styles in communion melodies.

10. McKinnon's whole premise behind *The Advent Project* is the seventh-century century creation of the Mass proper. At that time, the Vulgate was the standard, and any deviation from the standard text would have to be seen as a textual adjustment rather than an earlier translation.

11. Niedermeyer, "versus."

12. Gunilla Iversen. "Cantans-Orans-Exultans: Interpretation of the Chants of the Introit Liturgy" in Szendrei, Janka, and Hiley, David. *Laborare fratres in unum: Festschrift Laszlo Dobszay zum 60. Geburtstag* (Zuerich: Weidmann, 1995), 130.

13. Andreas Jungmann, SJ. *Missarum sollemnia—eine genetische Erklaerung der roemischen Messe* (Freiburg: Herder, 1958), 422: "Auf einer aelteren Stufe des Introitusgesanges muss das Hauptgewicht jedenfalls auf den Psalmen gelegen haben . . . Hier waehlte man einen Psalm, der als Ganzes, im Sinn der damaligen allegorisierenden Psalmenexegese, zur betreffenden Tagesidee passen mochte. Der einzige Psalmvers aber, der im heutigen Introitus erhalten geblieben ist—das ist in der Regel der erste Vers des Psalmes, oder aber der Vers, der auf den als Antiphon dienenden Anfangsvers folgt—zeigt nun oefter keinerlei sichtbare Beziehung zu einer solchen Tagesidee."

14. Ibid., 422: "Unsere Zeit, die auch dem Introitus seinen vollen Sinn zurueck-gewinnen moechte, zeigt Neigung, fuer festliche Gelegenheiten wieder den urspruenglichen Psalm aufleben zu lassen, und sie hat dafuer bereits die Billigung Roms erlangt" (Decret 1947 for Bayonne, also 1938 Choir Missal of Duesseldorf). To that we can add the post-Vatican II *Ordo cantus Missae,* which at least for the communion antiphon indicates several pertinent psalm verses.

15. James McKinnon. *Antiquity and the Middle Ages* (Englewood Cliffs, New Jersey: Prentice Hall, 1990), 132.

16. Joseph Dyer. "The Introit and Communion Psalmody of Old Roman Chant." *Chant and Its Peripheries* (Ottawa: Institute of Mediaeval Music, 1998), 130.

17. Ut Gloria Patri cum omni honore apud omnes canentur.

18. Ekenberg 35: et Gloria Patri ac Sanctus atque credulitas et Kyrie eleison a cunctis reverenter canantur.

19. Jungmann Missarum, 420.

20. Aurelian of Reome, tr. Joseph Ponte. *The Discipline of Music (Musica disciplina)* (Colorado Springs: Colorado College Music Press, 1968), 54.

21. See the discussion of Ordo I in the Appendix.

22. See appendix, under Pontificals. The RGP's treatment of the versus ad repetendum is very vague, but, judging from the appearance of the v.a.r. in Roman notated antiphoners shortly after this document's introduction in Rome, it is likely that this performance practice is represented in the RGP.

23. Described under "Monastic Influence."

Chapter 3

1. McKinnon Advent, 118.

2. Dyer Introit, 120.

3. Hiley, 493.

4. Taft, "Frequency," as quoted in Maxwell E. Johnson. *Between Memory and Hope: Readings on the Liturgical Year* (Collegeville, Minnesota: The Liturgical Press, 2000), 87.

5. Robert F. Hayburn. *Papal Legislation on Sacred Music* (Collegeville: The Liturgical Press, 1979), 3.

6. Ioanne Hanssen, SJ, ed. "Amalarii Episcopi Opera Liturgica Omnia." *Studi e testi*, 138 ff (Rome: Biblioteca Apostolica Vaticana, 1948–1950), ii:139, 433.

7. Hiley, 490: Hiley's interpretation of this text includes a repetition of the antiphon by alternating choirs after each psalm verse, which is sung by soloists. Amalar's comments really obscure the text, and it is sometimes difficult to see the detail through the fog.

8. Hiley, 491.

9. Dyer Monastic, 43.

10. Ibid., 59.

11. Ibid., 67.

12. Taft, 150.

13. McKinnon Advent, 212.

14. Ibid., 8.

15. McKinnon Antiquity, 89.

CHAPTER 4

1. P. M. Peebles. "Bible, 13. Latin Versions." *New Catholic Encyclopedia* (New York: McGraw-Hill, 1967), NCE XII:792.

2. Baldovin, 114, lists the presbyters of tituli who signed the "acta" for the Roman parochial synods of 499 and 595. In 499, about half of the 29 parishes have three presbyters, the rest fewer. In 595, the situation is direr: six of the parishes listed in 499 are not listed at all, 13 parishes report only one presbyter, and there is only one with three presbyters (St. Marcellus).

3. Niedermeyer, "schola."

4. McKinnon Advent, 62: "Later 4th century Mass psalmody, certainly, is lector chant, whereas the Roman Mass Proper of the 7th and 8th centuries is schola chant."

5. Ibid., 141.

6. Ibid., 10; the "project" being the compilation of the entire corpus of the Mass proper.

7. Alberto Turco. "Les Antiennes d'Introit du Chant Romain." *Subsidia Gregoriana* 3 (Solesmes: Imprimerie Saint-Pierre, 1993), 5: "La quasi totalite des antiennes d'introit peut etre datee de la periode que s'etend entre 492–496, epoque du pontifical de Gelase I, et 520–525." Alberto Turco. *Il Canto Gregoriano* (Rome: Edizione Torre d'Orfeo, 1987), 20: "I testi e le melodie di questi canti [introits and communions] sono stati composti interamente in un periode di tempo che va dalla fine del sec. V alla meta del sec. VI. Destinati alla schola, comportano uno stile compositivo elaborato."

8. Ekenberg, 38.

9. Hayburn, 3.

10. Turco Canto, 21.

11. Jungmann Liturgie, 210.

12. Hiley, 496.

13. James McKinnon. *The Temple, the Church Fathers, and Early Western Chant* (Aldershot: Ashgate, 1998), VIII:159.

14. Hiley, 484.

15. McKinnon Temple, III:77; also described in detail in VIII:160–164.

16. Ibid., VIII:165.

17. Hiley, 485.

18. McKinnon Temple, VIII:180.

19. Ibid., 182.

20. Ibid., 184.

21. James McKinnon. "The Fourth Century Origin of the Gradual."
Early Music History 7 (Cambridge: Cambridge University Press, 1987), 93.

22. Ibid., 92.

23. Ibid., 93.

24. Ibid., 98.

25. Paul F. Bradshaw. "Cathedral vs. Monastery: The Only Alternatives
for the Liturgy of the Hours?" in J. Neil Alexander. *Time and Community*
(Washington, D.C.: Pastoral Press, 1990), 127.

26. Jungmann Liturgie, 155. (Leitner, 132, mentions that the people's
repertoire at Arles included several psalms: 49, 50, 72, 80, and 118.)

27. McKinnon Advent, 37.

28. McKinnon Temple, VIII:185.

29. Duchesne, *Liber pontificalis I,* 230: Constituit ut psalmi David CL ante
sacrificium psalli antephanatim ex omnibus, quod ante non fiebat, nisi tantum
epistula beati Pauli recitabatur et sanctum evangelium.

30. Peter Jeffrey. "The Introduction of Psalmody into the Roman Mass by
Pope Celestine I (422–432)." *Archiv fuer Liturgiewissenschaft* (Regensburg:
F. Pustet, 1984), xxvi:164.

31. Jungmann Missarum, 416: ". . . dass in der Enstehungszeit dieser Schicht
des Papstbuches, vor der Mitte des 6. Jahrhunderts, der aus Psalmentexten
gebildete Introitusgesang schon laengst in Uebung war."

32. Leitner, 156: "Viel umstritten ist die Frage nach der Einfuehrung des
Psalmengesanges zur Einleitung der ganzen Opferfeier. Urspruenglich
begann der Gottesdienst mit der Lesung . . . Auch Ambrosius und
Augustinus kennen den Introitus noch nicht."

33. McKinnon Antiquity, 116.

34. One point that illustrates the extended period of composition of the
introits is the usage of Isaiah 9:6 in the Masses for Christmas Day (pre-336
feast) and Christmas Dawn (sixth-century feast). This is not to say that the
Christmas Day liturgy had an introit from the start, because introits may not
yet have existed. But it certainly would have been among the first feasts to
receive an introit and Christmas Dawn among the last. This would be a span
of at least 100 years, for reasons given later in this chapter.

35. Studiosus erat et capax in officio cantilena, prior cantorum pro doctrina est traditus.

36. McKinnon Advent, 87.

37. Michel Andrieu. *Les Ordines Romain du Haut Moyen-Age* (Louvain: Spicipegium Sacrum Lovaniense, 1948–1956), IV:195: Primum in qualicumque scola reperti fuerint pueri bene psallentes, tolluntur unde et nutriuntur in scola cantorum et postea fiunt cubicularii. Si autem nobilium filii fuerint, statim in cubiculo nutriuntur.

38. Peebles, II:443.

39. *Biblia Sacra Vulgata* (Stuttgart: Deutsche Bibelgesellschaft, 1994), xxx.

40. Ibid., xxx: "Alcuin, as part of his liturgical reforms, substituted [for the Hewbrew psalter] Jerome's earlier version of the Old Latin on the basis of the Hexapla, which was the psalter text in common use in Gaul in Alcuin's day, and Alcuin's influence was so strong that it soon became the regular psalter text in almost all later Vulgate manuscripts."

41. Peebles, II:441.

42. Dom Robert Weber. *Le Psautier Romain et les autres Anciens Psautiers Latins* (Rome: Abbaye Saint-Jerome, 1953), viii: "Le psautier "iuxta Hebraeos", comme les autres traductions des livres de l'Ancien Testament faites par S. Jerome directement sur le texte original hebreu, devrait faire partie de la Vulgate, et qui de fait, est insere dans de nombreux manuscrits anciens de celle-ci, s'en est trouve evince au IXe siecle au profit du Psautier dit "Gallican" de S. Jerome . . . L'introduction du Psautier Gallican dans la Vulgate est due a Alcuin."

43. Max Luetolf. *Das Graduale von Sta. Cecilia in Trastevere: Biblioteka Bodmer 74* (Cologny-Geneve: Foundation Martin Bodmer, 1987).

44. Peebles, II:446.

45. Theodor Klauser. *Das roemische Capitulare Evangeliorum* (Muenster: Aschendorff, 1972), preface: end of 5th c. St. Gall Stiftsbibl. 1395, Vulgate with Old Latin sections; 6th c. Cividale Bibl. Cap. CXXXVIII, Vulgate, Aquileia; 545 Fulda Landesbibl. 1, Capua; 678–715 Florence Laur. 1, Vulgate with Eusebian sections.

46. Ibid.

47. Hans Thurn. *Comes Romanus Wirziburgensis* (Graz: Akademische Druck- und Verlagsanstalt, 1968).

48. In his *Advent Project*, McKinnon lists "textual adjustments" for the introits of the Advent-Christmas, Easter, and post-Pentecostal seasons, 209–221.

However, he does not enter into the subject of translations. Textual adjustments, according to his definition, are significant alterations of the text when taken out of the context of a scriptural passage, and these actually apply to fewer cases than he claims. The rest are clearly due to a use of Old Latin.

49. Bonifatius Fischer. *Vetus Latina: Die Reste der altlateinischen Bibel* (Freiburg: Herder, 1951–), 25:681: "id est 'commendatum meum,' nam codices nonnulli non habent 'depositum,' set quod est planius 'commendatum.'"

50. Although the feast was celebrated in other rites already in the third century, it does not appear in the Philocalian Calendar. The Leonine or Veronese Sacramentary contains three Masses for the day, the Old Gelasian the present two.

51. The feasts of Saint Peter and Saint Paul are mentioned in the third century as separate celebrations on June 29: Saint Peter on Vatican Hill and Saint Paul on the Ostian Way.

CHAPTER 5

1. Vogel Medieval, 70.

2. Ibid., 146–147.

3. Ibid., 147.

4. Andrieu Ordines, iii:6.

5. Hayburn, 6.

6. Vogel Medieval, 148–149.

7. Ibid., 149.

8. McKinnon Lector, 209.

9. Ibid., 202.

10. Ob unanimitatem apostolicae sedis et sanctae Dei ecclesiae pacificam concordiam.

11. McKinnon Lector, 209.

12. Hiley, 493.

13. Vogel Medieval, 150.

14. Emma Hornby. *Gregorian and Old Roman Eighth-Mode Tracts* (Aldershot: Ashgate, 2002). Discusses the oral transmission of chant in detail, 14, 134–140, 221–223.

15. McKinnon Antiquity, 110.

16. Ibid., 133.

17. McKinnon Antiquity, 132.

18. Amalar of Metz, Prologus antiphonarii a se composti, Hanssen 138:1. Cum longo tempore taedio affectus essem propter antiphonarios discordantes inter se in nostra provincia, moderni enim alio ordine currebant quam vetusti, et quid plus retinendum esset nesciebam, placuit ei qui omnibus tribuit copia antiphonariorum in monasterio Corbiensi, id est tria volumina de nocturnali officio et quartum quod solummodo continebat diurnale, certavi a pelago curiositatis carbasa tendere ad portam tranquillitatis. 2. Nam quando fui missus Romam a sancto et christianissimo imperatore Hludovico ad sanctum et reverendissimum papam Gregorium, de memoratis voluminibus retulit mihi ita idem papa: Antiphonarium non habeo quem possim mittere filio meo domino imperatori, quoniam hos quos habuimus, Wala, quando functus est huc legatione aliqua, abduxit eos hinc secum in Franciam. 3. Quae memorata volumina contuli cum nostris antiphonariis, invenique ea discrepare a nostris non solum in ordine, verum etiam in verbis et multitudine responsoriorum et antiphonarum, quas nos non cantamus. Nam in multi rationabilius statuta reperi nostra volumina, quam essent illa. 7. Ubi ordo responsorium et antiphonarum in perspectis voluminibus dissonare videbatur ab ordine librorum de quibus sumpta sunt, et a cosonatia quae ratione adstipulatur, non dubitavi sequi in nostro antiphonario ea potius quae historiae et rationi istius vel illius festivitatis visa sunt congruere. 8. Ubi ordinabilius visum est mihi scriptum haberi in antiphonario romano quam in nostro, ibi scripsi in margine R, propter nomen urbis Romae; et ubi in nostro, M, propter Metensiem civitatem; ubi nostrum ingenium cogitavit aliquid posse rationabilius illis ordinare, IC, propter indulgentiam et caritatem. 12. Notandum est necessarium nobis esse ut alteros versus habeat noster antiphonarius quam romanus, quoniam altero ordine cantamus nostros responsorios quam Romani. Illi a capite incipiunt responsorium, finito versu, nos, versum finitum, informamus in responsorium per latera eius . . . 18. Notandum est volumen quod nos vocamus antiphonarium, tria habet nomina apud Romanos: quod dicimus gradale, illi vocant cantatorium; quid adhuc iuxta morem antiquum apud illos in aliquibus ecclesiis in uno volumine continetur. Sequentem partem dividunt in duobus nominibus: pars quae continet responsorios, vocatur responsoriale, et pars quae continet antiphonas, vocatur antiphonarius. Ego secutus sum nostrum usum et posui mixtim responsoria et antiphonas secundum ordinum temporum, in quibus solemnitates nostrae celebrantur.

19. McKinnon Antiquity, 133.

20. McKinnon Antiquity, 99.

21. Vogel Medieval, 150.

22. Hiley, 293.

23. Ibid., 479.

24. Vogel Medieval, 238.

25. Ekenberg, 40.

26. Iversen, 145.

CHAPTER 7

1. Webber, iv.

2. Nichol Grieve. *The Scottish Metrical Psalter (1650), A Revision* (Edinburgh: T. & T. Clark, 1940), v.

3. A.M.P. Dawson. *A New Metrical Version of the Psalter* (Croydon: Brighton, 1950), 3.

4. Austin P. Flannery. *Documents of Vatican II.* (Grand Rapids: Eerdmans, 1978), *Musicam sacram*, #3. *Institutio Generalis Missalis Romani* (Rome, 2000), English translation (Washington, D.C.: U.S. Catholic Conference, 2003), Institutio Generalis, #48. *The Music Documents: Music in Catholic Worship and Liturgical Music Today* (Portland, Oregon: Bishops Committee on the Liturgy, 1995), *Music in Catholic Worship*, #60.

5. Othmar Keel. *The Symbolism of the Biblical World* (New York: Seabury Press, 1997), 255.

6. S. E. Gillingham. *The Poems and Psalms of the Hebrew Bible* (Oxford: Oxford University Press, 1994), 192–193.

7. Ibid.

8. Grieve, vii ff.

9. Ibid., vii.

10. Dawson, 4.

11. All examples taken from *Psalter Hymnal, Doctrinal Standards and Liturgy of the Christian Reformed Church* (Grand Rapids: Board of Publications of the Christian Reformed Church, 1976), Psalm 95, #184.

12. Grieve, ix.

13. Ibid., ix, actually says that many references to Jewish ritual should be avoided, since they strike a wrong note in Christian worship. Since 1940, however, biblical thinking in this regard has changed in most Churches, and it would be better to educate the people rather than compromise the psalm texts.

14. Christopher L. Webber. *A New Metrical Psalter* (New York: Church Publishing, 1986), iv.

15. *Worship II* (Chicago: GIA Publications, 1963), #154 vs. 3.

16. D. A. Carson. *The Inclusive Language Debate—A Plea for Realism* (Grand Rapids: Barker Books, 1998), 27.

17. Ibid., 11.

CHAPTER 8

1. *Musicam sacram,* #32; *Institutio Generalis,* #48; *Music in Catholic Worship,* #60.

2. *Sacrosanctum Concilium,* #116.

APPENDIX 1: ORDINES ROMANI

1. *Sacrosanctum Concilium,* #230.

2. Erich Stapper. "Ordo Romanus Primus de Missa Papali." *Opuscula et textus Historiam ecclesiae eiusque vitam atque doctrinam illustrantia, Series Liturgica,* fasc. 1 (Aschendroff: Typis Aschendorff, 1933).

3. Dom Jacques Froger. "Les chants de la Messe au VIIIe et IXe siecles." *Revue Gregorienne* (Paris, 1947), xxvi:162.

4. Vogel Medieval, 159.

5. Andrieu Ordines, III:18.

6. Jungmann Missarum, 416, agrees with this interpretation, and also the performance practice of a continuous psalm which is not interrupted by repeats of the antiphon: "Der Papst verharrt noch kniend im Gebet 'usque ad repetitionem versus,' womit offenbar die Antiphon gemeint ist. Diese wurde also am Schluss des Psalmes wiederholt. Dass sie auch nach jedem einzelnen Vers zu wiederholen war, laesst sich fuer Rom nicht beweisen." Stapper concurs with this as well. Dyer (Introit, 116) suggests the following sequence: A [V1 A V2 . . . . A] D1 [A?] D2 [A] VadR A, making it similar to the practice of Ordo XV. There may be some validity to considering a versus ad repetendum, especially when comparing the words of Ordo I, "Et accedens pontifex orat super ipsum usque ad repetitionem versus" with those of Ordo IV," 18. Et dum dixerit scola versum ad repetendum, surgit pontifex ab oratione . . ." Both times the pontiff prays until the "repetitionem versu" (Ordo I) or the "versus ad repetendum" (Ordo IV), which, however, are not necessarily the same thing. The medieval interpretation of "antiphona" included the meaning "an alternating liturgical chant," and the word "versus", a "verse from the Bible," could mean a selected verse or refer to the particular verse of the antiphon. In all of Ordo I, the word "antiphona" is mentioned only twice, once at the beginning or the introit, and once at the beginning of the communio; this wording indicates rather strongly that "antiphona" here means the whole composition. As we have discussed above, there are substantial divergences in the choice of versus ad repetendum, pointing to non-Roman invention. Also, the antiphons in parentheses (Dyer, see above) and the split of the doxology are elements of Ordo XV. It is questionable whether a successor document can be used in this case to explain its source. In addition, it should be mentioned that there is no evidence in any of the ordines or pontificals that the antiphon was ever repeated between psalm verses.

7. McKinnon Antiquity, 92.

8. Vogel Medieval, 160.

9. Andrieu Ordines, II:158.

10. Vogel Medieval, 161.

11. Andrieu Ordines, II:211.

12. Vogel Medieval, 168.

13. Ibid., 153.

14. Andrieu Ordines, III:97 ff.

15. Andrieu, 120.

16. Vogel Medieval, 168–169.

17. Andrieu Ordines, III:178.

18. Vogel Medieval, 169.

19. Andrieu Ordines, IV:73.

Appendix 2: Pontificals

1. Vogel Medieval, 230 ff.

2. Cyrille Vogel and Reinhard Elze. *Le Pontifical Romano-Germanique du dixieme siecle* (Vatican: Biblioteca Apostolica Vaticana, 1963), 13 ff.

3. Vogel Medieval, 164.

4. Vogel Pontifical, ii:1 ff.

5. "Versus" could refer to a repeat of the antiphon or the versus ad repetendum. XCII of the RGP copied Ordo V, which uses the same terminology. XCIV:2

uses "versus" very clearly to refer to the antiphon. XCV refers to versus in the singular form (see answer); because this question falls between the questions about antiphon and doxology, we have to assume that the writer is referring to the psalm. Although this psalm verse is listed in singular form in XCV, we have to assume that several verses were sung, since the bishop still indicates with a sign that the Gloria Patri should begin (XCVIII:15).

6. Michel Andrieu. *Le Pontifical Romain au Moyen-Age* (Vatican: Biblioteca Apostolica Vaticana, 1938–1940), i.

7. Ibid., ii.

8. Ibid., iii.

9. Ibid., 553.

10. Ibid., 558 ff.

Bibliography

Part I. Origin and Early Development of the Introit

Andrieu, Michel. *Les Ordines Romain du Haut Moyen-Age.* Louvain: Spicilegium Sacrum Lovaniense, 1948–1956.
> Text of and detailed commentary on high medieval Ordines Romani.

Andrieu, Michel. *Le Pontifical Romain au Moyen-Age.* Vatican: Biblioteca Apostolica Vaticana, 1938–1940.
> Text of and detailed commentary on late medieval Roman pontificals.

Aurelian of Reome, tr. Joseph Ponte. *The Discipline of Music (Musica disciplina).* Colorado Springs: Colorado College Music Press, 1968.
> Good translation of this standard work of 843. Treats introit, offertory, communion, and office antiphons in a discussion of the modes.

Baldovin, SJ, John F. *The Urban Character of Christian Worship.* Orientalia Christiana Analecta 228. Rome, Pont. Institutum Studiorum Orientalium, 1987.
> Thorough treatise on the origin and development of the stational system in Jerusalem, Rome, and Constantinople.

Biblia Sacra Vulgata. Stuttgart: Deutsche Bibelgesellschaft, 1994.
> Scholarly edition of the Vulgate Bible with copious footnotes and a critical apparatus. Of special interest is a side-by-side psalter of the Gallican and Hebrew versions.

Biblioteca Apostolica Vaticana. *MS F.22. Archivo San Pietro.*
> Microfilm of thirteenth-century antiphoner of St. Peter's Basilica with musical notation.

Bibliotheque de Chartres. *Chartres 47: Antiphonale Missarum Sancti Gregorii.* Paleographie musicale 11. Tournai: Desclee & Cie, 1912.
> Facsimile of tenth-century antiphoner.

Bradshaw, Paul F. "Cathedral vs. Monastery: The Only Alternatives for the Liturgy of the Hours?" in J. Neil Alexander. *Time and Community.* Washington, D.C.: Pastoral Press, 1990.
> General overview of the question of the cathedral and monastic office, stressing also the distinction between urban and desert monasticism.

Butler, Alban. *Butler's Lives of the Saints,* edited, revised, and supplemented by Herbert Thurston, SJ, and Donald Attwater. New York: P. J. Kenedy & Sons, 1956.
> Standard multi-volume edition of eighteenth-century work, with saints arranged in chronological order of feasts, as they are arranged in the Roman calendar.

Cardine, Dom Eugene. "La Psalmodie des Introits. *Revue Gregorienne,* vol. xxvi and xxvii. Paris 1947 and 1948
> Practical application of Froger's treatise.

Dyer, Joseph. "The Introit and Communion Psalmody of Old Roman Chant." *Chant and Its Peripheries*. Ottawa: Institute of Mediaeval Music, 1998.
Excellent article about the introits and communions of Old Roman Chant, making heavy use of the ordines romani and tonaries.

Dyer, Joseph. "Monastic Psalmody of the Middle Ages." *Revue Benedictine* 99. Maredsous: Abbaye, 1989.

Einsiedeln 121: Antiphonale Missarum Sancti Gregorii. Paleographie musicale 4. Solesmes: Imprimerie Saint-Pierre, 1920.
Facsimile of tenth- to eleventh-century antiphoner.

Ekenberg, Anders. *Cur Cantatur?* Stockholm: Almqvist & Wiksell International, 1987.
Treatise on the art of singing in the Middle Ages.

Ferreres, SJ, P. Juan B. *Historia del Misal Romano*. Barcelona: E. Subriana, 1929.
Comprehensive but dated history of the Roman Missal.

Fischer, Bonifatius. *Vetus Latina: Die Reste der altlateinischen Bibel*. Freiburg: Herder, 1951–.
Incomplete multi-volume research source. Comprehensive study of all available Old Latin biblical books and excerpts. The balance of biblical material is available online through www.brepolis.net.

Froger, Dom Jacques. "Les chants de la Messe au VIIIe et IXe siecles." *Revue Gregorienne*, vol. xxvi. Paris 1947.
Discussion of performance practice of Mass chants in the eighth and ninth centuries.

Graduale Triplex. Solesmes: Abbaye Saint-Pierre, 1979.
Complete chants of the Mass proper for the liturgical year, including neumes of Laon 239, St. Gall 359, and Einsiedeln 121.

The Gregorian Missal for Sundays. Solesmes: Abbaye Saint-Pierre, 1990.
Current Mass repertoire of Gregorian chant for Sundays and feast days with English translations.

Hanssen, SJ, Ioanne, ed. "Amalarii Episcopi Opera Liturgica Omnia." *Studi e testi* 138 ff. Rome: Biblioteca Apostolica Vaticana, 1948–1950.
Complete annotated text of Amalar of Metz's liturgical writings.

Hayburn, Robert F. *Papal Legislation on Sacred Music*. Collegeville: The Liturgical Press, 1979.
Comprehensive volume. Commentary and fact-finding on early popes may be a bit too much influenced by medieval assumptions.

Hesbert, Dom Rene-Jean, ed. *Antiphonale Missarum Sextuplex*. Brussels: Vromant, 1935.
Side by side comparative study of the gradual of Monza (eighth century) and antiphoners of Rheinau (end of eighth century), Mont-Blandin (ca. 800), Compiegne (ninth century), Corbie (ca. 900), and Senlis (ninth century). Extensive introduction discusses the documents, their contents, and their dating.

Hiley, David. *Western Plainchant—A Handbook*. Oxford: Clarendon Press, 1995.
Comprehensive textbook on every aspect of Western plainchant, considered the standard for this type of study at the college and university level.

Hornby, Emma. *Gregorian and Old Roman Eighth-Mode Tracts*. Aldershot: Ashgate, 2002.

Iversen, Gunilla. "Cantans-Orans-Exultans: Interpretation of the Chants of the Introit Liturgy" in Szendrei, Janka, and Hiley, David. *Laborare fratres in unum: Festschrift Laszlo Dobszay zum 60. Geburtstag.* Zuerich: Weidmann, 1995.
 Discussion of the theology of the entrance rite as seen through medieval eyes.

Jeffery, Peter. "The Introduction of Psalmody into the Roman Mass by Pope Celestine I (422–432)." *Archiv fuer Liturgiewissenschaft,* vol. xxvi, 147–165. Regensburg: F. Pustet, 1984.
 Examination of the *Liber pontificalis* article on Pope Celestine with a special view to psalmody.

Johnson, Maxwell E. *Between Memory and Hope: Readings on the Liturgical Year.* Collegeville: The Liturgical Press, 2000.
 Collections of scholarly articles by Baldovin, Bradshaw, Connell, Johnson, LaCugna, McDonnell, Porter, Regan, Roll, Searle, Taft, Talley, White, and Winkler.

Johnson, Maxwell E. *The Rites of Christian Initiation: Their Evolution and Interpretation.* Collegeville: The Liturgical Press, 1999.
 In-depth examination of the history and character of the rites of initiation, covering Eastern and Western Churches as well as the Protestant Reformation.

Jungmann, SJ, Andreas. *Liturgie der christlichen Fruehzeit bis auf Gregor den Grossen.* Freiburg: Universitaetsverlag, 1967.
 Comprehensive treatise on liturgical aspects of the time; treating Eastern as well as Western rites.

Jungmann, SJ, Andreas. *Missarum sollemnia—eine genetische Erklaerung der roemischen Messe.* Freiburg: Herder, 1958.
 Thorough liturgical work on history and practice of the Mass. Outdated in many ways, but still a good reference.

Kellner, Dr. K. A. Heinrich. *Heortology: A History of the Christian Festivals from Their Origin to the Present Day.* London: International Catholic Library, 1908.

Klauser, Theodor. *Das roemische Capitulare Evangeliorum.* Muenster: Aschendorff, 1972.
 Comprehensive list and analysis of sixth- through thirteenth-century Latin Gospel Lectionaries.

Laon 239: Antiphonale Missarum Sancti Gregorii. Paleographie musicale. Tournai: Desclee & Cie, 1909.
 Facsimile of antiphoner of the ninth or tenth century.

Leitner, Franz. *Der gottesdienstliche Volksgesang im juedischen und christlichen Altertum.* Freiburg, 1906.
 Somewhat dated treatise on congregational song in Jewish and Christian antiquity.

Liber usualis. Tournai: Desclee & Cie, 1956.
 Tridentine Repertoire of Gregorian chant, encompassing Mass and office chants.

Luetolf, Max. *Das Graduale von Sta. Cecilia in Trastevere: Biblioteka Bodmer 74.* Cologny-Geneve: Foundation Martin Bodmer, 1987.
 Facsimile edition of Roman Graduale of 1071 with musical notation.

Maiani, Brad. "Approaching the Communion Melodies." *JAMS* vol. 53 No. 2, (Summer 2000).

Comprehensive look at the different types of communion melodies. Very clear tables and charts comparing communion chants of Frankish, German, Roman, and Beneventan sources.

Martimort, Aime Georges. *The Church at Prayer.* Collegeville: The Liturgical Press, 1988.

    Extensive treatise on the liturgy and rites of the Catholic Church.

McKinnon, James. *The Advent Project: The Later-Seventh-Century Creation of the Roman Mass Proper.* Berkeley: University of California Press, 2000.

    Comprehensive treatise on the origins of the various parts of the Mass proper. Seeks, by a kind of musical archaeology, to divine what went on in the crucible of seventh-century Rome.

McKinnon, James. *Antiquity and the Middle Ages.* Englewood Cliffs, New Jersey: Prentice Hall, 1990.

    Traces music history from ancient Greece to the fifteenth century. Draws very good connections to culture at the time.

McKinnon, James. "The Fourth Century Origin of the Gradual." *Early Music History* 7. Cambridge: Cambridge University Press, 1987.

McKinnon, James. "Lector Chant versus Schola Chant: A Question of Historical Plausibility" in Szendrei, Janka, and Hiley, David. *Laborare fratres in unum: Festschrift Laszlo Dobszay zum 60. Geburtstag.* Zuerich: Weidmann, 1995.

    Discusses in-depth various aspects of the possible establishment of the schola cantorum.

McKinnon, James. *The Temple, the Church Fathers, and Early Western Chant.* Aldershot: Ashgate, 1998.

    Forerunner of *The Advent Project;* seeks to prepare the scene for the seventh-century developments in chant. Consists of a series of independent articles and papers.

Morin, G. "Le plus ancien Comes ou lectionnaire de l'Eglise romaine." *Revue Benedictine* 27. Maredsous: Abbaye de Maredsous, 1910.

    Article discussing the mid-eighth-century copy of Roman document reflecting usage at the end of the sixth and beginning of the seventh centuries. Anglo-Saxon writing traits. Could have come to Wuerzburg by way of England. In Wuerzburg library since ninth century. This is only an epistles directory and does not include complete texts.

Morin, G. "Liturgie et basiliques de Rome au milieu du VIIe siecle d'apres les listes d'Evangiles de Wuerzburg." *Revue Benedictine* 28. Maredsous: Abbaye de Maredsous, 1911.

    See Morin above; this list includes Gospels only and reflects usage of the end of the seventh century. Again only a directory.

Niedermeyer, J. F. *Mediae Latinitatis Lexicon minus.* Leiden: Brill, 1984.

    Dictionary of Medieval Latin usage, giving examples from literature.

Nocent, OSB, Adrian. *The Liturgical Year.* Collegeville: The Liturgical Press, 1977.

    Four-volume set describing the theology of each season and describing the readings for each Sunday and feast day of the new calendar. Also contains some helpful historical information.

Ordo cantus Missae. Vatican: Typis Polyglottis Vaticanis, 1973.

Directory for the reordering of Gregorian chant according to the post–
Vatican II Lectionary cycles, with new chants where necessary. Also contains
oration and lection tones.

Peebles, B. M. "Bible, 13. Latin Versions." *New Catholic Encyclopedia.* New York:
McGraw-Hill, 1967.

Psalterium Romanum ad usum cleri basilicae Vaticane. Rome, 1593.
Breviary for all Roman basilical churches. Uses the Roman psalter
throughout.

Saint Gall 339: Antiphonale Missarum Sancti Gregorii. Paleographie musicale. Solesmes:
Imprimerie Saint-Pierre.
Facsimile of tenth-century antiphonale.

Saint Gall 359: Cantatorium. Paleographie musicale. Solesmes: Imprimerie Saint-Pierre.
Facsimile of Cantatorium of the ninth century.

Stapper, Erich. "Ordo Romanus Primus de Missa Papali." *Opuscula et textus Historiam
ecclesiae eiusque vitam atque doctrinam illustrantia, Series Liturgica,* fasc. 1.
Aschendroff: Typis Aschendorff, 1933.
Latin text and detailed description and interpretation of Ordo I. Takes
Wolfenbuettel 4175 as source document.

Taft, SJ, Robert. *The Liturgy of the Hours in East and West.* Collegeville: The Liturgical
Press, 1986.
Comprehensive treatise on the office, both from an historical and practical
perspective.

Talley, Thomas J. *The Origins of the Liturgical Year.* Collegeville: The Liturgical Press,
1986.
Comprehensive study, easy to read, many footnotes.

Thurn, Hans. *Comes Romanus Wirziburgensis.* Graz: Akademische Druck- und
Verlagsanstalt, 1968.
Facsimile edition.

Tract Society. *The Lives of the Popes.* London: Tract Society, 1799.
History of Rome from the viewpoint of the papacy.

Turco, Alberto, and Albarosa, Nino, ed. *Codices Gregoriani, Bibliotheque Municipale,
Verdun 759, Missale.* Verona: La Linea, 1994.
Facsimile and detailed description of early thirteenth-century French missal,
containing readings, chants, and prayers.

Turco, Alberto. "Les Antiennes d'Introit du Chant Romain." *Subsidia Gregoriana* 3.
Solesmes: Imprimerie Saint-Pierre, 1993.
Comparative study of introit antiphons found in Roman, Gregorian, and
Beneventan sources.

Turco, Alberto. *Il Canto Gregoriano.* Rome: Edizione Torre d'Orfeo, 1987.
Textbook on Gregorian chant.

Vogel, Cyrille, translated by William G. Storey and Niels Krogh Rasmussen, OP.
Medieval Liturgy: An Introduction to the Sources. Washington, D.C.: Pastoral
Press, 1986.
Comprehensive listing and discussion of the sources used in researching the
medieval liturgy.

Vogel, Cyrille, and Elze, Reinhard. *Le Pontifical Romano-Germanique du dixieme siecle.*
Vatican: Biblioteca Apostolica Vaticana, 1963.

Weber, Dom Robert. *Le Psautier Romain et les autres Anciens Psautiers Latins.* Rome: Abbaye Saint-Jerome, 1953.
  Study and text of the Roman psalter, with reference to Old Latin versions.

Part II. Metrical Psalters and Metrical Introits

John Ainslie, ed.: *The Simple Gradual for Sundays and Holy Days.* London: Geoffrey Chapman, 1970.
  English setting of the (mostly seasonal) proper of the Church year, giving mostly short refrain antiphons and several choices of psalm tones.
Carson, D. A. *The Inclusive Language Debate—A Plea for Realism.* Grand Rapids: Barker Books, 1998.
  Treatise on inclusive language, touching mainly on horizontal inclusivity.
Cooke, W. J. *Israel's Songs and Meditations.* Preston: R. Reed & Sons, 1924.
  Metrical psalter.
Dawson, A.M.P. *A New Metrical Version of the Psalter.* Croydon: Brighton, 1950.
  Good preface and good use of language in a new version made directly from the Bible and the Book of Common Prayer.
Flannery, Austin P. *Documents of Vatican II.* Grand Rapids: Eerdmans, 1978.
  A new authoritative translation of the conciliar documents, including post-conciliar papers and commentaries.
Ford, Paul F. *By Flowing Waters.* Collegeville: The Liturgical Press, 1999.
  English settings of the (mostly seasonal) proper of the Mass in chant style for congregational or monastic use.
Gillingham, S. E. *The Poems and Psalms of the Hebrew Bible.* Oxford: Oxford University Press, 1994.
  Treatise on the poetry of the Bible, with special emphasis on the psalms.
Grieve, Nichol. *The Scottish Metrical Psalter (1650), A Revision.* Edinburgh: T. & T. Clark, 1940.
  Thorough preface talks about every aspect of revision. Good use of language in a complete revision of 1650 Psalter. Multiple settings for some psalms, and greater variety of meters.
Institutio Generalis Missalis Romani. Rome, 2000. English translation Washington, D.C.: U.S. Catholic Conference, 2003.
  General Instruction of the Roman Missal.
Keel, Othmar. *The Symbolism of the Biblical World.* New York: Seabury Press, 1997.
  Treatise on Egyptian, Babylonian, and other elements that influenced Hebrew thinking and religion.
The Music Documents: Music in Catholic Worship and Liturgical Music Today. Portland, Oregon: Bishops Committee on the Liturgy, 1995.
Psalter Hymnal, Doctrinal Standards and Liturgy of the Christian Reformed Church. Grand Rapids: Board of Publications of the Christian Reformed Church, 1976.

Hymnal consisting of metrical psalms of different traditions. Preface summarizes the arguments for including particular settings, both textual and musical. The supplement contains a lengthy treatise on the use of psalmody in the Jewish and early Christian traditions, as well as under the Reformation.

The Psalter: A Revised Edition of the Scottish Metrical Version of the Psalms with Additional Psalm-Versions, Prepared and Published by Authority of the General Assembly of the Presbyterian Church in Ireland. Oxford: Oxford University Press, 1997.

Reprint of 1898 edition. Cleans up the language of the original 1650 Scottish Psalter while respecting biblical scholarship and providing more variety in meter. Also contains selected verses of other biblical texts.

Webber, Christopher L. *A New Metrical Psalter.* New York: Church Publishing, 1986.

Good preface justifying a contemporary language version of the psalter. Applies contemporary language to metrical psalter. Application to three-year Lectionary (Episcopal) indicated. Limited musical possibility, only three meters used.

Sources

The author gratefully acknowledges the following publishers for permission to use the following copyrighted material for this project.

Introit antiphons, verses, and doxologies by Christoph Tietze from *Introit Hymns for the Church Year.* Copyright © 2005 World Library Publications, 3708 River Road, Suite 400, Franklin Park IL 60131-2158; www.wlpmusic.com. All rights reserved. Used by permission.

The English translations of the Latin introit texts are from *The Gregorian Missal for Sundays,* Solesmes, Copyright © 1990 St. Peter's Abbey, Solesmes, and Desclee, Paris-Tournai.

Christopher L. Webber: *A New Metrical Psalter,* New York, Copyright © 1986 Christopher Webber. Published by Church Publishing Corporation, New York, New York: Antiphons: Lent 1, Ordinary Time 10 AC, 10 B, 16, 28, and 29.

Psalm Verses: Advent 3, 4, Christmas Vigil and Dawn, Holy Family, Epiphany, Lent 1, 2, 4, Holy Thursday, Easter 2, Corpus Christi, Ordinary Time 3 AB, 10 AC, 10 B, 11, 16, 23, 24, 26 BC, 27, 28, 29. Doxologies: Advent 1, 4, Christmas Vigil, Dawn, and Day, Holy Family, Mary, Mother of God, Epiphany, Baptism of the Lord, Lent 2, 3, 4, Easter 2, 4, 5, Ascension, Pentecost Vigil, Corpus Christi, Ordinary Time 3 AB, 5, 6, 7, 9, 10 B, 11, 13, 14, 15, 16, 18 BC, 24, 28, 31 AB, 32.

Index

About the Liturgical Institute

The Liturgical Institute, founded in 2000 by His Eminence Francis Cardinal George of Chicago, offers a variety of options for education in Liturgical Studies. A unified, rites-based core curriculum constitutes the foundation of the program, providing integrated and balanced studies toward the advancement of the renewal promoted by the Second Vatican Council. The musical, artistic, and architectural dimensions of worship are given particular emphasis in the curriculum. Institute students are encouraged to participate in its "liturgical heart" of daily Mass and Morning and Evening Prayer. The academic program of the Institute serves a diverse, international student population—laity, religious, and clergy—who are preparing for service in parishes, dioceses, and religious communities. Personalized mentoring is provided in view of each student's ministerial and professional goals. The Institute is housed on the campus of the University of St. Mary of the Lake/Mundelein Seminary, which offers the largest priestly formation program in the United States and is the center of the permanent diaconate and lay ministry training programs of the Archdiocese of Chicago. In addition, the University has the distinction of being the first chartered institution of higher learning in Chicago (1844), and one of only seven pontifical faculties in North America.

For more information about the Liturgical Institute and its programs, contact: usml.edu/liturgicalinstitute. Phone: 847-837-4542. E-mail: litinst@usml.edu.

Msgr. Reynold Hillenbrand
1904-1979

Monsignor Reynold Hillenbrand, ordained a priest by Cardinal George Mundelein in 1929, was Rector of St. Mary of the Lake Seminary from 1936 to 1944.

He was a leading figure in the liturgical and social action movement in the United States during the 1930s and worked to promote active, intelligent, and informed participation in the Church's liturgy.

He believed that a reconstruction of society would occur as a result of the renewal of the Christian spirit, whose source and center is the liturgy.

Hillenbrand taught that, since the ultimate purpose of Catholic action is to Christianize society, the renewal of the liturgy must undoubtedly play the key role in achieving this goal.

Hillenbrand Books strives to reflect the spirit of Monsignor Reynold Hillenbrand's pioneering work by making available innovative and scholarly resources that advance the liturgical and sacramental life of the Church.